List of

Photographs are kindly provid⸺ ⸺ ⸺⸺⸺⸺
unless otherwise stated in italics.

1. Cliff Palace, Mesa Verde, c.1190–1260 CE. *Rational Observer/ Wikimedia Creative Commons.*
2. Amerigo Vespucci, detail from a map of the New World by Martin Waldseemüller, 1507. *Pictures Now/Alamy.*
3. Secoton, Roanoke, 1585. Detail of an illustration by Theodor de Bry after John White, from Thomas Hariot, *A Briefe and True Report of the New Found Land of Virginia*, 1590. *Barry Lawrence Ruderman Antique Maps, Inc.*
4. Pocahontas, 1616. Portrait by English School after an engraving by Simon van der Passe. Private collection. *Peter Newark American Pictures/Bridgeman Images.*
5. The first Thanksgiving Day, Plymouth, 1621. Painting by Jennie A. Brownscombe, 1914. Pilgrim Hall Museum, Plymouth, MA. *GL Archive/Alamy.*
6. The trial of George Jacobs, Salem, 1692. Painting by Tompkins Matteson, 1855. Peabody Essex Museum, Salem, MA. *Bridgeman Images.*
7. Penn's Treaty with the Indians in 1683. Detail of a painting by Benjamin West, 1771–2. Oil on canvas, 191.77 x 273.68 cm (75½ x 107¾ in.). Pennsylvania Academy of the Fine Arts, Philadelphia, PA. Gift of Mrs Sarah Harrison (The Joseph Harrison, Jr Collection). Acc. No. 1878.1.10. *Courtesy of the Pennsylvania Academy of the Fine Arts, Philadelphia.*
8. A Virginia planter smoking tobacco while field workers toil nearby. Tobacco dealer's trade card, c.1725. *New York Public Library Digital Collections.*

A Short History of America

A Short History of America

From Tea Party to Trump

SIMON JENKINS

PENGUIN
VIKING

VIKING

UK | USA | Canada | Ireland | Australia
India | New Zealand | South Africa

Viking is part of the Penguin Random House group of companies
whose addresses can be found at global.penguinrandomhouse.com

Penguin Random House UK,
One Embassy Gardens, 8 Viaduct Gardens, London SW11 7BW

penguin.co.uk

Penguin
Random House
UK

First published 2025

001

Set in 12/14.75pt Dante MT Std
Typeset by Six Red Marbles UK, Thetford, Norfolk
Printed and bound by CPI (UK) Ltd, Croydon CR0 4YY

The authorized representative in the EEA is Penguin Random House Ireland,
Morrison Chambers, 32 Nassau Street, Dublin D02 YH68

A CIP catalogue record for this book is available from the British Library

ISBN: 978–0–241–74759–9

Penguin Random House is committed to a sustainable future
for our business, our readers and our planet. This book is made from
Forest Stewardship Council® certified paper.

To the memory of Gayle, a true Texan

Contents

Contents

Maps

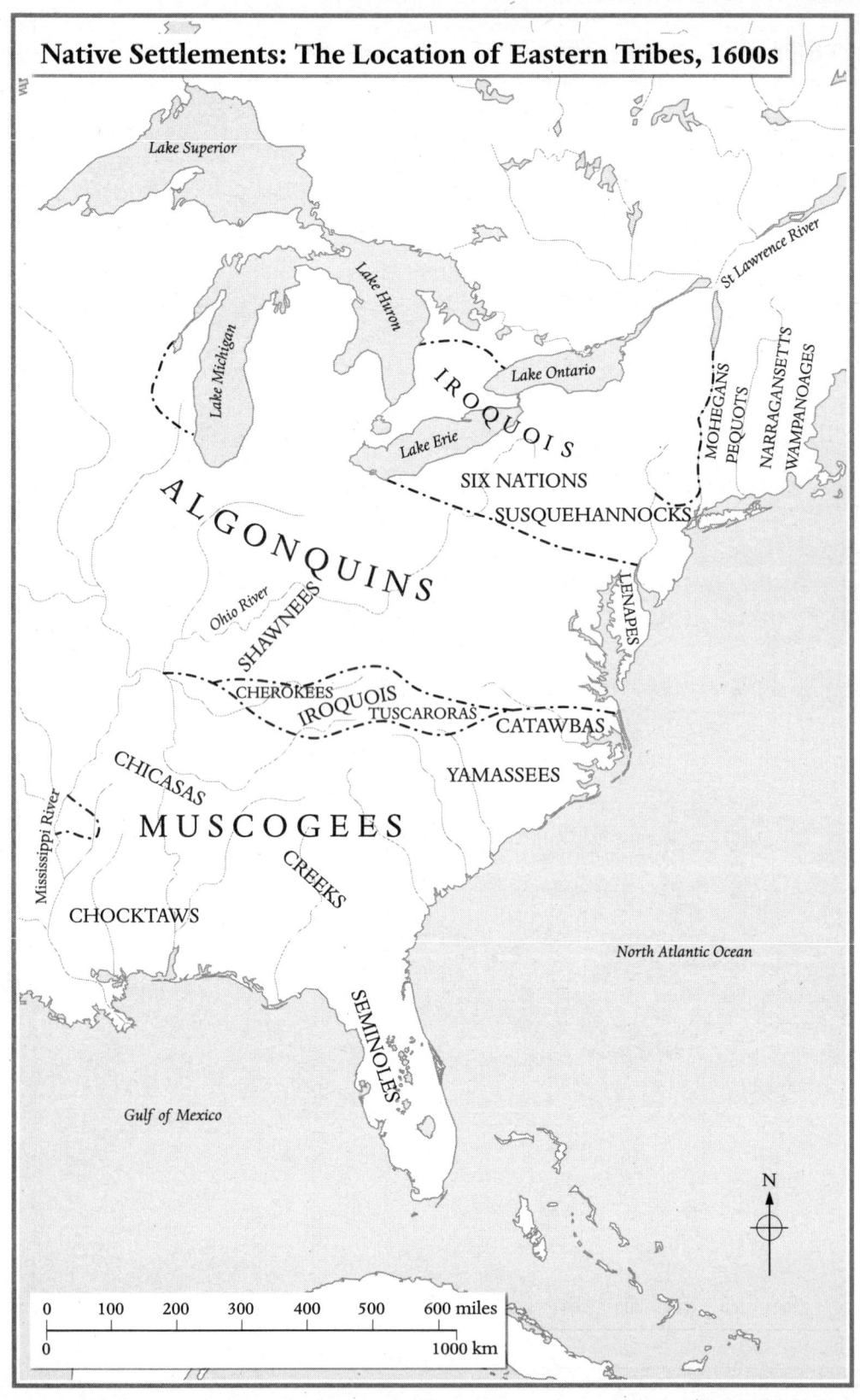

Native Settlements: The Location of Eastern Tribes, 1600s

Lake Superior

Lake Huron

Lake Michigan

St Lawrence River

Lake Ontario

IROQUOIS

Lake Erie

MOHEGANS

PEQUOTS

NARRAGANSETTS

WAMPANOAGES

SIX NATIONS

ALGONQUINS

SUSQUEHANNOCKS

Ohio River

SHAWNEES

LENAPES

CHEROKEES

IROQUOIS

TUSCARORAS

CATAWBAS

YAMASSEES

CHICASAS

MUSCOGEES

Mississippi River

CREEKS

CHOCKTAWS

North Atlantic Ocean

SEMINOLES

Gulf of Mexico

N

| 0 | 100 | 200 | 300 | 400 | 500 | 600 miles |

| 0 | | | | | | 1000 km |

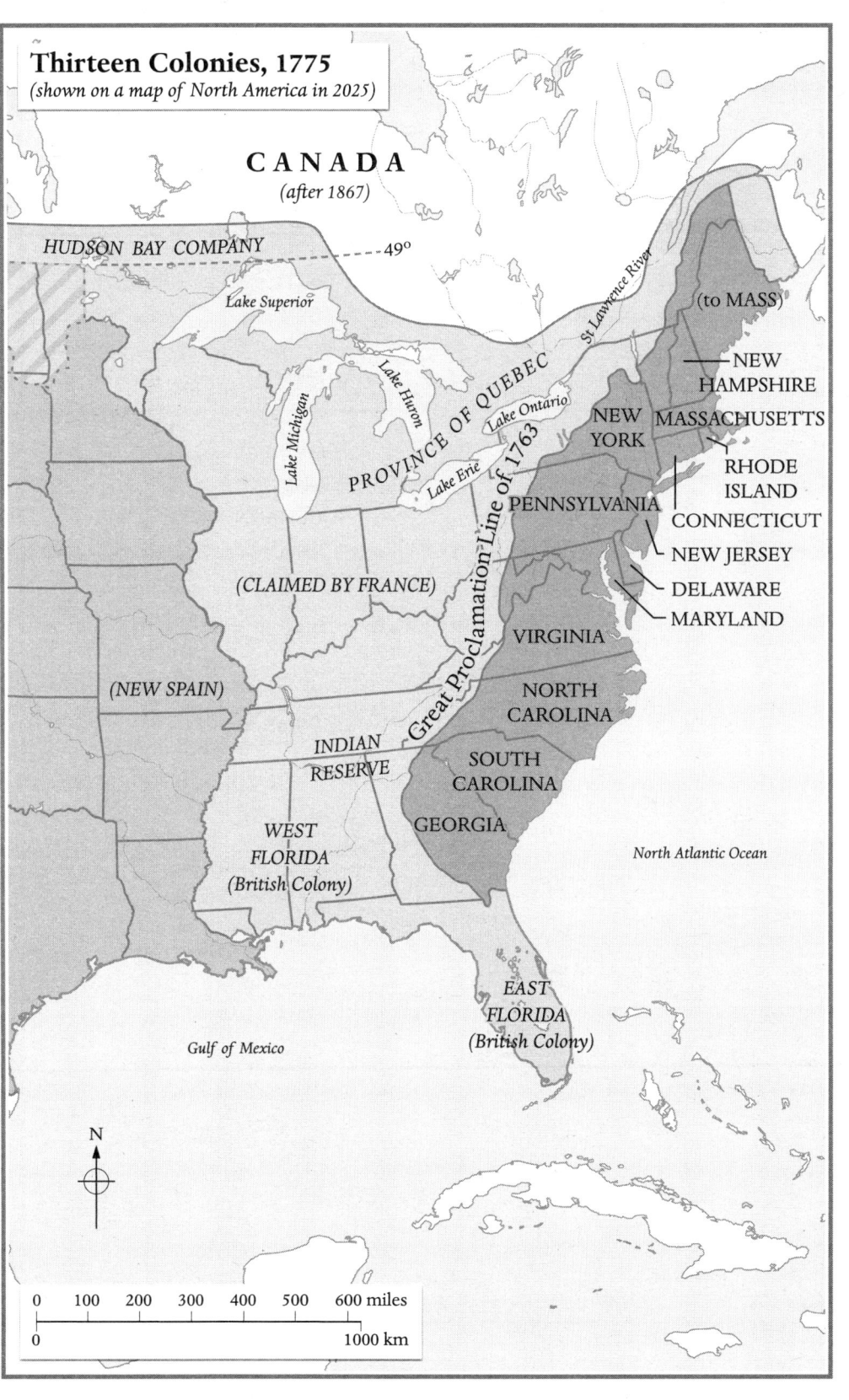

Thirteen Colonies, 1775
(shown on a map of North America in 2025)

CANADA
(after 1867)

HUDSON BAY COMPANY — — 49°

Lake Superior

(to MASS)

Lake Michigan

Lake Huron

Lake Ontario

Lake Erie

St Lawrence River

PROVINCE OF QUEBEC

NEW
YORK

NEW
HAMPSHIRE

MASSACHUSETTS

RHODE
ISLAND

CONNECTICUT

NEW JERSEY

DELAWARE

MARYLAND

PENNSYLVANIA

Great Proclamation Line of 1763

(CLAIMED BY FRANCE)

VIRGINIA

(NEW SPAIN)

NORTH
CAROLINA

INDIAN
RESERVE

SOUTH
CAROLINA

GEORGIA

WEST
FLORIDA
(British Colony)

North Atlantic Ocean

EAST
FLORIDA
(British Colony)

Gulf of Mexico

N

0   100   200   300   400   500   600 miles

0   1000 km

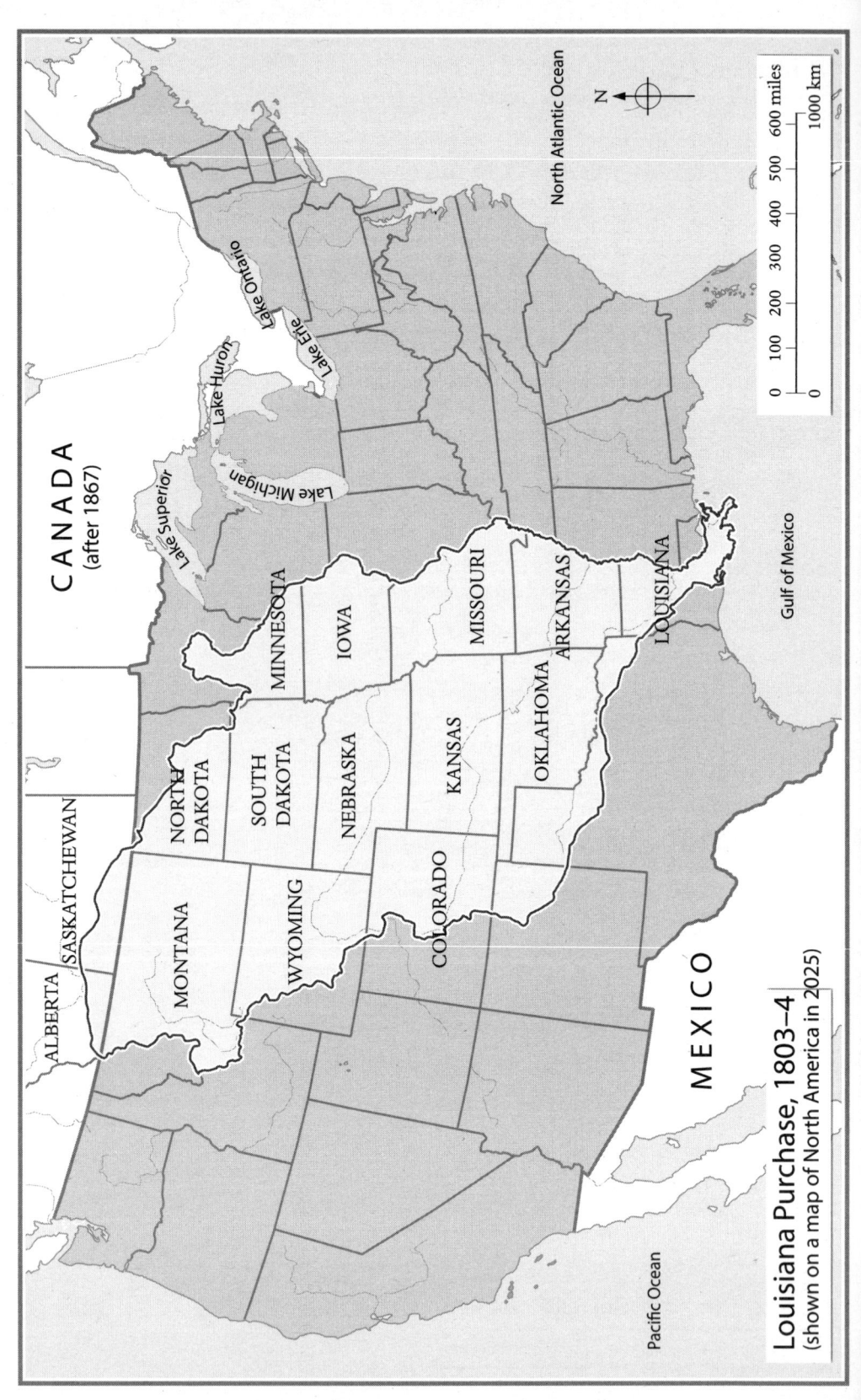

Louisiana Purchase, 1803–4
(shown on a map of North America in 2025)

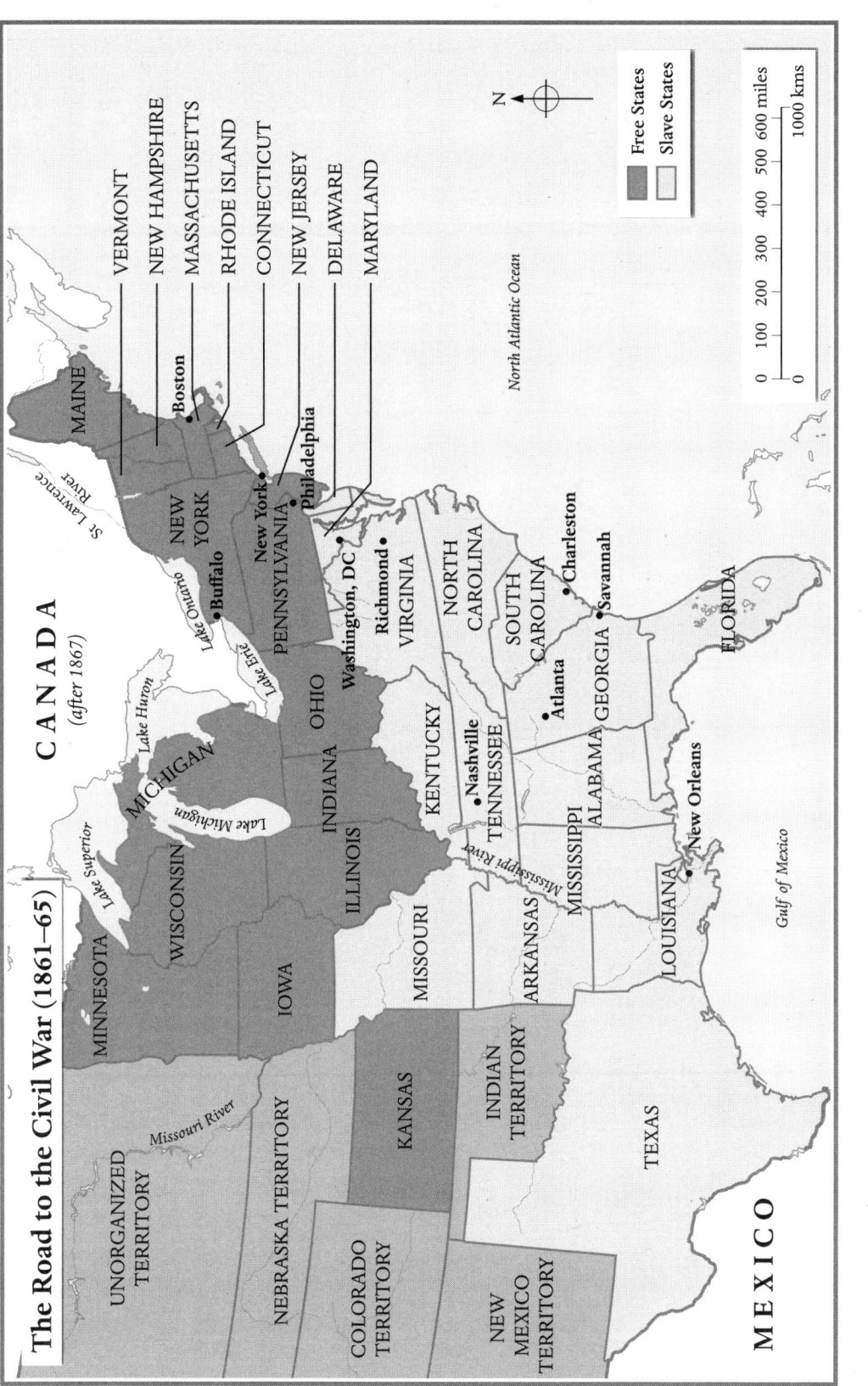

The Road to the Civil War (1861–65)

CANADA
(after 1867)

MEXICO

Free States
Slave States

N

0   100 200 300 400 500 600 miles

0   1000 kms

North Atlantic Ocean

Gulf of Mexico

VERMONT
NEW HAMPSHIRE
MASSACHUSETTS
RHODE ISLAND
CONNECTICUT
NEW JERSEY
DELAWARE
MARYLAND

MAINE
Boston
NEW YORK
New York
PENNSYLVANIA
Philadelphia
Buffalo
Washington, DC
Richmond
VIRGINIA
NORTH CAROLINA
SOUTH CAROLINA
Charleston
Savannah
GEORGIA
FLORIDA
Atlanta
ALABAMA
Nashville
TENNESSEE
KENTUCKY
OHIO
INDIANA
ILLINOIS
MICHIGAN
WISCONSIN
IOWA
MINNESOTA
MISSOURI
ARKANSAS
MISSISSIPPI
LOUISIANA
New Orleans
INDIAN TERRITORY
KANSAS
TEXAS
NEBRASKA TERRITORY
COLORADO TERRITORY
NEW MEXICO TERRITORY
UNORGANIZED TERRITORY

St. Lawrence River
Lake Ontario
Lake Erie
Lake Huron
Lake Michigan
Lake Superior
Missouri River
Mississippi River

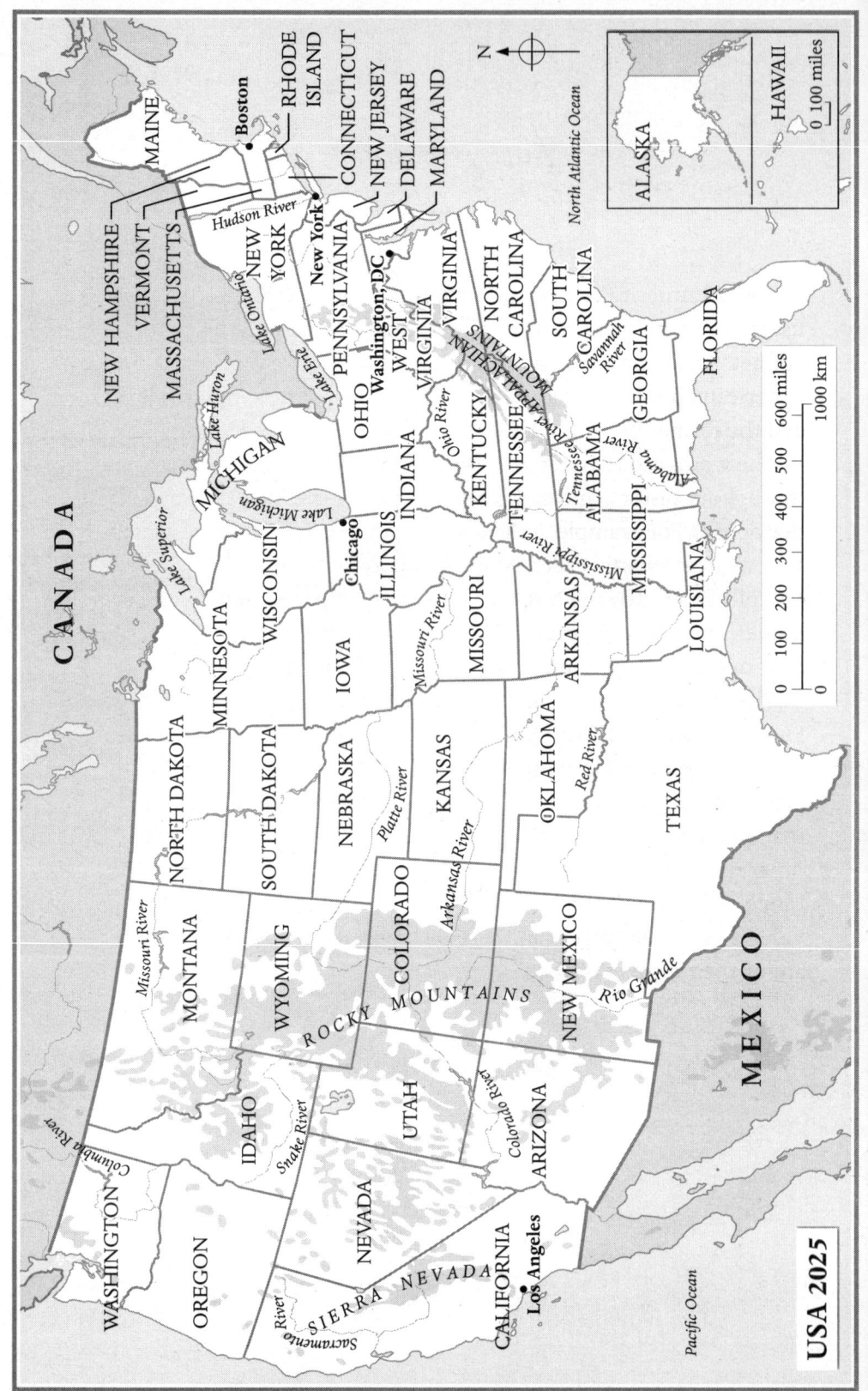

USA 2025

Author's Note

The word 'America' in my title and throughout this book is common usage for the United States of America. The same applies to the epithet American. The book also covers the story of the North American continent as a whole prior to the War of Independence and the formation of the United States.

The words used to refer to different races have changed many times throughout history, and today's most appropriate usage is not a settled debate. For example, indigenous tribes long referred to as Indians are now customarily called Native Americans, though their statistics are still gathered by the National Congress of American Indians. I use modern terminology unless I am quoting historical texts where the now-outdated term is integral to the intended meaning of the quote.

The book is written in British English not American English. Hence my use of British spellings and the absence of railroads, sidewalks and subways in their American meaning.

This is not an academic work and its sources are secondary rather than primary, but I have tried to indicate the authors of quotes and other material in the text. The Further Reading section indicates the range of books on which I have drawn. The dates of significant individuals are given, except in the case of presidents, where the dates are of their terms of office.

Introduction

The United States of America began life in the eighteenth century on a sliver of land on the North American continent. That continent had long been settled by peoples out of Asia and was not occupied by Europeans until the sixteenth century. The settlers came initially from Spain, moving up from the Caribbean, to be followed by the French to the north and the English along the Atlantic coast. By far the most numerous were the English, arriving in their thousands from a country they felt could not tolerate their beliefs or respond to their dreams. They came primarily as farmers and formed what became vigorous self-governing communities.

American history constantly reverts to these beginnings, to the ambitions of the early settlers and their so-called Founding Fathers. Emanating chiefly from the east-coast colonies of Virginia and Massachusetts, these individuals, some wealthy, others pious, wedded themselves to classical history and Enlightenment philosophy. Their intention was twofold: to formulate an ideology of political freedom and to create a constitution that would join their scattered settlements in a secure union.

The first, a eulogy of liberty and equality, was noble but partial. The Virginians were slave-owners and the colonists had scant respect for the Native peoples they were soon to drive into near oblivion. The second intention was specific. It was to enable thirteen self-governing colonies to combine in such a way as to form a confederacy yet retain their individual character and self-government.

The resulting document is a work of political architecture that I believe holds the single key to America's story. It contrived to bind together a group of small agrarian communities isolated far from their ancestral homes, and yet the same architecture was to sustain what became the most powerful country on earth. One of the constitution's creators, Alexander Hamilton, insisted it be called an experiment, designed to find a way of devolving power among the communities, or states, and with the centre that honoured local democratic autonomy. The result was a civil war. But the union has lasted to this day and could serve as a model to nations still sundered by the strains of political union. They include many in the Europe America was founded to escape, not least the United Kingdom.

To the rights awarded to states under the US constitution was added a further safeguard: the separation of powers within the central government. Its institutions were checked and balanced in a triumvirate of the president and two houses of Congress. Though the price was often inertia and stalemate, this curbed the centralizing tendencies that have dragged so many powerful states down the road to dictatorship. Even today, America has not taken that path. That is why I treat its constitution as the leitmotif of its history, even as it is under peculiar strain as I write.

As America came to draw population from a wide variety of nations and peoples, it has always coated its history in patriotism. It has elevated its heroic events and dressed them in myth, which in turn has opened them to controversy. From Jamestown and the *Mayflower* to the Boston Tea Party and Yorktown, the national story follows an often exhilarating course. Each age has been christened with a title, as in the City upon a Hill, the Frontier Spirit, the Gilded Age, the Roaring Twenties. Its early years are fleshed out with personalities, from Pocahontas and John Smith to George Washington and Abraham Lincoln. The very word 'America' evokes images of Pilgrim Fathers, cowboys and Indians, Mississippi steamboats, the Italian Mafia and the Hollywood sign.

Controversy has never been far behind. From the enslavement of imported Africans after 1619 to the extermination of the Pequot and other tribes in 1638 there is often another side to be told. Jefferson's 'empire of liberty' was to many a war of violent conquest. Traditional histories rarely mention George III's ban on trans-Appalachian expansion. The Civil War and Reconstruction require constant reinterpretation, as do the Mexican and Sioux wars. There was a dark side even to American prosperity, from the railway monopolists and robber barons to the handling of the Great Depression. In this history, I have tried to balance these still-sensitive issues.

What is incontrovertible is that by the turn of the twentieth century an America had emerged that was a global phenomenon. The laws of supply and demand, fuelled by a constant influx of labour, capital and raw materials, had begun producing wealth beyond the world's imaginings. At one point 80 per cent of all motor cars were being made – and driven – in America. For a brief spell during the presidency of Theodore Roosevelt, the country even began a tentative empire of its own beyond the borders of North America.

A growing self-confidence was boosted by America's participation in the twentieth century's two world wars and the subsequent Cold War. Their outcome projected the nation into an age when military power was newly defined and deployed. Though America was geographically secure, it felt the need for a defence establishment unrivalled on earth. It was to defend in alliance with others the values inherited from its Founding Fathers against 'the forces of evil' anywhere on the planet.

Following the USSR's defeat in the Cold War, Mikhail Gorbachev, the Soviet president, asked 'what America would do now for an enemy'. There have been many analyses of America's answer. The concept of policing a 'new world order' advanced by successive occupants of the White House has had a relatively brief life. It seemed at times as if America was judge, jury and executioner to the world, especially after the trauma of 9/11 and failures in Iraq and Afghanistan. Successive presidents have seemed deaf to the pleas of their founder, George Washington, to steer clear of foreign conflicts, even as one intervention after another ended in failure.

The struggle over whether and when to intervene has gone back to the birth of the United States. It has been a struggle between the isolationism of the early Virginians and the missionary ambition of their Massachusetts colleagues. It is easy to admire the latter, and their desire to export values of liberty and democracy to the rest of the world. The manner of doing so – with increasing belligerence – has been controversial. As it is, interventionists fight with isolationists, warriors with peacemakers, global philanthropists with those committed to the country's self-interest. The ever uncertain outcome of this argument is the essence of America's recent history, rarely more so than at the time when this book was written. I only hope that a better understanding of the past leads to the same of the present.

I.

Out of Asia

Before 1492

The scene is a muddy shoreline of a lake in White Sands, New Mexico, and the time is some 23,000 years ago. It is of the footprints of a woman leading, sometimes carrying, a child for at least a mile amid the prints of mammoths and sloths. The wonders of archaeology have enabled the pollen and other substances attached to the prints to be dated with relative precision. They are the earliest known traces of human occupation on the American continent.

These prints, discovered in 2009, are now inaccessible but moulds of them are displayed in an adjacent museum. Even detached from their setting, they convey an eerie intimacy. We appear to be walking alongside them, witnessing fellow human beings journeying through life and leaving their mark on the sands of time. To see them is intensely moving.

The history of the nation that now occupies that land – the United States of America – is known to a degree shared by few others, if only because it is so comparatively short. Its two and a half centuries are, for the most part, openly recorded, but of the continent on which that union settled and of its earliest peoples we know little. Until the turn of the twenty-first century it was generally thought that the two American continents, north and south, were first occupied between 15,000 and 14,000 years ago. The earliest signs of human habitation were traces of stone tools embedded in the datable skeletons of mastodons and mammoths. Their users were held to be immigrants from Siberia, crossing a previously frozen land bridge known as Beringia, where is now the Bering Strait, into

5

Alaska. Genetic archaeology has confirmed that the first Americans were unquestionably of Asian origin.

This period of occupation was associated with finds in the 1920s in Clovis, New Mexico, but the so-called Clovis culture has now been superseded as the continent's first. The sciences of radiocarbon dating and DNA sequencing have unearthed earlier activities associated with camps, animal traps, tools and seeds. From Idaho in the north to Chile in the south, evidence of human occupation is dated as far back as possibly 33,000 years ago. That date, currently the earliest recorded, applies to tools found in Chiquihuite, a cave in central Mexico, though it remains controversial. What we can say for sure is that the New Mexico footprints are the first traces of actual human beings so far discovered on North or South American soil.

The footprints have been attributed to 'a failed colonization which may well have left no genetically detectable heritage'. Some have even suggested they might have followed a migration by Polynesians (originally from Asia) journeying across the Pacific. As for the earliest known remains of an actual person, that title rests with the bones of a small boy found in Montana in 1968. Known as the Anzick child after the farm where he was discovered, he is just 12,600 years old. His DNA has been related both to Siberia and to South America. Anzick is the oldest known American.

These early inhabitants would have been groups of hunter-gatherers who moved south from Beringia either down the west coast of America – since dubbed the 'kelp highway' – or down an ice-free corridor to the south-western prairies east of the Rocky Mountains. Climate change would have led the newcomers ever further south, eventually into central and southern America. Here they evolved into the Maya, Toltec, Inca and Aztec peoples.

Those who turned east into North America were long a mystery. They would have moved in family groups in pursuit of wild game, with little need to combine into large tribes for reasons of succour or security. That is probably why the National Congress of American Indians has, with the aid of scholarship, managed to identify as many as 574 distinct Native American tribes inhabiting various parts of what is now the United States of America, of which 229 are in Alaska. Over millennia they made their way into the Great Plains and the Mississippi Basin, possibly driven by the gradual extinction of mammoths and other beasts on which they depended. Where they came across fertile soil they began to settle. They found copper and developed pottery and weaving.

Attempts to categorize the phases of American prehistory along the lines of Europe's variously distinct 'ages' of Stone, Bronze and Iron have proved elusive. All that is known is that human settlement was taking place across North America as early as thirteen millennia ago, with ever greater complexity. At Watson Brake in Louisiana, mounds and pits associated with static communities and religious ceremonies have been dated to 5,500 years ago. These are older than either Egypt's pyramids or England's Stonehenge and suggest that North America had communities that developed in parallel with their better-known counterparts in South America. These so-called 'mound cultures' were spread across the Mississippi Basin for thousands of years.

Ancient Americans may have lacked the three chief agents of change in European and Asian societies – iron, horses and writing – but this did not appear to impede their development of subsistence farming and territorial settlement. There remains an aura of suspense surrounding American prehistory, as we wait in hope for science one day to reveal people and activities as yet undiscovered. Of all the rights of the world's indigenous peoples, the most fundamental is the right to a history. But where that history resides only in mounds, pits, tools and seeds, the challenge of painting a detailed picture remains great indeed.

As we advance over time through what is termed the Common Era that began 2,000 years ago, one of the oldest and possibly the largest of North America's known settlements survives at Cahokia in Illinois. This is located at the junction of the Mississippi and Missouri rivers near the present city of St Louis. It dates from *c.*900–1350 CE and was clearly a major concentration of people. Research has yielded a 'built-up area' of some six square miles, spread round a

palisaded enclave. The city appears to have comprised 120 ceremonial earthen mounds and building clusters, some with courtyards
and even steam baths.

Cahokia was constructed on a grid pattern with no outer defences.
At its peak in c.1100, contemporary with Europe's Norman period,
it is estimated to have housed between 10,000 and 20,000 people.
The outer settled area may have embraced many more, possibly
double this number. At the centre, Cahokia's Monks Mound pyramid would have risen a hundred feet, half the estimated height of
Mexico City's lost Tenochtitlan. Its base was equal in size to that of
Egypt's Great Pyramid at Giza and overlooked what would have
been a plaza of fifty acres. Another, Mound 72, contained the 'bird-
man tomb', wherein a figure with bird-like mask and wings was
interred with dozens of apparent acolytes and shell jewellery c.950.
The inhabitants left no writing, but their funerary carving indicates
a talent for decoration.

There has been much debate over how stable was the hierarchy
that prevailed over Cahokia. Such a large settlement suggests a
complex society with a developed leadership. It is hard to believe it
was not preceded by other settlements now unknown. They clearly
indulged in human sacrifice, with some 270 victims over six epi-
sodes discovered in Mound 72. Such activities would have required
a degree of authority and order, not to mention an economy able
to produce and distribute food. Cahokia's pre-eminence may have
depended on the presence of its two rivers. Trade by water was
easier than trade by land. We know that copperware was exported
north to the Great Lakes and south to the Gulf of Mexico. What
is clear at least is that North America at the end of the first millen-
nium was host to a city bigger than London or Paris at the time.

The decline of this remarkable place was probably due to climate
change, possibly associated with the Little Ice Age in the fourteenth
century. There was a brief resurgence in the seventeenth century
when the settlement was visited by French explorers, whose more
pious element gave the Monks Mound its name by living next to it,
and they named the neighbouring colony after their king, Louis.

Even after Cahokia's abandonment, the Mississippi culture survived in the basin's Natchez and Choctaw peoples. The Natchez were remarkable for a language apparently unrelated to other Native tongues. They became allies of the French colonists of the basin. Relations deteriorated in the early eighteenth century and an uprising in 1729 led to widespread massacres by the colonists. The French transported thousands of Natchez into Caribbean slavery.

Though smaller than Cahokia, the settlement of the Pueblo branch of the Navajo people at Chaco Canyon in New Mexico has the advantage of stone structures still standing. Founded *c.*850, the population at its twelfth-century peak was estimated to be 15,000. The buildings are closely packed and circular, many two storeys high but ruined and roofless. They appear to be honeycombed with apartments, while below them are underground kivas or ceremonial chambers. The stone-walled Chetro Ketl appears to be one such kiva.

On the outskirts stands the semicircular Pueblo Bonito, apparently a palace compound containing some three hundred rooms. Inside were found the skeletons of nine of the city's matrilineal rulers. Another palace, Pueblo Pintado, appears to have been of sumptuous size, one of some 150 such great houses linked by roads in the surrounding desert. With their surviving walls and chambers, these are the most evocative ruins in America.

Chaco Canyon lies at the centre of what was once a road network extending for about sixty miles. As at Cahokia, this implies trading or pilgrimage activities of some sophistication, clearly comparable with those in South America. Again the cause of decline in the twelfth century would appear to be climate change and desertification. Today Chaco stands magnificent in its isolation, with no modern roads or buildings intruding on its antiquity. The absence of artificial light has made Chaco a popular destination for stargazers.

Another prominent survivor of the Pueblo culture lies in southern Colorado at Mesa Verde. This dates from the tenth century, a time when these landscapes must have been fertile and alive with people. With a population of some 20,000, its extraordinary troglodyte dwellings sprout from mountainside alcoves reached by steps and ladders. Cliff Palace has around 150 cliffside rooms carved from its surrounding rock. Mesa Verde too appears to have fallen victim to environmental change. It remains the most vivid of these ruined settlements, with rooms through which we can walk, and views out over the now barren desert.

Such survivors are few and far between, but these and lesser ones at Taos, Casa Grande, Canyon de Chelly and elsewhere are sufficient to suggest that the America 'discovered' in the fifteenth century was not the wilderness of 'savage' hunter-gatherers described by early European explorers. Native Americans had already inhabited, prospered and in some sense controlled much of this continent for thousands of years.

Their descendants managed to resist colonial invaders to the extent of retaining their identity into modern times. Of the 574 tribes still recognized today, no fewer than 147 languages have been distinguished. Nowhere in Europe is there a remotely comparable tribal or cultural longevity. The tribes' distinctive identities and histories were long ignored, to be researched and revealed only in the twentieth century. I like to think the obsession modern America has with localism – such as the refusal to combine smaller states into large ones – is a reflection of this prehistoric diversity.

There are few signs that pre-Columbian American society was ever naturally violent or warlike. Many tribes were ruled by matriarchies and most engaged in early cohabitation with Spanish, French and English colonists as they pushed north from the Gulf of Mexico, south from Canada or west from the east coast. Most of these sought trade, as of gold and furs. It was largely the British quest for land to settle that fuelled clashes down the east coast, such as with the Iroquois, the Lenape and the Powhatan.

Here even the British authorities were adamant that their colonists should not spread westwards over the Appalachian Mountains into what they defined as Indian territory. Charles II (r.1662–85) expressly forbade any such move. Only after the creation of the independent United States in the eighteenth century did its frontiersmen become conquerors of what was to become America's domestic empire. As we shall see, the tribes with whom they came into contact were increasingly driven westwards, to become ever more resistant.

In his *Indigenous Continent* (2022), the Finnish historian Pekka Hämäläinen has stressed the continuation of this resistance into the nineteenth century. He depicts the western tribes, particularly the larger Lakota, Comanche and Apache, as remaining in occupation of large tracts of land west of the Mississippi. Through his analysis of how far they controlled this territory, he shows that the completion of the European 'empire' of North America required military conquest down to the Sioux Wars of the 1880s. These were the final drive to exclude the Native tribes from their territory in the far west and confine them to reservations. Native numbers plummeted – some say from some 50 million at the time of first colonization to 7 million, including mixed race, today – though they are now on the increase.

Not a murmur would have reached the people of Cahokia about a modest camp erected in the tenth century far to their north-east in what is now Canada. In 986 a Viking sailor named Bjarni Herjólfsson lost his way off the coast of Greenland and sailed on westward. He eventually came across a 'flat and wooded land' backed by a glacier. He did not go ashore but returned to Greenland to tell of his discovery. Unlike his American contemporaries, Herjólfsson had the writers of sagas to record his experience. He was the first European known to have set eyes on America.

Fifteen years later, in 1001, another adventurer, Leif Erikson, decided to investigate Herjólfsson's report, apparently using the same boat. His father Erik the Red was an Icelander, driven into exile for murder, who had sailed west to found a colony on Greenland. It was from here that Erikson set off with thirty-five fellow settlers to found another colony. He is thought to have reached Baffin Island and from there went on to Labrador and down to the tip of Newfoundland. Here he came across a country of lush grass and salmon-rich waters, where he built a settlement of eight huts. The saga relates that Erikson called the land Vinland after the grapes or berries found there.

The site of the settlement was discovered in 1960 at what is now L'Anse aux Meadows. It yielded a hoard of some eight hundred Norse objects, dated to soon after 1000. The Norse saga tells of the settlers' encounters with local Native people, probably of the Mi'kmaq tribe, sometimes trading, sometimes fighting. The Native people were described as 'small, ill-favoured men with ugly hair on their heads. They had big eyes and were broad in their cheeks.' In one encounter the Native people attacked the Norse men, who promptly took flight, whereupon the Norse women reportedly seized their swords, bared their breasts and terrified the Native people into defeat.

The Vinland colony lasted some twenty years before a cold spell forced the inhabitants to return to Greenland. Back in Scandinavia, the Norse Vikings outgrew their cramped Fjords, but this time they ignored Vinland. Instead they turned east to Russia and south to the coast of Europe, to become the 'Northmen' or Normans. The American coast off Newfoundland was left to the French and other fishing fleets. The bounty of the northern seas was to the French what gold was to the Spanish.

Theories that a Prince Madoc, son of the ruler of Gwynedd, travelled to Florida or the Mississippi in 1170 and left fragments of Welsh in Native tongues are generally discounted as myth.

2.

Enter Columbus

In 1488 maritime Europe received dramatic news. A Portuguese sea captain, Bartolomeu Dias, had arrived in Lisbon after rounding the Cape of Good Hope and opening a new sea route to India. The Portuguese had long voyaged down the west coast of Africa, establishing island colonies on Madeira, Cape Verde and the Azores. By 1450 they had begun exporting sugar from Madeira.

Existing trade with Asia, primarily of spices and precious stones, was along the ancient silk routes from China and Indonesia through India, Mesopotamia and the eastern Mediterranean. Though lucrative it was slow, costly and unreliable and had long been controlled by Venice and other powers on sea and land. The possibility of a new and secure route round Africa was dramatic.

In the crowd that greeted him was said to be a man with a more ambitious idea of reaching those same shores. A Genoese mariner, Christopher Columbus (1451–1506), now believed to be of Spanish and perhaps Jewish extraction, had for eight years promoted the idea of an alternative route to the distant east. His ambition was to reach China by sailing across the Atlantic.

Based on Arab reports, Columbus believed that the earth was smaller than the circumference estimated, with remarkable accuracy, by the Greek Eratosthenes in third-century BCE Egypt. That distance was roughly 25,000 miles. Columbus and his sources claimed that this was a third too big. He thus viewed China as extending much further east than it did, and thought it could be reached in just a few weeks of sailing west.

13

Columbus sought sponsorship in the capitals of Europe, including at the courts of Italy and France. None was interested. In 1491 his brother travelled to England to see if Henry VII might give support, but he was captured by pirates and returned empty-handed. The last hope lay with Spain. The marriage in 1469 of Isabella of Castile to Ferdinand of Aragon had united Iberia under one kingdom. In 1479 the Treaty of Alcáçovas settled a long-running conflict between Spain and Portugal. It recognized Portugal's monopoly on trade in the Atlantic south of the Canary Islands, but granted Spain the Azores and the unknown seas to the north.

In 1489 Ferdinand and Isabella completed their unification of Spain as a Catholic kingdom by evicting the Moors from their centuries-old occupation of Granada and ordering the conversion or expulsion of Spain's remaining Muslims and Jews. They agreed to celebrate their ascendancy by backing Columbus. The one proviso was that he obey Alcáçovas and stay north of Portugal's Atlantic sphere of interest. The message was explicit: 'The limits signed in the sharing of Alcáçovas should not be overcome.'

Columbus now needed to convince a crew that his Asian destination was indeed just weeks away. Many were attracted, albeit for contrasting motives. To some his mission was mercenary. Most sailors were fortune-seekers, and there was no question that trade with the spice islands of the Far East was lucrative. While the sea route now plotted by Dias was a boon, it was also Portuguese. An alternative and possibly much shorter route would be welcomed by the Spanish.

Others saw opportunities for religious evangelism. Columbus might find, if not China, then a new country and a new heathen land fit for conversion to Christianity. Glory would attach to its achievement. To others still, the mystery of adventure was romance enough. As far back as when ancient Rome ruled, the writer Seneca had declared that 'an age will come when the ocean will loosen the chain of things and a huge land will lie revealed'. It was in this spirit that the first boy and girl born to Portuguese who settled Madeira in the 1420s are said to have been christened Adam and Eve.

By the spring of 1492 Columbus had assembled three ships, the *Pinta*, the *Niña* and the *Santa Maria*, and set sail, restocking in the Canaries in August before heading west. Two months later in October, with their crews on the brink of mutiny and demanding a return home, they saw land. A relieved Columbus called it San Salvador. He was so convinced that he had found Asia that, on his first landfall, he is said to have sent a Chinese interpreter ashore. He likewise called the Native people 'Indians' assuming them to be occupying what were then the East Indies of south-east Asia. The name stuck.

Columbus's perseverance was relentless. He went on from San Salvador, now the Bahamas, to set up a base on the island of Hispaniola, which now comprises Haiti and the Dominican Republic. There he left colonists and moved on to what is now Cuba – which he believed initially to be Japan – before sailing home to a hero's welcome. He returned to the Caribbean a year later with 1,500 colonists to find the Native people had destroyed and massacred his colony. He responded with a massacre in kind.

The result was to be a rush of voyages in Columbus's wake, leading to the development of what came to be called the Columbian Exchange. The Spanish brought with them horses, chickens, cows and cereals such as rice and wheat. They returned with gold, potatoes, chocolate, tobacco and maize. But the Spanish also brought annihilation in the form of smallpox, measles, cholera and influenza. These diseases shattered the indigenous populations of the Caribbean, also rendering them inefficient as slaves. Within thirty years, disease-resistant Africans were being imported in ever-increasing numbers by the Spanish to work the island plantations.

For all his endeavours, Columbus was not a popular figure. His tenacity was extraordinary but his crews found him stubborn and unpleasant. One biographer, Felipe Fernández-Armesto, admits that 'a lifetime of study has not led me to like Columbus: he was mendacious, egotistical, irrational, self-righteous, humourless, and mean'. He was brutal to the Caribbean natives and party to the creation of what became the world's most extensive slave economy. When he later brought five hundred Native slaves as a gift to Queen

Isabella in Spain – two hundred of them dying en route – she was so shocked she sent them home.

Columbus himself sailed the Atlantic four times. He visited one island after another, as well as the coasts of Honduras and Panama, but he never touched the North American mainland. He retained until his death a belief that he was somewhere in Asia, always searching for a new route west. He retired to Spain, complaining that he never received the treasure he felt was his due. He does not rank among history's most popular heroes.

Spain's discovery was enough to stir rival instincts across Europe. In 1494 papal mediation updated the Treaty of Alcáçovas with the Treaty of Tordesillas. This stipulated that any new lands discovered across the Atlantic would be Spanish west of a line down the middle of that ocean 'from pole to pole'. This was equidistant between Portugal's Cape Verde Islands and Columbus's landfall in the Bahamas. Any land east of the line would remain Portuguese. Just as Spain had been excluded from the coast of Africa, so Portugal was excluded from new worlds to the west. The 'line of Tordesillas' did have one unintended consequence. Unknown to its authors, the line of longitude to the south sliced through the eastern coast of Brazil, which accordingly fell to Portugal.

This was duly claimed by Pedro Cabral in 1500. Hence to this day Brazil's language is Portuguese while the rest of South America speaks Spanish. Indeed it was an Italian explorer, Amerigo Vespucci, who conducted a series of cartographic expeditions to South America for Portugal between 1497 and 1504. He mapped his journeys and recorded his discoveries with a vivid imagination. On one trip in 1501 he lost a sailor who went ashore and was killed and reputedly eaten by Native people, conveyed in gruesome illustrations to the map.

Vespucci freely assigned names to this 'New World'. At a loss what to call a Brazilian river estuary he named it after the date, Rio de Janeiro. To the north Lake Maracaibo so reminded him of Venice that he christened its location as Little Venice or Venezuela. His maps were published in an edition of 1,000 and became widely consulted. As for the continent, Vespucci signed his maps as was customary with his Christian name in Latin: Americus. Plausible legend gives to this practice the use of his name for the continent depicted. Rarely has a cartographer been so richly celebrated.

Portugal's example was soon followed by others. In 1497 England's Henry VII commissioned the Venetian John Cabot (1450–99) to explore a different westward route to Asia, following the Vikings beyond Greenland. Cabot organized his expedition from Bristol, whose sailors were England's most adventurous. They were known to have visited Persia to the east – the Bristol church of St Mary Redcliffe has a probably Islamic arch – and Iceland to the west. In the latter, Bristolians would have heard of lands across the Atlantic, such as those in the Greenland sagas.

Cabot reached the Canadian coast but failed to make contact with any Native people or establish a colony. He named his 'newfound land' for England, planting an additional banner for the Pope, and returned to a reward from Henry of £10. There were believed to have been further voyages by Bristol adventurers but with little result. With Henry VII's death in 1509 the venture expired.

Columbus's base on Hispaniola was rebuilt in 1502 and is considered the earliest European settlement in the Americas. Here the first bishopric was established and expeditions were launched to Puerto Rico, Cuba and Mexico. The largest Caribbean island of Cuba was settled in 1511, though two-thirds of the Native population was wiped out by smallpox and measles.

In 1519, just three decades after Spain's arrival in the New World, a Cuban official named Hernán Cortés (1485–1547) set out on an expedition into the American mainland to claim the Aztec empire for Spain. He was of a generation of young Spanish junior noblemen eager for adventure beyond the bounds of Castilian society. Their enterprise was extraordinary. These were wholly unknown lands and they were travelling with tiny numbers of soldiers – Cortés had just five hundred – to confront tens of thousands of potentially hostile indigenous people. Cortés was arrogant and disobedient, defying orders from the governor of Cuba, Diego Velázquez, to abandon his mission. When his army threatened mutiny and a return home, he scuttled his fleet off the Mexican coast.

Over the course of 1519 Cortés negotiated and fought his way across Mexico, finally subduing the Aztecs and destroying their capital, Tenochtitlan, which he rebuilt as Mexico City. The last king, Moctezuma, was killed. Such was the anarchy of the new Spanish empire that Cortés then had to fight off a challenge from Velázquez to his governorship of Mexico. It became New Spain.

In 1529 another conquistador, Francisco Pizarro (1478–1541), then mayor of Panama City, pushed into South America and a year later reached the gold-rich empire of the Incas, stretching down the Andes to Chile. Within two years and with an army of barely two hundred soldiers he defeated an Inca army reputedly of 50,000. His chief advantages lay in guns and horses. He held the emperor, Atahualpa, hostage in his Peruvian capital of Cuzco and, despite receipt of a ransom of a chamber filled with gold, executed him. Spain's empire was eventually to occupy all of Central America and a third of South America. To its conquistadors, it had seemed an easy supremacy over indigenous peoples who were poorly armed and vulnerable to new diseases.

That said and unlike later European colonists, relatively few Spaniards saw America as their new home. They did not seek land to farm or goods to trade. They were sailors, soldiers and priests, explorers and conquerors. They sought gold and glory, for themselves and for the Spanish monarchy in whose name their colonies were founded. Their priests were avid for converts to the Catholic Church. As a result, the North American coastline along the shore of the Caribbean and the Gulf of Mexico held little appeal. It appeared to offer no gold and only a possible supply of slaves.

None the less, in 1528 an expedition led by the conqueror of Cuba, Pánfilo de Narváez, landed in what was to become Florida with permission from Madrid to seize the coast westwards 'as far as the Pacific', wherever that might be. It was the first intended European conquest of North America. Yet Narváez met with one disaster after another. The Apalachee and Seminole tribes were sufficiently strong to wear down Narváez's party, its survivors becoming virtual slaves to the Native people. When a handful eventually escaped to Cuba they told of no gold and no empire like the Aztec to conquer. There was only a seemingly endless land occupied by small groups of Native people, some hostile, some not.

Occasional adventurers followed Narváez, but few with any success. The most concerted expedition was under Hernando de Soto (*c.*1500–42). In 1524, still in his twenties, he had taken part in the conquest of Nicaragua and joined Pizarro's expedition to Peru. Within ten years he had become governor of Cuzco. De Soto returned to Spain laden with a private fortune, and received a commission from the king to lead a new expedition to the North American mainland.

De Soto's enterprise was better prepared than Narváez's and was clearly an attempt to bring the northern territories under Spanish dominion. Setting off in 1539, de Soto led nine ships carrying more than six hundred soldiers, priests and even potential settlers. They were attended by a number of Aztec-European mestizos, who appeared to have better resistance than most Native people to western diseases. They landed at Tampa Bay and headed north into present-day Georgia, where they found a survivor of Narváez's expedition who became their interpreter. De Soto was vulnerable to what grew to be a ploy against the Spaniards by the Native people, who told them that quantities of gold lay somewhere over the hills to entice them away.

The expedition, now known as the 'de Soto's trail', lasted three years. It travelled through what is now Florida, Georgia, the Carolinas and Tennessee before turning south to Alabama and the Mississippi River. The going was severe and often violent. De Soto seized Native men as slaves and Native women to serve the soldiers. He fought two pitched battles, involving the massacre of two Native tribes, the Timucua of Florida and the Alabama Mabilans. The Battle of Mabila in 1540 was said to be among the most lethal encounters in Native American history. Some 3,000 people died, many in the burning of the fortified town of Mabila. A measure of the tribes' growing militancy was that the Spanish eventually lost two hundred men and much of their supply train.

De Soto dared not retreat for fear of humiliation back in Spain. He led his dwindling party across the Mississippi River, where he himself died of fever. The survivors travelled west until they reached present-day Texas. Here the Native tribes, the Comanche and Apache, famed for their warrior culture, proved too much for them. By 1542 three hundred or so Spaniards, many clothed only in animal skins, had retreated to Mexico. The expedition had found no gold to plunder and no empire to conquer.

This did not deter others. In 1540–42 another conquistador, Francisco Vázquez de Coronado, led an expedition inland from the Gulf of Mexico through present-day Arizona. He was the first European to explore the Colorado River, the Rio Grande and the Grand Canyon and reach what is now Kansas. These expeditions, including others up the Californian coast, aimed at matching those of Cortés and Pizarro into central and southern America. While they established Spanish interest in the territory – indeed including it in New Spain – they found little by way of gold. They brought soldiers and priests and built forts and churches, but they rarely imported the essence of the true colony: settlers, merchants and farmers.

The most lasting Spanish settlement was along the Florida coastline at St Augustine. Founded in 1565, it is claimed as the earliest European base in North America. It wiped out a neighbouring French Protestant Huguenot settlement for being 'a Satanic sect', but was itself overwhelmed by England's Francis Drake in a piratical raid in 1586.

At the end of the century in 1598 another Spaniard, Juan de Oñate, was determined to be a successful exception. He progressed up the Rio Grande through the lands of the Pueblo Native people and brought with him five hundred colonists. His intention was to found a permanent settlement led by the Franciscan order of priests. Oñate was married to a mestizo descendant of the Aztec emperor Moctezuma, and in each Pueblo town he would hold elaborate rituals of conversion and compulsory submission to Spanish authority. But the Native people had no interest in Oñate's missionary intentions, nor in his parading a naked body executed on a cross. They were devoted to their own worship of Corn Mother and Thought Woman, the first responsible for their maize crop, the seeds for which were given by the second, the founding goddess of their Acoma tribe.

The venture led to disaster. In the ancient town of Acoma Pueblo, reputedly five centuries old, a dispute led to a skirmish and the killing of a dozen settlers. Oñate's retribution was to put to death eight hundred Native people. He also ordered the twenty-year enslavement of every young male while every older male had a foot cut off. The Pueblos were stunned by the atrocity. Oñate's superiors, on hearing of it, instantly recalled him to Spain.

Spain's colonization, first of the south-east and then of the south-west of America, was everywhere incidental. It nowhere took root. That of the English and French in the American north-east was initially no more successful. French and British sailors had long fished the seas off the Grand Banks of Newfoundland. The French sent expeditions to what is now Canada down the Hudson River in 1524 and the St Lawrence in 1534. None led to substantial colonies, though they allowed France to declare the land Francesca after its king, Francis I. The French also attempted colonies to the south in Florida and Brazil, but both were wiped out, by the Spanish and Portuguese respectively. In short, northern America seemed to defy conquest.

All this activity did not pass unnoticed in England. A Tudor lawyer-geographer, Richard Hakluyt (1553–1616), was an early champion of American colonization. He wrote that his country was neglecting opportunities that could relieve an overcrowded England and add to its trading prosperity. The English should 'have the grace to set fast footing in such fertile and temperate places as are left as yet unpossessed'. It would also sow seeds of Protestantism where the Spanish were embedding Catholicism.

In 1578 the challenge was tentatively taken up by Elizabeth I. After initial scepticism she granted Sir Humphrey Gilbert a permit to 'discover and charter' anywhere that was 'not possessed of any Christian prince . . . agreeable to the forms of the laws and policies of England'. This would duly lead to the 'inhabiting and planting of our people in America'. In two voyages beset by misfortune Gilbert reached Newfoundland but failed to establish a colony. He died in the course of the second.

The next effort came from a more ambitious explorer. In 1579 an English sailor turned privateer named Francis Drake led a circumnavigation of the world, raiding anything Spanish that came his way. The remarkable voyage – only the second round the world in history – took him up the California coast to Marin County and then Oregon. These he claimed for England as New Albion, though he left little evidence of possession. Anglophile Californians have been claiming it for Britain ever since.

There now appeared another of Elizabeth's buccaneering favourites, Walter Raleigh. He had won his spurs in the contested English 'plantation' of Ireland, involving the settlement of English and Scottish Protestants in predominantly Catholic territory. In 1584 Elizabeth authorized him 'to discover, search, find out and view such remote heathen and barbarous lands, countries and territories . . . to have, hold, occupy and enjoy'. She would not let him go himself – he subsequently married one of her ladies-in-waiting to her fury. Instead Raleigh despatched seven ships and six hundred men on their own. They settled a colony on the island of Roanoke near Chesapeake Bay, off a land that Raleigh named Virginia after his 'Virgin Queen'.

The colony, which required three visits to establish, was wracked with dissent and inexperience at feeding itself. It was complicated by the absence of the expected gold and the ambition of some colonists to use it as a base to attack passing Spanish ships. A supply expedition in 1588 was crucially delayed by the Armada campaign in England. By 1590 the local Croatan and Secotan tribes had turned hostile and a final relief expedition found the colony wrecked and deserted. Legend surrounded the colonists' fate, including one that they had merged with the Native people and produced the first European Americans. Roanoke became England's 'lost colony'. Neither archaeological nor genetic evidence of it survives.

The failure of Roanoke dented Tudor England's enthusiasm

for America. Since the country had been at war with Spain over much of Elizabeth's reign, her courtiers found it more profitable to seek booty rather than settlement. So-called privateers were effectively pirates enjoying, or claiming to enjoy, authority from their monarch. They were content to attack any enemy of the state for their – and her – personal gain. They shared in the wealth of the New World by raiding Spanish galleons.

While this was to cause Spain much annoyance, it did little to dent its supremacy in the continent. By the end of the sixteenth century there was no argument. Seen from Europe, the Americas were the domain of Spain, even if it had shown little interest in their permanent settlement.

3.

The English Arrive

1607–1672

America's initial appeal to Europe lay in gold. That meant South America and access to it through the Caribbean and the land awarded to Spain under the Treaty of Tordesillas. The Spanish land to the north had already been christened New Spain. That dominance began to be challenged with the death in 1603 of Elizabeth I of England and her succession by the Stuart James I. A year later at the Somerset House Conference in London, James won Spanish recognition of England's Protestant crown in return for an end to the 'disruption' of Spain's transatlantic trade with America by English privateers.

The forward-looking James now turned his attention to the opportunities America might afford. Though North America was formally Spanish, its north-eastern coastline was treated as open to general colonization. In 1607 James authorized three ships to sail to Chesapeake Bay, north of the failed Roanoke settlement, where they were to found a new colony to be known as Jamestown.

While Spain's holdings were in the ownership of the king, England's were privatized under royal charter. Jamestown was thus financed by one of two Virginia companies of 'adventurers'. The Virginia Company of London was approved in 1606 by Parliament, and in 1609 its charter was extended to found colonies up the east coast from Chesapeake to present-day Canada. A second Company of Plymouth went to Maine and a third at Cuper's Cove in Canada was later abandoned. The Virginia Company's remit ran 'from sea to sea', supposedly the entire continent east to west. Early maps show all eastern America as 'Virginia'.

Jamestown's colonists were not ideal frontiersmen. Half were described as 'diverse knights, gentlemen, merchants and others', the 'others' being servants and labourers. Many were layabouts and almost all refused to work the land. There were no women until a Mistress Forrest and her maid arrived a year later. The intention was to convert the local Powhatan tribe to Christianity and live off their produce. One colonist stated that the ambition was 'to recover out of the arms of the Devil a number of poor and innocent souls wrapt up unto death in almost invincible ignorance'. The Native people were sure to be grateful and generous in return.

The Jamestown colonists were thus no more prepared for the harshness of colonial life than those of Roanoke before them. They brought inadequate supplies while the Powhatan proved unwelcoming hosts and disinclined to offer food. Conditions were terrible and within six months half the colonists were dead, mostly of malaria and starvation. A conflict with the Native people then culminated in the capture of the colony's leader, John Smith. Legend has it that his clubbing to death was averted only by pleas from the daughter of the Powhatan chief, a thirteen-year-old named Pocahontas (*c.* 1596–1617). Whether Smith and Pocahontas were personally close seems doubtful, though such became the stuff of legend. Smith was later injured and returned to England.

Jamestown received three convoys over two years but they merely burdened it with more mouths to feed. One ship was wrecked on the uninhabited island of Bermuda, its crew settling it and rendering it a British territory to this day. By 1609 Jamestown's now five hundred colonists were effectively at war with the Powhatan and on the point of collapse. That winter was known as the Starving Time. Only sixty people survived, and excavated burials have revealed signs of cannibalism.

By the spring of 1610 the colonists had had enough and resolved to go home. They embarked and were already sailing downriver when they met another relief convoy led by the company's newly appointed governor and principal investor, Lord De La Warr. Accompanied by a platoon of soldiers, he turned them round and restored the colony, though he stayed barely a year before falling sick and returning home. The local river and later the adjacent state were named Delaware after him.

Jamestown was now stabilized under a new leader, Samuel Argall, though relations with the Powhatans remained hostile. In the course of one raid in 1613, Pocahontas was seized by the colonists as a hostage. She was later baptized into the Protestant Church and married a settler, John Rolfe (c.1585–1622), giving birth to a son. Rolfe was an inventive farmer who succeeded in producing the first soft and sweet type of tobacco to be grown in South America.

The arrival of Rolfe's tobacco in England caused a sensation and established the Virginia Company with a monopoly in its supply. This gave the colony the serious commercial boost it had so far lacked. In 1616 the company invited Rolfe and Pocahontas to England to promote further investment. They arrived with a small retinue of Powhatans to be feted as symbols of concord between England and the New World. Pocahontas met King James, attended a royal masque and was depicted in Stuart dress. Tragically, the girl's life came to an abrupt end when she died a year later at Gravesend on her way home, aged just twenty-one.

Pocahontas's son Thomas did return to Virginia, where his daughter created a dynasty sufficiently plentiful to enable countless Virginians to claim descent. Pocahontas thus ranked among the early 'founding Americans' and her fanciful relationship with Smith, rather than Rolfe, was elevated into a symbolic bond between old America and new. She was the first Native American to appear on a US stamp (in 1907). In 1995 a Disney cartoon propelled her to even greater fame. No Americans were to become as celebrated as the Order of the First Families of Virginia, descended from these earliest Jamestown settlers.

Lest Rolfe set a trend, in 1619 the company sent a ship from London carrying ninety young women to ease a chronic shortage of wives. The right, officially to their labour, was sold on the Jamestown quayside to male colonists, to repay the cost of their passage. Given the colony's absence of cash, the going price was said to be

125 pounds of tobacco. While these presumably volunteer women were being 'sold into marriage', poor male migrants paid for their own transhipment by indenture to the plantation owners. They would agree to work from four to seven years to pay for their crossing before being freed of their bond.

There was soon no way the supply of migrants could meet the demand for labour from the tobacco plantations. Native people were rarely employed, as they were found to be acutely vulnerable to European diseases. The Caribbean market to the south now offered an alternative. African slaves had for some time been trafficked to the islands' sugar estates. In 1619 Rolfe recorded the arrival in Jamestown of 'a Dutch man-of-warre that sold us 20 negars'. These people had been brought not from Africa but from markets in the Caribbean. Those in Jamestown were initially employed on similar terms to indentured labourers from England. Some slaves were later freed and were even able to buy land. By 1621 Virginia was sending England 370,000 pounds of tobacco annually.

At the same time Jamestown's corporate governance went in a different direction from that of the Spanish colonies, which were essentially under military rule. The new settlement was granted a substantial measure of autonomy. Below the appointed governor was a 'general assembly' of six councillors and twenty-two burgesses who would be elected by the owners of plantations covering fifty acres or more. They adopted a code of civil discipline on such matters as Sabbath observance, modesty in dress and hard work. The assembly also acted as a judicial court for the colony. There was no reference to royal or imperial prerogative. From the start, Virginia's development was for Virginians to decide. The colony's assembly, now proudly declared to be 'the oldest law-making body in the western hemisphere', first met on 30 July 1619. To some Americans this marks the foundation date of the nation, both as the dawn of democracy and as the year of the arrival of the first African-Americans.

Meanwhile other European states were showing an interest in this quarter of the New World. Chief among them were the French, now sending three hundred ships annually to fish the Grand Banks.

Only when the newcomers strayed inland in search of fur did the local Native people resist. When in 1608 Samuel de Champlain matched the English by founding a French colony at Quebec on the St Lawrence River he was exceptional in believing success would lie in building close relations with the Native people. He adopted three girls of the Montagnais tribe, naming them Faith, Hope and Charity, and he allied himself to the Wyandots in their running battles with Mohawks. Conflict was mostly over access to the fur trade.

The result was that the French colonies in what became Canada were unlike those of the English and Spanish to the south. From the start they acknowledged the status and the rights of the Native people. Critical was the rise of the Iroquois 'Five Nations' League, including the Mohawk and the Seneca, on a wide sweep of territory between the Appalachians and the Great Lakes. Over the course of the seventeenth century this league became strong enough to subjugate lesser tribes and extend its power across much of the north-east. A feature of the subjugation was the so-called mourning wars, usually ordered by clan matriarchs to avenge lost offspring and reinforce the ranks of the tribal armies, now increasingly devastated by European diseases resulting from contact with colonists.

By the middle of the century, the Iroquois League could field 2,000 men armed with flintlock guns traded for fur. To Hämäläinen, 'no other indigenous nation or confederacy had ever reached so far, conducted such an ambitious foreign policy or commanded such fear and respect'. They strove to take control of the fur trade and 'blended diplomacy, intimidation and violence, creating a measured instability that only they could navigate'. It was a coherent resistance, potentially strong enough to reverse the advance of European colonization. The small and scattered French settlements were at its mercy.

Champlain's attempted colonization of the St Lawrence initially failed. New immigration was negligible, with just a few hundred French occupying Quebec. A second colony was founded at Montreal in 1642 and a formal treaty with the Iroquois was reached in 1653. This changed with the reign of Louis XIV (r.1643–1715), when migration resumed. In 1663 Louis sponsored the importation of eight hundred young French women to boost the population; called *les filles du roi*, they were awarded dowries by the king. They had been carefully selected, chosen via recommendations from local priests and some coming from impecunious noble families. The ships called at the three colonies on the St Lawrence with the first, Quebec, reputedly gaining the pick of the crop. The venture worked and Quebec's population reached 6,700 in a decade.

Other newcomers were the Dutch, settling on the Hudson River in 1624 and also seeking good relations with the Iroquois. They based a trading station at Fort Orange, later Albany, in what is now upstate New York. Two years later the Dutch West India Company bought the island of Manhattan from the Lenape people for $24. This became the extensive colony of the New Netherlands, embracing a small Swedish colony, New Sweden, down the coast. Under persistent Mohawk harassment neither established a firm foothold, more a network of trade stations and alliances.

Soon, European wars were deciding the fate of some colonies. In the 1660s a series of conflicts between the Dutch and the English led the English to seize New Amsterdam. Under the 1667 Treaty of Breda, England then agreed to exchange possessions in the East Indies and Surinam in South America for the entirety of the New Netherlands. The territory was renamed New York after Charles II's brother, the Duke of York (the future James II), who bought personal ownership of it. Many Dutch remained. An attempt to rename the settlement of Haarlem in Manhattan as Lancaster failed, though an 'a' was dropped. English colonies soon lined the American coast as far south as the Florida border.

Back in England, new push factors were developing behind migration. The English Protestant Church might have broken with Roman Catholicism, but the Gunpowder Plot of 1605 indicated that its position was by no means secure from Catholic reassertion. The Church's hierarchy also remained hostile to many emerging Puritan sects. So-called Separatists, eager to break away completely from the hierarchy, were persecuted and in 1608 four hundred fled from Nottingham to Leiden in Holland, where freedom of worship was permitted. In time they found life among the Dutch intolerable and the threat from Catholic Spain in what is now Belgium ever present. In 1620 they and other Separatists in the English West Country liaised in a plan to cross the Atlantic and set up a new colony in Virginia in the manner of Jamestown.

They set out with the confidence of pilgrims. Aware of the suffering of Roanoke and Jamestown, they believed God would see them safe to 'a new Israel'. America was a 'spiritual Jerusalem', a promised land. If they did not succeed it would be God's decision. Two ships were intended to make the crossing, the *Mayflower* leaving from London and another, the *Speedwell*, leaving from Holland to join it in Plymouth. The *Mayflower*'s departure quay survives in Rotherhithe, marked by a modest sign in a neglected and strangely moving corner of east London.

There followed a chapter of mishaps. In Plymouth the *Speedwell* proved unseaworthy and the two ships twice had to turn back for repairs. The *Mayflower* eventually departed alone, carrying 102 passengers. Fewer than half of them were pilgrims, thirty-seven of them from Leiden, with the others being servants and hangers-on. The delay had meant that summer had turned to autumn and the crossing was rough. Desperately short of supplies, the *Mayflower* made landfall in November not, as intended, in Virginia but to the north on Cape Cod in Massachusetts. It went no further.

Shortly before disembarking, some forty 'heads of household' gathered below decks and drew up the 'Mayflower Compact', dictating how they would run their new settlement. There was no mention of any king, governor or church authority and the members declared God as their 'co-signatory'. They were radical Congregationalists, committed to being self-governing and subject to no outside authority, political or religious.

The Mayflower Compact was to become a sacred document on America's path to independence, awarded quasi-biblical status by some American historians. One of these, E. W. Bishop in the 1920s, reflected that 'the entirety of a new church, a new commonwealth, a new nation, all of which were to bless the world, were confined within the limits of the *Mayflower's* hold'. A more recent British historian, Rebecca Fraser, points out that their self-government was not so much ideological as practical. A collective consent 'was necessary in order to bind the community together; it was revolutionary by chance'. It would have to ensure cooperation in what promised to be a grim first year for their community. Congregationalism was their discipline, their glue.

The *Mayflower* moored at what was named New Plymouth after their port of departure, but the winter ice was bitter and the pilgrims had no alternative but to remain on board. Crops could not be sown and the newcomers depended for food on local Patuxet people of the Wampanoag tribe. An attempt was made to build huts on the ruins of an old native village, but by spring only fifty-three pilgrims, roughly half the original complement, were still alive.

A critical Native contact was made through a young man, Tisquantum, who had been enslaved by a previous British explorer, sold in Spain and reached London, possibly as a servant. From there he had somehow managed to return to the Patuxet. Nicknamed Squanto, his ability to speak English made him a crucial go-between. When the tribal leaders were inclined to evict the pilgrims, Squanto calmed relations and taught the colonists to grow crops and otherwise survive.

The Plymouth Colony struggled on. After twelve months, in November 1621, the pilgrims celebrated the anniversary with the Patuxet in what was later to become America's national day of Thanksgiving. As extreme Separatists, they were joined by few new migrants and, unlike Jamestown, did not prosper from a tradable product such as tobacco. Plymouth also lacked a royal charter. It was brought under the new Massachusetts Bay Company in the 1690s, headquartered not in London but in Boston.

These early colonies were born of an often desperate hope and were testaments to the survival of the fittest. For all their tribulations, their survival and prosperity made them legends back home.

To an England rife with religious intolerance under Charles I, America offered freedom of worship and a new beginning. England was hardly the most oppressive of European states. Its hardships were mild in comparison with the religious conflicts, starvations and massacres of the continental Thirty Years War (1618–48). But England's emigrants could afford to leave, and America held out a freedom nowhere in Europe could offer. The result was that in the 1630s alone no fewer than two hundred ships brought 20,000 English colonists to settle in New England, though the name had been first coined by John Smith in Virginia.

Whereas Jamestown had drawn a motley band of adventurers and speculators, the communities of the north-east appealed to a quite different migration, one imbued with Puritan religiosity and self-reliance. The Plymouth Colony itself was too exclusive to prosper, and nine years later it was overshadowed by a settlement fifty miles to its north. Boston was founded in 1630 by Isaac Johnson and William Blaxton and named after Johnson's Lincolnshire home, an abbreviation of St Botolph's town. The two men's alma mater, Cambridge University, gave its name to an adjacent settlement, bought from a Massachusetts matriarch for the price of £23 and a new coat every winter. The colony took its name from her tribe. Within six years a college was founded there to train clergy for this 'church in the wilderness', named after its earliest benefactor, John Harvard.

Boston's governor for twelve of its first twenty years was a Puritan lawyer and preacher, John Winthrop (1588–1649). His ego and fundamentalist rhetoric bestrode the colony's growth. He likened himself to Moses leading the Israelites out of Egypt and his preaching produced much of the phraseology of America's birth. To him England was a nation lost in hell, while the colony was the 'the light of the world' and the 'city upon a hill'. Colonists should be aware that 'all the eyes of the world will be upon us'. Winthrop asserted that God 'hath smitten all other churches before our eyes'. Like Noah's Ark, America alone was 'to be saved out of His general calamity'. The message was much influenced by Calvin's doctrine of the salvation of the chosen. The language fed itself into the oratory of successive American presidents, from Woodrow Wilson to Ronald Reagan in the twentieth century.

Another preacher and for twenty years president of the new Harvard College rejoiced in the name of Increase Mather. To him the sufferings of the *Mayflower* pilgrims had been proof of 'divine Providence, by the greatest miseries to prepare for the greatest mercies . . . Without doubt the Lord Jesus hath a peculiar respect unto this place and for this people.' America was uniquely blessed with God's covenant. This concept of exceptionalism was to run deep in America's sense of identity. It gave the New England colonists a self-confidence bordering on arrogance, not least when contrasted with their Virginian contemporaries.

Winthrop built himself a mansion in Boston and acquired a 600-acre farm. His leadership of the Massachusetts community stepped away from the collectivism of the Mayflower Compact. He was elected annually by a cabal of voters whom he selected from his church circle for their 'Godly behaviour'. Winthrop opposed any general assembly and saw democracy 'as the meanest and worst of all forms of government'. He even opposed the writing down of laws as 'repugnant to the laws of England'. Magistrates should be the law, and brutal punishments were ordered of those who offended his theology.

This led Winthrop to display precisely the characteristics of religious persecution that thousands of colonists had fled England to escape. Catholics and Anglicans were banned from Boston. A man was shipped back to England for erecting a maypole. A decade after Winthrop's death, three Quakers were executed and became the 'Boston martyrs'. In 1661 Charles II explicitly forbade the killing of Quakers but they remained to be whipped.

One colonist who disagreed with Winthrop was Roger Williams. He had settled in the town of Salem in 1631, where he became a missionary to the Native people, even learning the local dialect of Algonquian. He protested Winthrop's intolerance, authoritarianism and mistreatment of the indigenous population. Eventually expelled from Massachusetts, Williams bought land from the Narragansett

tribe to the south and set up a tiny colony on Rhode Island, adjoining Massachusetts.

Rhode Island was designed to be a haven of genuine rather than
professed tolerance. Williams insisted on Native rights and invited
to settle 'anyone molested, punished, disquieted or called in question for any difference of opinion in matters of religion'. Williams
became governor of Rhode Island in 1654 and kept his tolerance
intact. The colony defied all threats to its existence and remains the
smallest state in the union today.

4.
King Philip's War and the Hunger for Land

1672–1700

On one matter the colonies shared a common ambition, their need to expand. The Appalachian chain stretched from north to south down most of America's eastern seaboard, forming a natural western boundary for European settlement. That was indeed how the London authorities saw it. At this early stage in the growth of empire, its central purpose to England was trade. Hence as far as London was concerned there was no need for the American colonies to extend more than a few dozen miles inland. Governors arriving from London were forbidden to venture further west. In particular they were not to trespass on land already claimed by Spain or France beyond the Appalachians, nor were they to jeopardize relations with the Native peoples. If for no other reason, England could not afford to send soldiers to police contested territory. Never throughout the colonial period did London see its American colonies as more than coastal possessions.

Yet the colonists were hungry for land. Newly arrived farmers and land speculators were pushing westwards. Inevitably they met Native resistance. Relations could be good, as with the Pilgrims at New Plymouth, but they were often bad and rarely stable. Worse, where tribes fell out with each other, the colonists found themselves taking sides. Thus in 1636–8 a conflict between the Massachusetts Pequots and the adjacent Narragansetts and Mohicans saw the colonists side with the latter. They almost annihilated the Pequots with a brutality that shocked Native people and settlers alike, killing hundreds of women and children and selling others into slavery on Bermuda.

In 1675 the last concerted uprising of the New England tribes broke out across Massachusetts, New Hampshire, Connecticut and Rhode Island. It was known as 'King Philip's War' after the English name for Metacom, the *sachem* (chief) of the Wampanoag tribe, now in alliance with the Narragansett and others. Some Mohicans and Mohawks sided with the colonists. The main issue was the constant seizure of Native farms and villages, but others were harassment by Christian missionaries – including forced conversion – and a refusal by colonists to negotiate with women. Many Native tribes throughout America were matriarchies. One such matriarch, Quaiapen, led an attack on Rhode Island to recover a lost Narragansett corn cache. She was captured and killed and her followers were enslaved.

King Philip's War lasted from 1675 to 1678 and involved multiple guerrilla raids on colonial towns, with retaliatory colonist attacks on Native villages. Both sides became ever crueller. More than half New England's towns were attacked and twelve were destroyed, including the Rhode Island capital, Providence. The colony's governor, Williams, though long a friend of the Narragansett, saw his house destroyed in flames. After two years of conflict, at least 1,000 colonists and an estimated 3,000 Native people had been killed. Large numbers were enslaved locally or sent to slave markets in Bermuda and the Caribbean. At no point did the colonists receive military aid from England. More significant, this was the first time the individual colonies collaborated as a fighting force.

King Philip's War was the most traumatic event in New England's early colonial history. Its brutality – or at least that of the colonial soldiers towards the Native people – shocked the Christian conscience of many. One colonist, Mary Rowlandson, had been a captive of the Native Nipmuck. On her release she wrote a book, *The Sovereignty and Goodness of God*, in which she attempted to relieve the colonists of what she saw as their shame. They had so offended God that he had 'nourished the Indians to be a scourge to the whole land'. The book was widely read. Increase Mather had no doubt of the war's cause: 'that farms and merchandising have been preferred before the things of God'. The people of New England had departed from God's doing and descended into greed and moral failure.

Virginians to the south initially greeted King Philip's War with a certain glee, contemptuous of the religiosity of the Massachusetts Congregationalists. The governor of Virginia, Sir William Berkeley, declared the New Englanders so otherworldly that 'they might as well have been expected to be invaded by the Persian or the Mogul as by the Indians'. He spoke too soon. No sooner had New England been engulfed in violence than in the same year of 1675 tension erupted between the Virginians and the local Susquehannock. Native bands terrorized plantation houses, and were killed in retaliation. Colonists lived in fear for their lives.

This briefly led to dissident settlers demanding a war of extermination against the Native peoples. Their leader, Nathaniel Bacon, accused Berkeley of having 'protected, favoured and emboldened the Indians against His Majesty's loyal subjects . . . with invasions, robberies and murders committed upon us'. This led to a major civil war, with Bacon actually capturing Jamestown. Not until 1677 was peace restored, with Bacon dying and his co-conspirators hanged. The Susquehannock agreed to honour England's king in return for their land being respected and enslavement no longer being used as a punishment.

By 1680 the English colonists had all but suppressed Native resistance, at least on the coastal side of the Appalachian divide. In New England they were crucially assisted by an earlier smallpox epidemic probably brought by fishermen and wiping out some 90 per cent of the Native Americans. With the conversion of the New Netherlands into New York, the two groups of English colonies to its north and south were now united, from Boston to Delaware Bay. But while they were joined geographically, they became ever more divided socially and ideologically. The split was to dominate America's history into the nineteenth century.

At first the new colony of New York, or at least its owner, the Duke of York, had no truck with New England's tentative democracy. The duke refused to allow his domain an assembly. To him 'assemblies were of dangerous consequence . . . destructive to the peace of the government wherein they are allowed'. His own colonists disagreed and refused to pay the taxes he imposed. Without any means of enforcement, the duke was forced to back down. The result was a New York assembly called in 1683 to fashion probably the most democratic constitution at the time in the western world. It contained a bill of rights and a franchise extending to virtually every settled male citizen, though not to slaves.

Virginia's constitution had evolved in a different direction. Berkeley, appointed in London to govern the colony, advertised Virginia to Britons as specifically a place of refuge for Stuart victims of England's Civil War. Virtually all Virginia's leading families – forming an oligarchical council under Berkeley – were sons of English landed gentry who had crossed the Atlantic during the Civil War and Commonwealth. As the colony grew ever more prosperous from tobacco, its plantations took on the character of English country estates.

The colony also showed a loyalty to the English monarchy that was largely absent in New England. This was well illustrated in the choice of place names. The map of the South blossomed in variants of Stuart and then Hanoverian monarchs, Charles, James, Caroline, George and Charlotte. When in 1633 a group of English Catholics had considered settling in Virginia, they asked Charles I for a colony of their own across the Potomac. Their leader, the Catholic Lord Baltimore, duly founded a city that took his name. The colony was named Maryland in honour of Charles's Catholic queen, Henrietta Maria.

Meanwhile the North rejected monarchs in favour of the mostly Dissenter towns of East Anglia and the West Country: hence Boston, Stamford, Yarmouth, Exeter, Dartmouth, Barnstaple and Taunton. At the same time the richness of English nonconformity took comfortable root in denominations and sects across the Atlantic. There emerged Seekers, Ranters, Diggers, Levellers, Anabaptists, Soul Sleepers and Muggletonians. Some were tolerated as cohabitants, others sought refuge in enclaves of their own. The most controversial, and often the most persecuted, were George Fox's Quakers, their faith being in a God who abided within each individual with no priestly mediation.

Among their number was the young William Penn (1644–1718), whose father was a sea captain and an associate of Charles II. One day at court the king noticed that Penn's son had followed the Quaker belief in equality and failed to remove his hat in the king's presence. Rather than have him punished, the jovial monarch removed his own hat, explaining that 'it was customary in my presence for at least one person to be bare-headed'. He at least was not for persecuting Quakers.

Others were less tolerant. The young Penn was soon spending time in and out of jail for attending Quaker meetings. Then in 1681 he personally turned to the king for help in founding a Quaker colony in America, on the possibly tenuous grounds that the monarch owed his father money. Charles was generous, though he was not averse to ridding himself of troublesome Quakers. He granted Penn a large expanse of land in royal ownership to the north of Maryland and adjoining New York. Much of it was occupied by contesting Dutch and Swedish colonists. Though it included Native territories it amounted to 45,000 square miles. The king demanded as rent a proportion of any gold found on the land, an unlikely prospect.

Penn had trouble assembling a party of colonists sufficient to meet this challenge, and advertised the new settlement widely in Europe, notably in Germany. Apart from Quakers he welcomed Huguenots, Mennonites, Jews, Amish and even Catholics. In 1682 he sailed for Chesapeake Bay with 250 colonists and reached an early treaty with the Native Lenape tribe, later celebrated in a fine depiction of the signing by Benjamin West. This granted them the right of assembly, hunting and fishing in their traditional areas. Pennsylvania's liberal-minded assembly was also rare in declaring that land across the Appalachian Mountains should be left to the Native peoples in perpetuity. The pledge was not honoured.

The governorship of Penn's sylvan estate went to Penn himself, with sovereign power over the territory. He copied the northern colonies in instituting an elected bicameral assembly, as well as freedom of worship and trial by jury. Imprisonment was to be minimal, with rehabilitation and early release preferred. The principal settlement, Philadelphia, was to be, in Penn's oft-quoted words, a 'city of brotherly love' in a 'holy experiment of tolerance'. Its design reflected the grid of London's western suburbs, rich in greenery. One neighbourhood spoke German, another Welsh. Philadelphia was exceptionally popular and soon became the largest city in pre-revolutionary America.

Penn travelled back and forth to England while his handling of his business affairs grew ever more distressed. At one point he tried unsuccessfully to sell Pennsylvania back to the English crown. He eventually died penniless in one of England's Home Counties. Penn's grave at Jordans Meeting House near Chalfont St Giles in Buckinghamshire is a modest memorial to a man who did much to define America's character. His Pennsylvania sought at this early stage to bridge the emerging cultural divide between the northern colonies and the South.

Something Penn's new colony was unable to avoid was its proximity to the slave-owning South. This was already a rampant feature of the southern economy. Following Jamestown in 1619, only fifteen of the 150 plantations in Virginia had slaves, with a total numbered in the hundreds. By the end of the century there were an estimated 60,000 in America as a whole. Penn needed settlers and, though Quakers strongly opposed slavery, he knew he could not ban Pennsylvanians from owning them. At one point he owned some himself.

Slave-owning had begun in Jamestown as an extension of the indentured labour system, but owners soon began to acquire slaves not as potential citizens but as property. That was controversial enough. What appalled newcomers was how the slaves were treated. The worst conditions appeared to arise from slave managers recruited from the sugar plantations of Barbados, where slaves were considered little better than animals. In some places Native Americans were also enslaved, despite this being specifically outlawed by Charles II 'on any occasion or pretence whatsoever'.

A secretary to the London commission that vetted the new colonial charters and constitutions was none other than the liberal philosopher John Locke (1632–1704). He edited the approved constitution for the new province of Carolina, south of Virginia, in 1669. The document allowed settlers to expropriate Native land on the grounds that Native people occupied and hunted over it but were not strictly farmers. As for slaves, 'every freeman of Carolina shall have absolute power and authority over his negro slaves'. Locke himself took his payment in the form of shares in the slave-trading Royal Africa Company.

The Carolina constitution clearly conflicted with Locke's liberal principles as later set out in his *Two Treatises on Government*, a work that was to influence the shapers of America's constitution a century later. He did not defend slavery and went on to obstruct the licensing of slaves after the Glorious Revolution of 1688. He also defended slaves' rights against repression. Locke's apologists have pointed out that in the 1660s he was a lawyer approving the terms of a document. He was conforming to England's acceptance of slavery as custom and practice in a country far from home. Slavery was not at the time banned even in New England. There were slaves in New York and Boston's Mather family owned at least one slave.

The eleven American colonies at the turn of the eighteenth century shared a characteristic unfamiliar in many imperial territories of quasi-autonomy. Their governments had been shaped in the 1640s and 50s at the time of England's Civil War when England itself had debated what was once considered undebatable: democracy, or at least self-rule. The Putney Debates of 1647 discussed civil rights, universal franchise and parliamentary sovereignty. One speaker, Thomas Rainsborough, famously said that 'the poorest he that is in England hath a life to live as the greatest he', and should be free to consent to his form of government.

The reality was that England in mid-century had enough on its plate without being overly concerned by the form of government of its overseas possessions. The politician Edmund Burke (1729–97) later described this as 'a wise and salutary neglect'. Colonies began to elect governors from among their leading citizens. Democracy in America might have been in its infancy but it was developing fast.

Even so, the colonies remained reliant on and subject to London for their defence and foreign relations. Where relevant, those relations included trade and customs duties. On these matters, the colonies had no spokesmen in London. This meant that every decision that an English government was to make about America in the coming century would be made largely in ignorance of conditions on the ground. That ignorance was exacerbated by the weeks it took for messages to cross the Atlantic.

On trade, England's regulations were entirely self-interested. Some required that American exports be sent exclusively to England, others that they not be sent there, for fear of undercutting local producers. The latter applied particularly to fish. Meanwhile the colonies were suffering from an absence of financial management. They had no currency other than the rare silver-based Spanish peso or dollar coin, known as the 'piece of eight'. Mostly they had to depend for business on a chaotic barter economy. Technically illegal bills of credit were commonly exchanged. In the South tobacco warehouse receipts became a form of tender. As wives had been sold for tobacco in Jamestown, so a student at Harvard asked if he could settle his college fee with a cow.

In 1686 James II, still proprietor of New York, made a radical decision. His brother Charles II had indicated a wish to bring the colonies more under his control. Now James proposed that all those in New England come under one 'dominion of New England'. Their individual autonomies would end. It was significant that the supposedly loyalist southern colonies were left out of the dominion. James moved an official, Sir Edmund Andros, from governor of New York to Boston as the new dominion's governor. He also nominated the Church of England as America's Established Church – an explosive choice in Massachusetts.

Andros did not consult locally and was wholly insensitive to colonial opinion. Within two years he had the colonies up in arms, with even their militias refusing to obey him. Increase Mather, still a leader of Massachusetts opposition, took ship to London to petition James to reconsider. He arrived in October 1688 just as James was being toppled in the Glorious Revolution. Rumours that Andros intended to take his cause – and his new dominion – to join the ousted king in Paris caused a full-scale revolt in Boston. Andros was seized and imprisoned. He was later released and became governor of Virginia.

Both King Philip's War and the Boston Revolt suggested that the New England colonies were starting to think as one. During the war they had been forced to combine their militias against a collective Native insurrection. In the case of the revolt, the coalition was not military but political, against a threat to their colonial autonomies. But the colonies were at least united in the need to suppress Native opposition to their territorial expansion and in their desire to retain a diversity independent of the English crown.

For all this diversity America was still a frontier society struggling to find cultural depth. It found early roots in the colleges that were to proliferate across the colonies, training a new generation mostly of lawyers and clergymen. Harvard in 1636 was followed by Virginia's William and Mary College in 1693 and Yale in 1701. Based in large part on Oxford and Cambridge, they were steeped in theology and the classics, but they became influenced by the more progressive learning of the Scottish Enlightenment, in particular by David Hume and Adam Smith.

Printing and publishing were scarce and chiefly consisted of Bibles and religious material. The first book to be printed in America was one of psalms in 1640. Newspapers began to appear in Boston in the eighteenth century. The first, the *Newsletter*, founded in 1704, was full of news of Catholic misdeeds in Britain but almost nothing of America. There was a stark lack of music and paintings. Music was heavily reliant on folk and classical traditions imported from Europe. As for painting, great excitement greeted the arrival from London in 1728 of an artist named John Smibert (1688–1751) to open a studio in Boston. A pupil of England's leading portraitist, Sir Godfrey Kneller, he became the colony's first and leading portraitist. He came at the invitation of another newcomer, the British philosopher Bishop Berkeley, showing the power of the colony to attract a more diverse intelligentsia.

A grimmer cultural vitality broke out at the end of the seventeenth century in the Massachusetts town of Salem. In 1692 the town became obsessed with two girls aged nine and eleven who had screaming fits and were declared agents of Satan. As many as two hundred women and some men were soon being accused of practising witchcraft. The result was a court of inquiry and trials for witchcraft, leading to nineteen victims being hanged as witches. A man was crushed under stones. The judge declared that the people of Massachusetts 'should look upon themselves as under a divine probation'. Later research suggested that Salem at the time was afflicted with family feuds lurking beneath the hysteria.

Writing later in the nineteenth century, the author Harriet Beecher Stowe described the prevailing Calvinism of the time as 'one of profound, unutterable and therefore unuttered melancholy, which regarded human existence itself as a ghastly risk'. New England society might have been democratic but it was a democracy suffused with theological fear. In the case of Salem, the Massachusetts assembly took control and in 1711 declared the witch trials null and void. Compensation was even paid to the victims' families. The Salem trials were over in a matter of months, but they were a lasting warning of the danger of mob rule, particularly for American liberals.

Increase Mather's son, Cotton, played a leading role in the trials and was himself an embodiment of the Puritan spirit. He had a furious energy. He championed the rights of women, Native people and the enslaved, and was said to have authored 388 books. But his belief in witches and the Devil was his undoing. Over the course of the early eighteenth century Boston grew out of its Puritan roots to become intellectually the most dynamic as well as the most prosperous of American cities. Cotton Mather ended his days as its Savonarola. He bewailed the decay of Puritanism and laid the blame on money. He wrote that 'religion brought forth prosperity and the daughter destroyed the mother'.

5.

The Roots of Empire

For two centuries after Columbus a curtain had been slowly rising on a 'new' hemisphere as seen from Europe. Onto the stage had strutted one nation after another to claim the spotlight and flex imperial muscles. Nothing about the future was certain. The star player was still Spain. It was in command of virtually the whole of Central and most of South America. As for North America, the Treaty of Tordesillas had given Spain legal claim to the entire continent but its presence was near invisible. Conquistadors had established footholds in the south-west, though they barely strayed inland over territory inhabited by hundreds of indigenous tribes. It was the north-east coast that had seen the most colonial activity, being the focus not of Spanish but of French, Dutch, Swedish and most emphatically English colonization. Though the overwhelming majority of Europeans in North America now spoke English, they occupied only a narrow strip of territory. In this age of competing empires, the remainder of the continent seemed there for the taking. To anyone looking at a map of the Americas at the end of the seventeenth century, the prospect was mouthwatering.

With the turn of the seventeenth century Spain had become more active. Its sole colony at St Augustine in Florida, established in 1565, had spent half a century defending itself against Muscogee Creek resistance to colonial occupation of their land. In 1610, Spain decided to build a new town far to the west at Santa Fe near the Rio Grande under an enterprising new governor, Pedro de Peralta. It was an attempt to redeem Juan de Oñate's discredited colonization of the valley a decade earlier. Although no gold had been found, there were rumours of 7,000 Native people who had been converted to Christianity and were in need of protection.

Peralta brought with him eight Franciscan priests and laid out a spacious settlement. It consisted of houses round a plaza with a governor's palace, chapel, prison and arsenal. Santa Fe was the oldest Spanish city west of the Mississippi and its palace the oldest building. In this corner of New Spain, Christianity was considered as effective a tool of authority as the sword. Spain thus staked its claim to the American west.

Over the course of the next few decades, further Spanish expeditions ventured up America's western coast, whose fertile soil might have made it Spain's answer to England's eastern colonization. Missions and forts were established in Baja California. Military bases were built at San Diego, Monterey and San Francisco. Yet the region never saw development of any intensity outside these centres. Indeed, Peralta's orders at Santa Fe were to confine his activities strictly to the religious conversion of Native people.

At no point did Spain seek to create in this part of America the equivalent of another New England or another Virginia. As already noted, the reason must lie in the absolute control over these colonies of Spain's royalist and ecclesiastical hierarchies. There seemed little urge to generate the popular enterprise that colonies needed in order to prosper. But then, as we shall see, the key to imperial outreach lay in the ambition of the people in whose hands colonization was placed.

Spain's chief rival in any advance across America was France. Despite their difficulties with the Iroquois, the French still laid claim in the north to the basins of the St Lawrence and Ohio rivers. They could dream of a territory stretching from Canada across to the Great Lakes and down the Mississippi to the Gulf of Mexico. This would dwarf the size of England's coastal strip and open up land that would eventually serve as a breadbasket of the world.

In 1669–70 an explorer, René-Robert La Salle, travelled from Quebec into Ohio and the upper waters of the Illinois River. Then, in 1682, obsessed with Columbus and finding a new route to China, he led a flotilla of canoes across the Great Lakes. Guided by the Seneca people, he discovered the Niagara Falls and built forts along the way. He reached the Chicago River and headed south, eventually reaching the Mississippi and founding Memphis. He confirmed that it flowed south towards Mexico, not, as he had fondly hoped, west to the Pacific.

La Salle claimed the entire basin for France, naming it La Louisiane after his king. It notionally covered territory from the Appalachians to the Rocky Mountains and from Canada to the Gulf of Mexico. The Mississippi was the natural highway of the American interior and was later to carry its agricultural wealth to the outside world. La Salle set a stone at its mouth declaring Louis XIV as in 'possession of all the nations, peoples, provinces, cities, towns, villages, mines, minerals, fisheries' of what he called New France. Here was indeed the making of a spectacular imperial domain, fit to compare with Spain's to the west and south.

As it was, on returning to France, La Salle found the king displeased. Louis thought the explorer mad to have travelled to such an inaccessible and potentially hostile place. In 1684 he was told to lead a second expedition to the Gulf of Mexico and settle a secure colony accessible to the sea on the coast of what is now Texas. This expedition failed even to find the mouth of the Mississippi. La Salle became increasingly unhinged, facing hostile Native people and a mutiny from his own men. He was eventually killed by one of them, and only a handful were ever seen again. France did not give up. It returned to the Gulf in 1718 and founded the settlement of New Orleans, named after Louis' younger brother, the Duke of Orléans.

For all that effort, Louisiana failed to develop into a French answer to England's Virginia. The requirement that settlers be loyal Catholics deterred the independence of spirit that had galvanized the English settlements. By the middle of the eighteenth century Louisiana's non-Native population was no more than 4,000 white and 5,000 black people, many of them freed slaves. Yet France remained in notional possession of a great crescent of the continent, sufficient to leave the coastal English colonies vulnerable to encirclement.

The emerging personality of those English colonies now came into focus. They had swallowed smaller Swedish and Dutch settlements but they remained disparate entities. They had no superior government, no collective authority or military force. They enjoyed no coherent defence against external threats, such as from the Native peoples. Their most urgent collective need was for the regulation of trade, but that was out of their hands in London, where their needs and interests were unrepresented and largely neglected. Spanish and French monarchs had been proud agents of colonization. To England, America was a land founded by enemies of its church and state. From the earliest times the American colonies could feel they were on their own. This had both disadvantages and advantages.

In the opening decades of the eighteenth century the English colonies saw tidal waves of immigrants. They became the continent's largest colonial population, the 260,000 in 1700 doubling every twenty-five years. One reason is that in New England they were formally welcomed not as tokens of great-power projection but as founders of a new nation. They were not there to seek gold or convert Native people; they were there to procreate, sow and harvest, to pray, learn and forge communities. Above all, they were there to stay.

In Massachusetts a local court would assemble new arrivals into groups each assigned to designated parcels of land up-country, arranged around new market settlements. They would be sworn in as citizens, the men told they would be liable for military service. Plots were allocated to each family and the local church and minister stood in place of a manorial lord. The colonists were then given equipment with which to start growing crops. Singles were discouraged from farming, as families were considered essential to the practice. Ten or more children were often the norm. New England could hardly have been less like New Spain or New France. No Founding Fathers emerged in Santa Fe or Quebec City.

The colonies were individually deep-rooted but collectively they were anything but stable. The New Englanders held fast to the traditions of their founders, but were vulnerable to the disputes familiar among those with passionate convictions. Leadership came from church elders, with an emphasis on religious observance, discipline and the sovereignty of the congregation. This created divisions which in turn led colonies to divide. Massachusetts at various stages spawned New Hampshire, Rhode Island and Vermont, while further south New Jersey, Delaware and Maryland went their separate ways. Connecticut was severely intolerant, with hanging ordained for twelve biblical sins, including bestiality, adultery and blasphemy. Counterfeiting money led to ear-cropping and the pillory.

There were frequent outbreaks of religious fervour. In the 1730s a movement called the Great Awakening saw thousands drawn to evangelical preaching. Yale University's eloquent Jonathan Edwards spoke of sinners as 'loathsome insects . . . held in the hand of God over the pit of hell. The Devil is waiting for them, hell is gaping for them, the flames gather and flash about them.' Migrant communities from Germany, the Netherlands, Sweden and Finland understandably preferred to settle in more placid upstate New York or in Pennsylvania.

In 1735 there arrived the English preachers Charles Wesley and his brother John, still in their twenties. Charles had an unfortunate time in Georgia, falling in love and being rejected. They were followed in 1738 by George Whitefield, who went on a year-long tour of America. He specialized in addressing large congregations outdoors, rousing his audiences to a near frenzy. What was to become American Methodism was a church whose popularity straddled the colonies and, coupled with the Great Awakening, embedded a lasting piety in American communities.

On a visit to South Carolina, Charles Wesley was traumatized to hear of a black woman thrashed unconscious and then scalded with hot wax, just for overfilling a teacup. He deplored such treatment and described the slaves as 'the outcasts of men, trodden down as dung upon the earth'. He was equally shocked by the owners, at the 'diabolical cruelty which these men (as they call themselves) daily practise upon their fellow creatures'. The colony's Slave Act laid down such punishments to slaves for misbehaviour as castration and loss of limbs or facial features. In addition no enslaved person could give evidence against a white person.

To many in England, Virginia and its neighbouring colonies remained pre-eminently British American colonies. Yet it was slavery that emerged as a dominant issue, capable sooner or later of tearing the English settlement of America in two. To the south a crisis arose as new settlers pushed down from Carolina into the territory soon to be known as Georgia, once contested between English and Spanish colonists.

Georgia had been settled as a trustee colony by an idealistic English MP, James Oglethorpe, in 1732, for 'worthy poor' English migrants, largely from debtors' prisons. It was intended as a buffer colony between Carolina and Spanish Florida, with which the English were in regular conflict throughout the 1740s. Oglethorpe was a reformist disciplinarian. He refused to allow slaves in Georgia. Liquor and even lawyers were banned as signs of degeneracy. This could not last. Pressure from Georgia's new colonists soon forced the trustees in London to change their minds, and the House of Commons reversed the colony's charter in 1750. No fewer than 18,000 slaves were imported into Georgia in the next twenty-five years, explicitly permitted by London.

As for where the North ended and the South began, Pennsylvania found itself torn. In 1763 confusion arose over the colony's border with Maryland, Delaware and Virginia due to an inaccurate map used by Charles II to assign land to William Penn. Two English surveyors, Charles Mason and Jeremiah Dixon, were appointed to plot a boundary from the sea to the Appalachians. This border, fixed in 1767, was named the Mason–Dixon Line and acquired significance as the notional divide between slave states and what became 'free' states. Such a boundary was rendered ever more controversial as it was later extended westwards.

North of the Mason–Dixon Line colonies remained free to treat slaves as their self-governing assemblies chose. Some, such as Vermont,

Pennsylvania and Massachusetts, voted for abolition. Slaves tended to be little different from house servants and some black people were free. Some northern slave-owners were to free them in their wills. In New York freed black people eventually outnumbered those that were enslaved. The reality was that English America was starting to look like not one potentially united colony – or nation – but two.

As for the Native peoples still occupying large areas of the Appalachian hinterland, they remained a destabilizing presence. While the north-east Algonquian, Lenape and Mohican tribes had mostly succumbed to land purchase or seizure by the colonists and moved away, this was less true of those further south. Here the Cherokee, Choctaw, Chickasaw, Creek and Seminole became known as the Five Civilized Tribes. They grew crops and developed their own townships, and many began to read and dress in the style of the occupiers. Some became Christians and some even kept slaves. But there was no law or constitutional provision to protect them should settlers invade their land.

Relations with the Native peoples remained a source of conflict between the colonies and Great Britain, now so named after England's union with Scotland in 1707. London was firmly and explicitly against the rest of continental America becoming part of its emergent empire. Its primary concern, and it was ever more urgent, was with the activities of the French moving down from Canada and now building forts and other bases in Ohio. The French were also finding ready allies among Native tribes opposed to the colonists' westward expansion across Appalachia – in defiance of London – for the simple reason that they sought land and the French did not.

In any prospective war between Britain and France, the Ohio valley was the obvious theatre for an imperial contest on the American continent, with tribal loyalty a factor in any conflict. It was precisely the predicament Britain's chief minister at the time, William Pitt, wanted fervently to avoid. It was also a predicament in which, for the first time, the colonists could see a joint interest in collective action.

6.

The Path to Revolution

1756–1775

If the creation of the modern United States can be attributed to any single event it is to the Seven Years War of 1756–63. It began as a European conflict fuelled by territorial ambitions and dynastic alliances. The expansionist Frederick of Prussia fought Austria, with hostilities spreading to embrace Russia, France, Spain and even Britain. William Pitt had, like Sir Robert Walpole before him, struggled to stay out of such conflicts, Britain having no territorial issue in European disputes. But overseas was a different matter. The age of trading empires was stirring new ambitions and the fighting spread ever further round the globe. Historians have called this the true 'first world war'.

London could not ignore the French presence on the Ohio River, hovering over the horizon from Britain's New England. The French had built a fort at Duquesne commanding the western flank of the Appalachians. They were there in alliance with the Algonquin Wabanaki Confederacy north of the Massachusetts colony, and with the Lenape and the Shawnee. Given an impending state of war between the two imperial powers, this constituted a serious threat.

In 1754 London sent troops to drive the French out of Ohio, a territory to which Britain had no claim. The force was primarily composed of local colonial militias, each separately structured. It had the support of the Iroquois, always ready to take up arms against their Algonquin foes, but on this distant frontier command was difficult and Britain's largely amateur militias lacked the professionalism of the French forces. The operation was a failure and the British had to retreat. One officer in the Virginia militia was a twenty-two-year-old plantation owner named George Washington (1732–99).

An initial consequence of the defeat was the summoning in 1754 of an Albany Congress. This was a meeting of the seven mostly New England colonies north of Maryland to discuss alliances with the Native peoples, notably the Mohawk, and their collective security against France. It also discussed for the first time the idea of a Plan of Union of the colonies. This was put forward by a talented and articulate young delegate from Pennsylvania named Benjamin Franklin (1706–90). He was a writer, publisher, scientist and political ideologue typical of the cadre of second-generation English immigrants who were to line the path to American independence. The plan proposed the formation of a united assembly of delegates from all thirteen colonies under a president appointed by the crown in England.

Franklin's plan was clearly radical and was approved by those attending the congress, though that did not include the southern colonies. It was later rejected by individual colonial assemblies as infringing what they saw as their independence, and it made no further progress. Franklin later reflected that, had it done so, it might have forestalled the revolutionary war and even retained British sovereignty over a self-governing union for many years. But the Albany Congress was an event in history, a dry run for the independence congresses to come. It brought the northern colonies together but also gave a foretaste of the arguments, and the compromises, that were to be the stuff of American independence.

Four years on, in 1758, the British returned to Ohio when the French were under renewed pressure on all sides in the Seven Years War. The French abandoned Duquesne and retreated. The fort was renamed Pittsburgh after the British chief minister. The young Washington was afterwards furious not to be given a commission in the British (rather than Virginian) army, feeling he had been treated like a colonial peasant. He never forgot the slight.

Britain's war with France was fought in India, the Caribbean and Canada and reached a climax in 1759 at the Battle of the Plains of Abraham outside Quebec. Here General James Wolfe defeated the

French and captured the colony, though he died in the course of the battle. Montreal fell shortly afterwards. The year was hailed as Britain's imperial *annus mirabilis* and effectively ended its war with France. There followed a rising of the Great Lakes tribes who had fought on the side of France. Called Pontiac's War after one of the chiefs, it reputedly saw a British attempt to infect Native prisoners using smallpox-impregnated blankets.

The Treaty of Paris in 1763 awarded Britain the French settlements of Canada and the Ohio valley, with Britain giving France in return the lucrative Caribbean sugar islands of Martinique and Guadeloupe, and keeping Grenada, St Vincent, Tobago and Dominica. France also lost the Mississippi's Louisiana territory to Spain, regaining it briefly under Napoleon in 1800 in exchange for part of Tuscany. In the south, Britain gained the Spanish colony of Florida in return for surrendering to Spain the island of Cuba, which it had occupied during the war. Many of Florida's Native people fled west, fearing an occupation by British settlers on their land.

Thus did Europe's powers in the mid-eighteenth century carve up the world to reflect their respective strengths and interests. In America, where the Seven Years War was known as the French and Indian War, the consequence was seismic. Despite acquiring Louisiana from France, Spain's North American empire remained little more than a dispersed scatter of forts and missions in land long occupied by substantial tribes such as the Apache and Comanche. France had entered the war with a North American empire twice the extent of Britain's and the possibility of great things to come. It was now effectively expelled.

The continent now appeared open to the dominant presence on the eastern seaboard, that of the newly enhanced British Empire. Yet this empire was more than reluctant. In the Ohio valley, the Native tribes could no longer rely on French assistance in resisting British colonial expansion. But they could hope to rely on a British government that was opposed to any such advance. That government and its colonists were now set on radically divergent paths.

In London, just as the war was coming to a conclusion, half a century of the Whig Party's supremacy under Walpole and Pitt ended with the death in 1760 of George II. The throne now passed to his grandson George III, aged just twenty-two. The atmosphere at Westminster changed dramatically. The Whig leadership had treated the first two Hanoverian kings almost as foreign implants, and they had responded with a degree of deference. The new king was adamantly British and determined to put his stamp on the government of the day. He had taken an intense dislike to Pitt, calling him 'the blackest of hearts'. In 1761, with the war not yet over and Pitt eager to attack Spain, George opposed him with the support of a number of members of the Cabinet worried at the expense.

The king eagerly accepted Pitt's resignation from the Cabinet, and made his tutor, the Earl of Bute, a man with little experience of office, his chief minister. The result was that, at the very moment when London needed the most sensitive handling of America, it was led by men of inexperience and incompetence. George was to see five chief ministers come and go in as many years, each struggling to win parliamentary support, which they did through the corrupt buying of MPs' votes in the Commons.

Relations with America swiftly deteriorated. Britain's national debt had doubled in the war and the Cabinet resented the fact that it had received neither taxes nor thanks for defending the colonies from the French. Britons at home were being taxed an average of twenty-five shillings a year, while Americans paid just sixpence. The principal tax was customs duty, and that was often costing more to collect than it raised. George regarded the colonists, none of whom he had ever met, as disobliging children.

The first task was to stop any move by the colonists to advance into the formerly French territory of Ohio, where they risked inciting the remaining French and the Native peoples to resist, resuming the war. In 1763 George III issued a Great Proclamation, declaring that America to the west of the Appalachians was 'for the Indians'. Colonists were forbidden to settle in 'any lands beyond the heads or sources of any of the rivers which fall into the Atlantic Ocean from the west or north-west'. To press home the message, any settlers who had in the past strayed over that line must 'forthwith remove themselves'. If any outside state was going to behave imperially in post-war America, it was not Britain.

The proclamation was unenforceable. The king seemed out of touch and unaware that hundreds if not thousands of colonists had already crossed the relevant mountains. A Virginia newspaper declared that 'not even a second Chinese Wall, unless guarded by a million soldiers, could prevent the settlement of the lands on the Ohio'. It was inconceivable that colonists already farming there would up sticks and return east. But what should happen now?

Crucial to America at this period is that it was not a single, co-ordinated political entity. There were officially thirteen 'Americas'. They were clearly at odds with their imperial masters, who would now be disinclined to defend them against potentially hostile Native people. In addition the colonies, as we have seen, were further diverging in character. The slave areas of the South were hardly on uniting terms with their northern counterparts, though they too were eager for expansion. What the South did have was a cadre of personalities in their thirties and forties, mostly sons of first-generation landed immigrants. These men were open minded, well educated and politically ambitious for the future country to which they now devoted their lives. They did not regard themselves as inferior colonials. Three were Virginians and almost all of genteel if not aristocratic descent. They were not instinctively belligerent rebels.

The names of the seven leading lights of this cadre were to echo down American history. They were George Washington, Thomas Jefferson, John Adams, Benjamin Franklin, Alexander Hamilton, John Jay and James Madison. They were to be graced with the title of Founding Fathers, and four were to serve as president. They might disagree with each other, both over relations with Britain and over how the colonies should collaborate in a future union, but the calibre of their arguments and the skill with which they resolved them were unique in nation formation. Nothing in political history merits more admiration than America's progress to independence.

The spotlight now turned to London. Here, many politicians such as Edmund Burke and Charles Fox were sympathetic to the American cause. They were in opposition to George III's government, which, under Bute, was set on raising colonial taxes and asserting control over apparently dissident settlers. Various measures were introduced under a succession of chief ministers, including a tax on sugar so incompetent that it raised a mere £2,000 per annum but cost £8,000 to collect. Then in 1765 came a proposal for a taxed stamp on all legal transactions, documents and newspapers throughout the colonies. It could hardly have been more provocative, targeted at the colonies' most articulate occupations: lawyers, merchants, businessmen and newspaper owners.

Of the leading Americans at the time the most impressive – and personally engaging – was Franklin, his English parentage leading him frequently to visit London. During a visit in 1757 he brought with him to his Craven Street house two of his domestic slaves, though he was later a fierce opponent of slavery. In Europe he soon became the colonies' unofficial envoy, which he combined with his talents as a writer, chess master, scientist and inventor. It was said to be then that he created an 'oil for pouring on troubled waters' after an experiment in London's Green Park. Franklin travelled to Scotland, where he stayed with the philosopher David Hume in Edinburgh, declaring it 'six weeks of the densest happiness I have met with in any part of my life'. Shocked at British ignorance of American affairs, he strongly advised the Commons against the Stamp Act. But it was to no effect and the bill passed unchallenged through Parliament.

The measure was deeply inefficient. It required teams of revenue men to collect from widely scattered American communities, officials who soon went in fear of their lives. The tax proved uncollectable and was abandoned a year later, but the damage was done. It led to an event not seen since the Albany Congress of 1754: a gathering of nine colonial representatives, all except one from the North. They assembled in New York in 1765 under the title of the Stamp Act Congress and issued a declaration of 'rights and grievances' to be sent to Parliament in London.

The central demand was the familiar colonial complaint, that there should be 'no taxation without representation'. There was much argument over whether the demand should be deferential or confrontational. One delegate even challenged another to a duel, though it was not fought. Virginia's absence from the congress was significant and was regarded in London as a sign of disunity.

There were some attempts at conciliation. At first ideas were canvassed for a compromise, for a new relationship between Britain and its American colonies. Franklin warned London that its oppression of New England – here distinct from Virginia – was like 'setting up a forge in a magazine of gunpowder'. He revived his Albany Congress proposal for a Grand Council of the Colonies, composed of representatives of each colony numbered according to its tax revenue. The council would deal with defence, frontiers and the Native tribes. Otherwise the colonies would remain independent of Britain and of each other. It was a proposal welcomed in London, but not in Massachusetts, where traditionally Dissenting Boston was emerging as a centre of anti-monarchist rebellion, in marked contrast to Virginia.

The British government, now led by Pitt, lost patience. Defied over the stamp tax, in 1767 it imposed a series of five so-called Townshend duties – named after the Chancellor of the Exchequer, Charles Townshend – on specific cargoes entering the American colonies. Customs duties were easier to collect on landing than had been stamp taxes and were strongly resented. In 1770 soldiers were sent to Boston to contain the protests. In a street confrontation the soldiers killed five rioters. What in London was reported as 'an incident on King Street' in America was 'the Boston Massacre'.

Opposition to the Townshend taxes increased and a number were withdrawn, but Westminster turned increasingly hostile. Politicians demanded the colonists be 'taught a lesson'. Even Pitt declared that 'this is the Mother country and they are the children: they must obey and we prescribe'. The government was confused over whether and by how much to tax its overseas possessions and how far to privilege its merchants. Prime among the latter was the East

India Company, exclusive importer of tea from China and by the 1770s almost bankrupt. A result was the 1773 Tea Act, which confirmed the East India Company in its long-standing monopoly of tea exported to America.

Boston was America's principal import centre but its regulation was anarchic, with corrupt customs officers and smugglers galore. The effect of the Tea Act was both to infuriate the smugglers and to reassert the Townshend duties. It also stressed the primacy of the British Parliament. As Townshend had once said, 'The superiority of the mother country can at no time be better exerted than now.' The company's first ships to carry tea to America under the new act arrived, one each at New York, Philadelphia and Charleston and three at Boston. The first met determined resistance and had to turn back to England. But in Boston the governor refused to let the ships leave and held his ground.

On the night of 16 December 1773, a crowd of some 5,000 people gathered in Boston's Old South Meeting House and spilled onto the streets. A gang of sixty men from a group called the Sons of Liberty disguised themselves as Mohawk Native people, with axes and 'copper-colour'd countenances'. They claimed to represent true Americans against the hated British, possibly the only time the colonists had cited Native people in aid. They raced to the docked tea ships, boarded them and threw three hundred bales of tea into the harbour. The gesture became known as the Boston Tea Party.

Boston was elated but Britain, as reports reached home, was outraged. In 1774 Parliament passed what were called the Coercive Acts, though in America they were labelled 'intolerable'. Boston port was closed. In order to penalize its business, London switched Boston's trade privileges to the newly British Quebec. This further anglicized the formerly French province – it had become British under the Peace of Paris in 1763 – and led many New Englanders loyal to George III to migrate north. The province became the colonies of Upper and Lower Canada in 1791.

The Boston Tea Party was the climax to the American colonists' demand to determine their own taxes. It was resisted by Britain because colonists were regarded as being in a lower category than full citizens. A subsidiary reason was that London wanted taxes to pay for colonial governors itself, lest they turn pro-colonist if paid by the assemblies. Few Americans were truly anti-British, but they were insistent on fiscal autonomy. The Boston Tea Party thus went to the essence of their rebellion. John Adams, the Massachusetts Founding Father, declared the incident 'so bold, so daring, so firm, intrepid and inflexible . . . that I cannot but consider it an epoch in history'. Americans stopped drinking tea in protest and have done so, more or less, ever since. They took to coffee instead.

Meanwhile, a quiet-spoken scholarly lawyer from Virginia's House of Burgesses, Thomas Jefferson, began to formulate ground rules for what was clearly a looming crisis. In his tract *A Summary View of the Rights of British America* he drew heavily on the Enlightenment learning of his college generation. He was well versed in Plato, Aristotle, Cato and Cicero, with Locke on democratic legitimacy and Hume on pragmatism in government. The tract's most relevant and elemental statement held that 'every society must at all times possess within itself the sovereign powers of legislation'.

The result was that when in 1774, a year after the Tea Party, the first so-called Continental Congress of some fifty colonial leaders met in Philadelphia, they had a common hymn sheet from which to sing. Only Quebec and the royalist colony of Georgia were absent, though Georgia did later join. Florida, Nova Scotia and Newfoundland were also absent. The Philadelphia congress passed a Declaration and Resolves which, in the most scholarly terms, was revolutionary. It condemned the king for his measures and demanded the colonies be granted the right to pass their own laws and raise their own taxes.

The congress agreed to boycott British trade and organize and train local militias, ready to 'mobilize at a minute's notice'. They were thus to be known as minutemen. One theatrical delegate, Patrick Henry, announced himself as 'no longer a Virginian but an American'. He imitated an enslaved person breaking his bonds and leaping free. Loyalist views were also certainly heard and a

Pennsylvania proposal to form a union of 'Great Britain and the Colonies' was rejected only narrowly, by six votes to five.

Back in London, Franklin was acting as virtual ambassador. He assiduously courted ministers and visited Burke and the ageing Pitt, pleading for compromise. He was unsuccessful. In February 1775 the British Parliament formally voted Massachusetts to be 'in a state of rebellion'. Soon afterwards a company of British soldiers in Boston was ordered to disarm the colony's militia and arrest its leaders. The city descended into turmoil. The British governor, Thomas Gage, had some 3,000 regular troops but no enthusiasm to use them. His wife was a known sympathizer with the colonists, now called Patriots.

The search for weapons took seven hundred soldiers up country to Lexington and Concord and led to a series of confused skirmishes. Local people had been warned – including it was said through the governor's wife – and the weapons were well hidden. There was no need for a battle, but everyone was on edge. There were confrontations and then shots were fired. Much research has been devoted to who fired first, a Briton or an American, but the British complained that the Patriots, whose numbers gradually rose to 16,000, refused to fight in the open. No weapons were found and the soldiers were driven back to Boston, harassed by ambushes. The British eventually lost seventy-three dead, the Patriots forty-nine. The British were then besieged for nearly a year in their Charlestown base across the river from Boston before escaping north to Nova Scotia.

Among the warnings reaching Lexington of the British soldiers' approach was a supposed midnight ride from Boston by a silversmith, Paul Revere, and two friends. They activated a series of signals and even encountered British units on the route. Scepticism later enveloped the ride, but, whatever occurred, 'The ride of Paul Revere' entered the canon of America's founding legends. A semi-fictitious poem on the journey was written by Longfellow with its 'cry of defiance and not of fear'. A new nation craved heroic events.

To America's philosopher of freedom, Ralph Waldo Emerson

(1803–82), the first gun fired at Lexington was 'the shot heard round the world'. A colonial revolution against royal oppression was mutating into a war for a nation's soul. As for what that soul really was, Emerson admitted nobody knew. He declared, 'I simply experiment, an endless seeker, with no past at my back.' It might have been the revolution's uncertain motto.

7.

The War for Independence

1775–1783

The city of Philadelphia in the 1770s had the appearance of an English county town. It looked anything but revolutionary. Penn's dignified layout was one of handsome civic buildings and red-brick Georgian terraces along the river front. Located equidistant between the North's turbulent Boston and the South's conservative capital of Richmond in Virginia, it was well suited to play host to America's new age.

The city's State House, later Independence Hall, was thus the natural meeting place for the second Continental Congress assembled just weeks after the Lexington skirmish in May 1775. The prospect before the fifty-six delegates could hardly have been more troubling. The twelve colonies, later joined by Georgia, faced open war with the might of the British Empire. Many were doubtful. They had no collective government, no organized army or general, no budget, not even a headquarters or capital city. They certainly had no idea what independence might involve. The outspoken John Adams wrote that 'there is no knowing where these calamities will end'. He could only agree that 'power and artillery' were now 'the most efficacious, sure and infallible conciliatory measures'.

The nearest to a government in embryo was the Congress itself. It arranged to assemble an army from its various militias and raise resources from the colonies to support it. Trade embargoes on Britain would be imposed. The ubiquitous Franklin busied himself with foreign relations. As Britain's perpetual enemy, the French were potentially a useful ally and Franklin departed for Paris with that in view.

It was one thing to fight for independence, a different matter to decide what it meant. Thirteen colonies if freed from British rule needed to know what was to take its place. Would each be independent and sovereign, as some such as Rhode Island had felt itself already to be? Or would they risk as a union creating a new superior authority that might prove even more oppressive? Virginia and Georgia were known to be appalled at being in bed with Massachusetts. They did not want to pass out of a frying pan into a fire.

In July 1775 the Congress sent George III an 'olive branch petition' pleading for peace, which he refused to read. It then issued a formal 'declaration of the causes and necessity for taking up arms'. This did not demand independence, since some colonies were still opposed to so radical a move, but the king nevertheless declared all thirteen colonies to be in rebellion. This clearly indicated war.

As for who should lead the Congress's Continental – later Patriot – army, the answer was clearly its most senior soldier, George Washington, already noted as a veteran of the Seven Years War. He was a tall, notoriously shy southerner whose troublesome teeth left him in constant pain and affected his speaking. Washington was a prosperous Virginian gentleman with a natural loyalty to the crown. He also owned more than a hundred slaves. But he offered to raise a Virginian militia of 1,000 men at his own expense. When the Congress offered him the command he was so proud he burst into tears.

Washington's experience in the Seven Years War had left him aware of the need for clear leadership, which in that war had come from William Pitt in London. America had only a fractious part-time Congress that had given itself power to borrow but not to tax. Throughout the coming war Washington would have to rely on the goodwill of the separate colonies to supply him with men and resources. The army itself was largely conscripted. It might be patriotic but it was inexperienced and lacked training and discipline. As for the possibility of allies, this was by no means certain. Franklin had set up a 'committee of secret correspondence' to seek help from foreign states, but of this there was as yet no sign.

The atmosphere in Philadelphia, Boston and New York became ever more belligerent. It was stirred in part by an upsurge in local newspapers, a feature of booming American towns in advance of anything seen in Europe. To this was added a pamphlet published in January 1776 by a British radical, Thomas Paine, a quarrelsome barrack-room militant with a gifted pen. Already in London and Paris he had been in trouble for advocating revolts against the established government. Arriving in Philadelphia in 1774 he edited the *Pennsylvania Magazine* and wrote a pamphlet in support of the revolutionary cause entitled *Common Sense*.

The pamphlet was electric. Strewn with myths of British savagery against Americans, including rape, child killing and town burning, it dismissed the king and said any American who did not stand up and fight 'had the heart of a coward and the spirit of a sycophant'. Paine's rousing payoff line was 'The blood of the slain, the weeping voice of nature cries "'Tis time to part."' The diatribe immediately sold 120,000 copies, and eventually half a million. Paine's next pamphlet, *The American Crisis*, was another best-seller. Historians have no doubt these works were critical in driving public opinion to war. For an entire generation of Americans, 'even the naked and untutored Indian is less a savage than the King'.

Amid this rising tempo, the Congress appointed five of its members to write what was to become the Declaration of Independence. They deputed Jefferson to prepare a first draft. John Adams was by no means wholehearted, stating, 'Independency is a hobgoblin of so frightful mien that it would throw a delicate person into fits to look it in the face.' But it could not be avoided. The objective was no longer for a confederacy or congress of colonies. It was for a singular union. This would have somehow to accommodate colonies such as Virginia, which were in favour of general independence but averse to any close union. It even passed a resolution that the old colonies 'ought of right to be free and independent states'. The trouble was that a union of independent states was a contradiction in terms. At least for the time being, all that was clear was that the United States were emphatically plural.

Jefferson's declaration avoided constitutional details and was rather a statement of political ideology. The preamble's second clause famously asserted, 'We hold these truths to be self-evident, that all men are created equal, that they are endowed by their Creator with certain inalienable rights, that among these are life, liberty and the pursuit of happiness.' The professor of Communication Arts Stephen E. Lucas called this 'the best-known sentence in the English language' – though it was virtually a verbatim quotation from Locke's *Second Treatise on Government* – and it was imitated in similar independence declarations around the globe. But what did it mean in practice?

The declaration went on to list the grievances of the colonies against the king, his offences against the rights of free citizens and the just cause those citizens had in rising in rebellion against such oppression. The British 'have been deaf to the voice of justice and consanguinity' and accordingly 'with a firm reliance on the protection of divine Providence, we mutually pledge to each other our lives, our fortunes and our sacred honor'.

The text was edited by Adams and Franklin, but we know only that 'self-evident' was a replacement for Jefferson's 'sacred and undeniable'. Over subsequent weeks the document was much battered by members of the Congress, losing a quarter of its length. Controversy was usually avoided by excision. But the surviving solemnities were signed by all the delegates and were to ring loud and clear through the chambers of American history. The declaration now sits in a bullet-proof shrine in the rotunda of the National Archives in Washington, as if holier than any Bible.

The Declaration of Independence had to handle glaring hypocrisies. It eulogized equality, liberty and the pursuit of happiness in a nation that held over a quarter of its inhabitants, 600,000 people, in legal bondage. The wording clearly implied that every enslaved person should be freed on independence. Yet this was flatly rejected by half the colonies. After much argument, the solution was a funk. All reference to slavery was omitted. As for the other 'equally created' occupants of their shared continent, the Native tribes, they were bizarrely described merely as 'merciless Indian savages'. Abraham Lincoln was to explain away the hypocrisies on the grounds that the declaration was a moral standard towards which the union need only strive. As for any rights for women, there was never a mention.

On the 4th of July 1776 the document was officially adopted and read out in Philadelphia's State House yard. That is the date customarily cited as Independence Day, a federal holiday and the annual occasion for much national celebration. The following year, the Congress published its Articles of Confederation, supposedly setting out relations between the new states and the union. These were tentative in the extreme. Franklin's trenchantly echoed dictum was, 'Well gentlemen, we must now all hang together or most assuredly we shall hang separately.' Yet references to decisions in which 'the states have a common interest' were not specified. Article II, inserted by North Carolina, stipulated that each state 'retains its sovereignty, freedom and independence, and every power, jurisdiction and right which is not by this confederation expressly delegated to . . . Congress'. For a nation embarking on war, the vehicle of its union could hardly have been more vague or its destination more uncertain.

The next stage of initiation into statehood was for each colony formally to break its ties with Britain and become a sovereign entity, prior to moving into union. Most had so far been governed through either corporate or royal charter. Each had to decide if it wanted an upper and lower house of assembly – almost all opted for both – and how much power to grant to an executive governor and how much to retain for its assembly. A complication was that the concept of governor was itself a leftover from the representative of the monarch. A strong feeling was that the office should not enjoy prerogatives similar to those it replaced. To be 'another George III' was to be a common criticism of future presidents.

One colony, Georgia, was clearly a reluctant rebel, as were to a lesser extent the Carolinas and Virginia. They felt, like many individuals loyal to the British crown, that some link with Britain should be retained, not least to guard the union's future security. This view was shared with colonies in the Caribbean and in Canada, none of which was present at the Philadelphia congresses and all of which were excluded from subsequent moves to independence. Another reason was that the southern colonies assumed, on past experience, that London might be more tolerant of slavery than a congress dominated by northern abolitionists.

A result was that thousands of loyal colonists, mainly from the South, were to fight in the coming war on the British side, while many more, both North and South, were quiet sympathizers. These people plausibly regarded a coalition of semi-autonomous states as an invitation to anarchy. Meanwhile, slaves were offered their freedom by Britain if they fought as loyalists. Hence for many the War of Independence that began in 1775 was tinged with a realization that it might be the prelude to a later conflict between the colonies themselves.

Fighting was initially concentrated around New York and Boston. The resident British army abandoned Boston and took control of New York in 1776. Their general, William Howe, then forced Washington's army south towards Delaware and Philadelphia. After a series of minor encounters, in 1777 the British defeated the Americans comprehensively at the Battle of Brandywine outside Philadelphia. One of those involved on the American side was a young French soldier of fortune, the Marquis de Lafayette. He had only recently joined the American cause and became close to Washington, who treated him like a son. Though wounded, Lafayette was to play a crucial role in the later conduct of the war.

The British now occupied Philadelphia unopposed. All of its church bells had been removed and hidden for fear of being melted down for British bullets. For the time being the American cause looked hopeless. Yet the British had difficulties. After Brandywine they faced a largely guerrilla war requiring flexibility and quick decisions. Yet orders and supplies from London were long delayed and often out of date through being communicated by sea. England's feel for the insurrection was minimal, the war having been initially regarded as an imperial disturbance. Nobody knew how victory over the colonists would be expressed, or even who was the real enemy and who were loyalists. Britain was fighting not one but many foes dispersed over hundreds of miles.

The war changed abruptly in October 1777 when a second British army based in the colony of Quebec moved south into New York under its general, John Burgoyne. As he moved to confront rebel forces in the Hudson valley, confused messages led to his losing touch with his reinforcements. This in turn culminated in a series of battles at Saratoga, outside Albany, in which Burgoyne was comprehensively defeated. His army was forced to surrender and was imprisoned by the Americans. The impact of Saratoga when reported in London and Paris was sensational, cancelling out the American defeat in Pennsylvania. Britain's prime minister, Lord North, now suggested a peace settlement but refused to concede independence. When this news reached the Continental Congress it was rejected.

In Paris, the news of Saratoga was cheered by the French. Franklin, rebuffed by London, had arrived in Paris as ambassador and champion of revolutionary freedom. Here he was welcomed as an authentic American hero against the hated British. Franklin adopted a touch of what would now be termed rebel chic. A French aristocrat referred to his clothing as 'rustic, his bearing simple but dignified, his language direct, his hair un-wigged and unpowdered'. He was seen in the context of the classical revival, of Cato and the Roman Republic, then fashionable in French intellectual circles. It contrasted with the rococo effeminacy of much of eighteenth-century Europe.

Franklin's performance in Paris was remarkable. His likeness appeared on medallions and snuffboxes. Ladies would demand 'la coiffure à la Franklin', imitating the fur cap he wore in place of a wig. He rose to the occasion. His memoir of this period in France recalled his nine indoor servants and a cellar with 1,000 bottles of wine. The cost to the American treasury, however met, was controversial but the diplomatic impact was brilliant. Louis XVI agreed to an alliance with the rebels and in February 1778 a treaty was signed and war formally declared by France on Britain. The writer

Beaumarchais led an appeal for money and supplies. Nantes became a logistical base, with ships sent across the Atlantic filled with munitions. A French naval unit in the Caribbean was put on standby.

On land there were now three British commanders seemingly at a loss about what to do. Indecisive battles were fought over large expanses of territory during 1778–80. New England defied both victory and defeat. The chief British hope was that Washington's conflict with the Congress for money and supplies would eventually wear him down. It was a plausible tactic. The American army was often close to mutiny, its militias deserting to tend their crops. Washington complained that he commanded not one army but thirteen. In addition, most amateur militiamen were usable 'only for light parties in the woods'. It was nothing but Washington's firmness of purpose that kept an American force in the field.

In 1780 it was France that transformed the war. Two years after Franklin's treaty, a French army of 5,000 landed in Rhode Island under Washington's now established colleague, Lafayette. In the summer of 1781 he moved south and joined Washington's forces outside New York. There followed a disagreement over whether to attempt to capture the city from the British or head south. This was resolved by news that the French Caribbean fleet was sailing north to Chesapeake Bay, where a British army of 8,000 under Lord Cornwallis had built a fort at Yorktown. His hope was that Virginia and Georgia might switch to the loyalist cause.

A combined Franco-American force of 17,000 under Washington and Lafayette now laid siege to Yorktown. When in September a British fleet arrived to relieve Cornwallis, it was driven off by French ships. The Americans now had artillery sufficient to batter Yorktown's defences and overwhelm his outposts. With half his troops stricken by malaria, the British commander had no option but to surrender.

Cornwallis was so humiliated by his failure that he refused to attend the surrender ceremony, and his sword of defeat had to be handed over by one of his brigadiers. Reluctant to recognize Washington's 'army of provincials', the British brigadier gave the sword to a French officer, who in turn insisted it go to Washington. When Washington refused it, the sword was finally accepted by one of his aides. Almost as if war was a professional game, the French officers gave a banquet for their defeated British opposite numbers, but they were said to have largely ignored their American allies.

In the following settlement, Washington refused to accept a British demand that slaves who had served in the loyalist army be granted their freedom. Washington rounded them up and sent them back to their owners. One account has the shocked British remarking that the Americans were not patriots but mere 'slave-catchers'. Also remarkable was the number of Germans involved, on the British side as mercenaries, on the American as prominent immigrants. They were estimated as a third of the total combatants.

Yorktown stripped London of any further enthusiasm for the war. It shocked George III, whose hard line in rejecting peace moves from the rebels was largely responsible for the defeat. On being told the outcome he cried, 'America is lost. Must we fall beneath the blow?' He was defeated, he said with more than a measure of truth, 'by a Presbyterian rebellion'. His prime minister, Lord North, lost a vote of censure in Parliament and resigned, making way for a Whig coalition that included the pro-Americans Burke and Fox.

Tripartite negotiations were held during 1782–3 in Paris by the British and French governments and by Franklin for the colonists. They covered fishing and trading rights, the restitution of confiscated loyalist property and the removal of British troops. They also included a clutter of issues left hanging from the Paris treaty ending the Seven Years War, also involving the Dutch and the Spanish. (The latter were then at war with Britain over Gibraltar.)

One issue on which the British refused to concede was Quebec's continued status as a British colony. Of some 80,000 loyalists who had fled their American homes during and after the war, most went to Canada. Their long and hazardous trek illustrated the deep divisions within the colonies over independence. One consequence was to strengthen Canada's links with Britain, the American negotiators accepting Canada's continued colonization.

The Ohio valley and related territories between the Appalachians and the Mississippi, which had gone to Britain after the Seven Years War, now passed to the very Americans King George had banned from settling them. American 'land-grabbers' thus could now cross the Appalachians, advance into Kentucky and Tennessee and even reach the Mississippi. The land beyond that river went to Spain, which also regained Florida, partly in return for Britain keeping Gibraltar.

There was no reference in the so-called Peace of Paris to the Native people who still occupied most of the lands being discussed. It was as if they were mere ghosts. Britain's delegate, Lord Shelburne, afterwards remarked that 'the Indian nations were not abandoned to their enemies; they were remitted to the care of neighbours', that is, the Americans.

The Peace was the culmination of what came to be termed the American Revolutionary War of Independence. As a revolution it was not social or economic, rather a rebellion against the political conduct of a particular imperial power, the British. That is why prominent Whigs such as Burke and Fox had been sympathetic to the rebels from the start, and why America's new status was widely welcomed in Britain. Burke, in a letter of congratulation to Franklin, openly regretted Britain's past treatment of the colonies. He remarked that 'providence has not done its work by halves. You have Success, and you have added and may yet add more to what success is unable to bestow.'

When a Frenchman present at the Paris talks remarked on what he saw as Britain's generosity to the new American union, he added a prediction that its people would one day 'form the greatest empire in the world'. A British delegate retorted, 'Yes, Monsieur, and they will speak English, every one of 'em.' But such bravado only went so far. A celebratory sketch of the Paris negotiations by the American artist Benjamin West was left unfinished down one side. The British delegates had been too ashamed to pose for it.

8.

Birth Pains of a Republic

1783–1796

On 23 December 1783, three months after the Peace of Paris, at a congressional meeting at Annapolis in Maryland, George Washington handed in his commission as commander of the Patriot army, and with it his sword. He shook hands with every delegate and rode through the night to spend Christmas at his Mount Vernon farm in Virginia. Under his leadership the American colonies had rid themselves of one overlord. But who would be their next? In particular, should it be one ruler or many?

Britain's American colonies had long been an imprecise grouping. The war's thirteen combatants had included no British colony in the Caribbean or Canada. The putative union was of a tiny slice of North America, though it would now be in possession of the expanse of the Ohio territory as far as the Mississippi. What that possession of as yet undefined territory meant was uncertain. Some of the former colonies were tiny; all faced at least the possibility that some other imperial power might choose to take them under its wing.

Colonists also faced the hostility of Native tribes, some of whom had supported Britain against them, including the Cherokee, the Creek and the Iroquois League. Many were now told by the Congress that their siding with Britain during the independence war meant they had wiped clean any treaties or agreements that had been made with them. Relations between the new union and the lands west of the Appalachians were thus anything but stable.

The concept of a new union had been embodied – almost

personified – in the so-called Continental Congress, a conference of colonies linked solely by their English origins and their membership of the British Empire. Each was now legally sovereign. The war had been fought under the umbrella of Jefferson's Declaration of Independence, with individual colonies donating money and men to victory. That had lent plausibility to unity and Washington's personal leadership had added to it. This still left open what that unity might involve.

A collective institution had to be established, and that meant an executive with a staff and financial resources. It needed urgently to regulate its borders, administer justice and determine trade and relations with the Native tribes. Most pressing, Washington's army remained in existence, leaderless, underpaid, ill-resourced and facing widespread desertion. Some soldiers went to Washington and pleaded with him to return to office and take charge, 'to take the crown'. Like General Monck facing similar pressure to assume Cromwell's autocracy in 1660 England, Washington refused. He was a professional soldier thrust by circumstance to the forefront of politics. Like Monck, in declining absolute power he saved his country from turmoil and from the possible autocracy that consumed the also soon-to-be independent South America.

Hovering at Washington's side in the matter of union leadership was his forceful associate Alexander Hamilton (1755–1804). An orphan who had been brought up on Nevis in the Caribbean, he had migrated to New York and studied law at what became Columbia University. On the outbreak of war he had joined Washington's headquarters staff, soon handling liaison with the indecisive and cash-poor Congress. Hamilton had, like Washington, despaired at the Congress's impotence. It had offered no guiding strategy during the war and supplied no continuing resources for the army or navy. The result might well have been chaos and defeat.

Hamilton's personality was that of an intelligent if argumentative New Yorker with a zest for power. He was everything the genteel southern elite who surrounded Washington were not. To him, America needed an emphatic central command, a driving force

1. The first Manhattan: Cliff Palace, Mesa Verde, Colorado, built by Ancestral Puebloans *c.*1190–1260 CE, abandoned by 1300.

2. Vespucci's claim to have mapped a 'New World' led cartographer Martin Waldseemüller to recognize his accomplishment in 1507 by applying his Latinized first name, Amerigo, to his first map of the region.

3. Engraving of John White's depiction of the village of Secoton, Roanoke, 1585, showing tobacco, corn and pumpkins being grown by Indians in Roanoke, present-day North Carolina.

4. Pocahontas, portrait by English School, after engraving by Simon van der Passe, 1616.

5. *The First Thanksgiving at Plymouth*, 1621; painting by Jennie A. Brownscombe, 1914.

6. Salem witches: *The Trial of George Jacobs*, 1692, as imagined by Tompkins Matteson, 1855.

7. William Penn signing Penn's treaty with members of the Lenape tribe on the Delaware River in 1683. Detail of *Penn's Treaty with the Indians* by Benjamin West, 1771–2.

8. A Virginia planter smoking tobacco while field workers toil nearby. Tobacco dealer's trade card, *c.*1725.

9. John Winthrop, governor of Massachusetts Bay Colony, led a group of English colonists to the New World in April 1630, founding a number of communities on the shores of Massachusetts Bay, later Boston.

10. *Mrs John Freake and Her Baby Mary, c.*1671. One of the earliest portraits of the New England mercantile classes, artist unknown.

11. The skirmish known in America as 'the Boston Massacre' between British soldiers and citizens of Boston on 5 March 1770. Print by Paul Revere.

12. The Boston Tea Party, 1773. Protestors tip bales of tea into Boston Harbor. Engraving by W. D. Cooper, 1789.

13. The Declaration of Independence in the US Capitol, 1776. Detail of a painting by John Trumbull, 1818. This scene of John Adams, Roger Sherman, Robert Livingston, Thomas Jefferson and Benjamin Franklin does not represent a real ceremony; the characters portrayed were never in the same room at the same time.

14. *Washington Crossing the Delaware* by Emanuel Leutze, 1851. In December 1776 George Washington led the Patriot army across the Delaware River to a surprise attack on so far superior British troops, a manoeuvre crucial to revolutionary morale.

15. George Washington, Founding Father and the first president of the United States, serving from 1789 to 1797. Portrait by Gilbert Stuart, 1795.

16. James Madison, Founding Father and fourth president of the United States from 1809 to 1817. Madison was regarded as the 'Father of the Constitution' for his pivotal role in its drafting and early amendment. Portrait by Gilbert Stuart, c.1821.

invulnerable to reactionary colonials. He called that force 'federalism'. In strong opposition to the Virginians Jefferson and Franklin, Hamilton completed the trio of Founding Fathers under Washington who did most to forge what became the United States.

In most revolutionary societies, rebellion ends in tears and dictators. France in 1789 had the Terror and Russia in 1917 had Lenin and Stalin. The tensions that surfaced in America in the 1780s could well have seen serious conflict between the Founding Fathers and the Patriot armies, rebellious slaves and Native tribes. The Continental Congress renamed itself the Confederacy Congress and continued to meet and talk, but it had no leader. When delegates returned home each colony reasserted its previous autonomy. Nothing was done to meet the Congress's war debt of some $75 million, or even honour its interest payments. The colonies merely rejected all proposals to levy a tax. It was as if they had had enough of taxes from the British.

Unionism now dithered close to collapse. In May 1787 the Congress reassembled in what had become America's de facto capital, Philadelphia, and pleaded with Washington to return as its chairman. On the table were two documents, Jefferson's 1776 Declaration of Independence and the Congress's 1777 Articles of Confederation. Neither offered a constitution for a union government. Such a government had to be formed. There was an army seething and unpaid, at the potential service of a new leader. The prospect so dismayed tiny Rhode Island that it refused even to send a delegate, fearing a union constitution would be its death knell.

America had to become a republic but the Founding Fathers, steeped in a classical education, were acutely aware of republican history. The best-known example, ancient Rome, had endured a turbulent existence before lapsing into often bloodthirsty dictatorship. Now, in four months on the banks of the Delaware River, delegates had to trawl through the trials and mostly errors of the past and draft something more robust. They had agreed to oppose monarchy and they called themselves 'states', but beyond that all they seemed to harbour were differences.

Delegates from New England were still tinged with religious fundamentalism and the blessings of God. But Boston was losing prominence to New York, whose materialist inhabitants like Hamilton were eager to move on from agriculture towards manufacturing and trade. To them strength lay in union. On the other hand, delegates from the South were concerned above all with autonomy. They were adamant that any union should not have the power to interfere with their trade or with their increasingly controversial slavery.

The Congress now turned for guidance to yet another Virginian, James Madison (1751–1836). Like Jefferson he was a slight, shy man of scholarly interests, the son of a wealthy planter and slave-owner. Educated at what became Princeton University, he had studied classics and law and was steeped, like Jefferson, in Locke and Adam Smith. As Jefferson had been impresario of the Declaration of Independence, so in 1787 Madison became that of the new American constitution.

The central issue was easily stated as plural versus singular. Was Madison creating a United States or a United State? Would populous Pennsylvania and Virginia now rule tiny Delaware and Maryland, much as George III had done before? Or worse, would the smaller states be able to outvote the big ones in an assembly of equals? Many of the colonies had previously debated Locke's 'elective despotism' and had curbed the authority, indeed the tyranny, of their governors with elected assemblies. Surely such curbs should be retained.

Madison had to find answers that were philosophically robust and yet pragmatic. His guiding principle was that no power should be absolute, and all should be subject to checks and balances. His central answer was a competitive trinity, composed of an elected presidency, a Congress composed of two separately elected houses and a separate supreme court of judges appointed for life. How these entities should be composed to prevent any one of them exerting too much power was the challenge.

Delaware's delegate, Gunning Bedford, put the case bluntly to the Virginian patricians. 'I do not, gentlemen, trust you. If you possess the power, the abuse of it could not be checked; and what then would prevent you from exercising it to our destruction?' Indeed, Bedford concluded, 'Is it come to this, then, that the sword must decide this controversy, and the horrors of war must be added to the rest of our misfortunes?'

The interjection, crude at the time, illustrated the threat of a descent into violence that hung over the birth of the union. But the fact that it was openly debated was also its strength. It contrasted America with the forms of rule in virtually all other nations on earth. In the eighteenth century they were mostly still discretionary monarchies, unconstrained by constitutions of any sort. America had won itself the option of a written constitution and was determined to honour it. But the essence of it was to be compromise within the trinity, not the sword.

As he charted America's future that summer of 1787, Madison's first compromise was between the two houses of Congress. The upper house, the Senate, would represent the historical union of semi-sovereign states, big and small, with two senators chosen from each of the thirteen former colonies. It was collective but hardly democratic, and it gave undue power to the smaller states. There was to be no question of states merging. Still today one senator from California represents 20 million people, one from Wyoming 300,000. To balance that, the lower House of Representatives was democratic, elected by free American males as individuals, from districts of equal population. This meant that populous states could easily outvote smaller ones owing to having more delegates.

Given the distortion of power in the Senate, Madison insisted that all federal laws should have to pass both houses. The role of the Senate would be to protect the autonomy of states from congressional tyranny. The role of the House of Representatives would be to prevent a Senate tilted towards the smaller states from forcing its will on the majority. It was a recipe for peace. It was also a recipe for stalemate.

There remained the question of the federal executive, the presidency. Here battle royal was joined. Washington's army had been traumatized by the inadequacy of central support during the war. From this emerged the desire for strong leadership, an obsession of Hamilton's. Matters such as foreign affairs, defence, the currency, a federal treasury and international trade could not be left to the conflicts and compromises of a legislature vulnerable to stalemate.

Hamilton won from Madison an 'emergency' right of presidential veto over Congress. It was essential if so disparate a nation as America was to act as one, not least in war. The southern states none the less accused Hamilton of wanting an 'elected monarch'. This was met by yet another compromise, that the presidential veto could itself be overridden by a vote of two-thirds of both houses of Congress. This measure was to prove vital in the country's emergence from civil war. The limit of two presidential terms, as practised by Washington, became a convention, but was formalized in the twenty-second amendment in 1951, after Franklin Roosevelt's twelve-year presidency.

Madison's final innovation was to make it exceptionally difficult to amend his constitution once it was passed. Any amendment would require the backing of two-thirds of each house of Congress, followed by the assent of three-quarters of the state assemblies. It made the American constitution the most rigid in the world. Apart from an initial burst of ten amendments during its passage, the American constitution has since been amended just seventeen times, hardly ever substantively.

Underlying Madison's creation lurked one relentless issue: the survival of slavery in the southern states. In 1772, before independence, a common-law judgment had been handed down by a British judge, Lord Mansfield, that slavery 'is so odious that nothing can be suffered to support it but positive law'. The implication was that legalization was unthinkable. Yet as Britain's Dr Johnson put it at the time, 'How is it that we hear the loudest yelps for liberty among the drivers of negroes?'

Some states were now legislating against the practice. In the two decades following 1787, slavery was abolished in Massachusetts, Rhode Island, Pennsylvania, Connecticut and New Jersey. It was also banned in the new Northwest Territory acquired from Britain in the Paris Treaty, the future so-called Great Lakes states of Ohio, Indiana, Illinois, Michigan, Wisconsin and part of Minnesota. Some states also allowed manumission or the freeing of slaves by their owners. By the end of the century 20 per cent of slaves had been freed, though the rest were still 'owned' even in northern states such as New York.

In the South a new cotton economy was developing alongside tobacco and rice, but it too required armies of manual labourers. Slave-owning farmers were pushing west from Virginia and the Carolinas into the new lands of Kentucky and Tennessee, which became states in 1792 and 1796 respectively. With their economies built on slavery, the southern states were adamant that they should decide its legal status for themselves, as should the new western states. It was not for a newfangled union to decide such crucial matters for them.

The pragmatist in Madison, himself a slave-owner, realized that this issue was critical to the union. Indeed it was existential: was slavery more important than the union? To him and most of his Virginian colleagues the answer was no. As in Jefferson's Declaration of Independence, the compromise was to leave slavery unmentioned. The constitution merely stipulated that 'the migration or importation of such persons as any of the states . . . think proper to admit shall not be prohibited by the Congress prior to 1808'. This presaged the formal ending of the international slave trade, but even where states voted for abolition, as did Pennsylvania, its enforcement was to be postponed for twenty years.

A measure of the South's power was its final extraordinary demand that the southern states could boost their 'population' in fixing their presence in the House of Representatives by counting their slaves as equalling three-fifths of a free person. This was treating a slave as neither a voter nor a citizen but as property. A New York delegate was outraged at the 'sordid deal'. Yet it was passed by Congress. The word was not compromise but concession.

As he proceeded with his constitution, Madison was at all times straining for a middle way. He agreed on the need for a strong centre, but the areas in which the centre should enjoy discretionary power were to be 'enumerated'. All other governmental functions would remain with the states. As the southern delegates said time and again, they had just rid themselves of one prerogative king; they did not want another. This put a stop to one of Madison's more radical proposals, that Congress should be able to veto state laws.

The constitution was festooned with lesser checks and balances. The president could not serve in the legislature. Senators would serve terms of six years, hopefully inclining them to take a long view. They would be selected by whatever means a state decided, not necessarily elected. The federal judiciary was under a Supreme Court whose members would sit in perpetuity, detached from both the executive and state judges. This was intended to establish an overarching judiciary as guardian of the constitution. In fact it created a reactionary, at times geriatric, blockage at the heart of federal government.

A final check was Madison's proposal that the president would not be elected directly by the people but through an electoral college of state delegates. It was seen as a protective layer of collegiate oversight against the threat of populist rule. A state's members might or might not be mandated to vote for the candidate who won that state's popular vote. In the event, in every state other than Maine and Nebraska, the electors were so mandated, except that the winning candidate took all the states' college votes. It meant that the elected president did not necessarily have to win the most votes nationally. This manifest unfairness was to become a festering constitutional wound. Though only five presidents have won fewer votes than their rival, two of them have been since 2000, George W. Bush (2000) and Donald Trump (2016).

An immediate objection to Madison's draft came from a number of states, complaining that the document included no articulation of America's civil rights. It did not specifically honour the aspirations of the Declaration of Independence. In response, Madison proposed a series of immediate amendments, of which ten were passed, which he described as a Bill of Rights. The first enshrined freedom of speech and freedom of religion. The controversial second amendment conferred the right to keep and bear arms, though it specifically related this to a militia necessary 'for the security of a free state'. The tenth amendment was crucial and explicit. 'Powers not delegated to the United States by the constitution . . . are reserved to the states respectively.'

The constitution had to be confirmed by a plebiscite of the entire union electorate. This was informed by a remarkable intellectual edifice, a collection of eighty-five essays titled *The Federalist*. Fifty or so of them were written by Hamilton and most of the rest by Madison and John Jay. All were initially pseudonymous, by 'Publius', as if emphasizing the classical backdrop of the exercise. The contents were learned and occasionally disagreed with each other. Most were initially published in three New York newspapers in 1787 but circulated across the states and they all appeared in book form the following spring, as did a version in French. The American constitution was an exercise not only in revolution but also in public education.

Madison's 1787 constitution together with Jefferson's Declaration of Independence became foundation stones of America's political culture. At one level they seemed a mishmash of liberal ideas, even platitudes, distorted by compromises on states' rights, but they offered Americans a secular faith, a focus on the conceptual architecture of what, for almost all of them, was a new home. Schoolchildren would stand, hand on heart, to learn the sacred phrases that united the nation in time of internal or external strife.

Since the states regarded themselves as partly autonomous democracies, many passed their own bills of rights. Some even restricted the freedoms supposedly guaranteed by the union, most glaringly the equality of man. They might punish Quakers, limit property rights, ban certain sexual acts and restrict voting rights. The South's slavery codes were racially dictatorial. They limited the movement of black people, their worship, marriage, parenting and leisure activity, all in flagrant defiance of the constitution. As for what should be the federal sanction on such defiance, the answer was silence. A crisis was postponed, a can was kicked down a long road.

The constitution was signed in Philadelphia's State House on 17 September 1787 by a safe majority of thirty-nine out of the fifty-five delegates. The union's first president was accepted by all parties to be George Washington, creator and founder of the republic and formally elected in 1789. He was reluctant to take the post but was the one figure favoured by all sides. On 23 April that year Washington was escorted to his inauguration across the harbour of New York, temporarily capital of the union, in a ceremonial barge. He told a friend he went 'with feelings not unlike those of a culprit who is going to the place of his execution'. He was the man for the moment.

The United States approached its future like a pupil at a new school, the academy of nationhood. Uniforms had to be chosen, prefects appointed, rules learned, fees collected and lodgings found. As for an emblem, a version of the Stars and Stripes had fluttered over the American headquarters during the War of Independence. Its design had been borrowed from the East India Company, a British institution the Americans had admired for devolving power to India's local states. The company flag had horizontal red and white stripes and a Union Jack in one quarter. America's version had thirteen stripes for the colonies and the Union Jack was replaced by thirteen stars on a blue background. The star-spangled banner acquired a sanctity that made abusing it a crime. When during the 1982 Falklands War Americans saw British marines photographed in Union Jack underpants, they were shocked at such disrespect for their own flag.

Under Washington's presidency argument deepened between Jefferson and Hamilton. Introvert and extrovert, localist and centralist, conservative and radical, they disliked one another intensely. Washington shrewdly kept both men close as his advisers. Hamilton became treasury secretary, Jefferson secretary of state, responsible for overseas affairs. Battle was immediately joined over the funding of the $75 million wartime debt. Jefferson thought the original lenders should be repaid their bonds at face value, despite their real value having soared with peace and inflation. Hamilton argued that investors – many of them fellow New Yorkers – had taken a risk and were entitled to the rise in value. If the marketplace was not respected by the union, America's infant capitalist economy would die. Jefferson founded the Democratic-Republican Party, Hamilton the Federalist Party.

As in many of the arguments of the early years, the outcome was a compromise or trade-off. Washington, though a Virginian, came down for Hamilton, who created a national bank, the First Bank of the United States. It received taxes, managed the national debt and printed currency. Jefferson, Madison and their Virginian colleagues were enraged. 'The Bank' came to embody the emergent 'money power' rooted in the North and threatening the landed interests of the South.

The issue was then how the South should be appeased. A bone of contention at the time was where the union's political centre should be located. Throughout the 1780s the federal authorities moved between Philadelphia, Annapolis and New York. Following the national bank's formation in Philadelphia, notionally in the North, the South demanded the honour of hosting the capital. As to its precise site, the decision was delegated to the new president, Washington.

He compromised, choosing a location on the informal border between North and South, between Maryland and Virginia at the then port of Georgetown on the Potomac River. It sat conveniently just fifteen miles north of his own home at Mount Vernon. The river was also the outlet of a route from the interior through the Cumberland Gap in the Appalachian Mountains. Jefferson said it would 'pour into our lap the whole commerce of the western world'. The city would be renamed Washington in the great man's honour, and sit in a mini-state of its own, the District of Columbia, in honour of America's 'discoverer', though it would lack representation in Congress.

The great question was how the new capital should look. Architecture is the privilege – and fantasy – of those in power, lending solidity to their authority. New capitals rarely acquire character or popularity. They reflect authority, not markets. They mutate into bureaucratic suburbs, as with Ottawa, Canberra, Bonn and Brasilia. Washington's location was not ideal. It was far from any existing city and had a torrid climate, especially in summer. As for style, the neoclassical revival was then in full flood in Europe, and especially in revolutionary France. To the Founding Fathers, the architecture of democratic Athens and republican Rome and of their own recent allies in Paris brooked no argument.

The president had met a young engineer with the French army during the war, Pierre L'Enfant. He was inculcated with the Beaux Arts style that was to enhance Napoleon's empire. L'Enfant's geometrical plan took its lead from the Rome planned by Pope Sixtus V in the sixteenth century but only partly built. It was to become a model for town planners into the twentieth century. Here it involved a hundred-square-mile grid of streets, cut across by diagonal avenues meeting at *rond-points*. They were wildly extravagant in road space and are confusing to Washington motorists to this day.

At the plan's heart lay a majestic boulevard lined with government offices linking Congress's Capitol on one hill with a presidential palace on a lesser slope a mile away. It was bereft of townscape detail, shops, residences or pavement activity. The palace itself was intended to be five times the size of the present White House and was never built on that scale. Parallel to the boulevard were two miles of grassed mall leading to the river. The distances between these structures, particularly in an age of pedestrians and horse-drawn vehicles, was absurd.

For decades the building of Washington was a fiasco. It was condemned as pompous, too big and too expensive. The climate was hot and no one wanted to buy plots for houses. But foundations were soon laid for the Capitol and a presidential mansion and no one had the courage or authority to cancel them. For decades the site was a sea of mud with half-finished buildings reached on wooden planks. It looked more like the ruin of ancient Rome than the start of a new one. Congress and the Supreme Court met for only a few months each year and then dispersed. America's serious business was conducted in New York and Philadelphia. Washington remained a part-time, one-industry town well into the twentieth century.

While France's critical role in the American revolution is not in doubt, much debate surrounded the United States' role in the revolution in France. Aid to support the War of Independence had near bankrupted the tottering French monarchy. The storming of the Bastille in 1789 took place just over two months after Washington's inauguration. But America's war had shown that even the power of a great empire was vulnerable to usurpation. Monarchy had no divine right to survive. A republic could supplant it, based on reason, the teaching of philosophers and the will of the people.

What France did not learn from America was how to interpret those teachings and how to discipline their debates and decisions. Paris had no Jeffersons, Madisons or Hamiltons to mediate between its rampaging mobs and the rattle of the guillotine. The dull reality is that constitutions and their creators matter. Revolutions may be awesome in their power to destabilize, but constitutions are essential to reconstruct. And they must have mechanisms to secure consent.

True, in America this constitutionalism did not embrace Native Americans or slaves, but it did include a sufficiency of citizens to establish Congress's sovereignty and accept a single presidency. France's ruling culture was that of monarchy and the Catholic Church, one of hierarchy and authority. When they tumbled there was only the mob to replace their authority.

George Washington served two terms as president and his obsession was with concord and unity. His plea for 'one people under an efficient government' and his manner of achieving it was to stand as the glory of his office. His final obsession was to dissociate America from its past. In his farewell address of 1796 he begged Americans to stay detached from the old world. They should play no part in Europe's controversies and conflicts, 'the causes of which are essentially foreign to our concerns'. Trade might be necessary but the overriding task 'in extending commercial relations with the outside world, is to have with them as little political connection as possible'. That was the lesson of geography and now should be the lesson of history.

Washington was a fanatical isolationist. His advice was destined to torture America's foreign policy for all time.

9.

Shaping a Continent

Washington's successor as president was his vice-president, John Adams (1797–1801). He was a lawyer and articulate federalist in the Hamilton mode, sharing with him a background not from the South but from Massachusetts. He owned no slaves. His term of office was uneventful. But Adams was a sophisticated diplomat and man of the world. He had negotiated the Treaty of Paris and was pro-British, going out of his way to refuse to side with France in the Napoleonic Wars.

Adams was followed in turn by Jefferson (1801–9), his vice-president and friend. There was an element of a private club to the Founding Fathers, as if the White House was theirs by right. Jefferson shared with many colonial intellectuals an extraordinary breadth of talents. Above all they were open-minded. Jefferson was a supreme polymath. To his biographer James Parton he could 'calculate an eclipse, survey an estate, tie an artery, plan an edifice, try a cause, break a horse, dance a minuet and play the violin'.

From his Virginia mansion at Monticello, Jefferson gazed out to the distant Blue Mountains, then the union's western limit, and pondered the limitless empire that lay beyond. Its size and nature were to be his prime concern as president. On his inauguration he was eager to set aside the divisions of recent years. He vowed that South and North, he and Hamilton, were at heart Americans. 'We are all Republicans. We are all Federalists,' he said. All believed in the sovereign rights of states, but all in the need for presidential

87

power. He brought originality and scope to what a president might achieve. He was truly the architect of the new America.

Unlike Adams, Jefferson was an ardent Francophile, having been minister to France in 1785–9 and seen the horrors into which chaotic rebellion could drive a nation. In 1803 he took the opportunity to negotiate with Napoleon the 'Louisiana Purchase' of France's vast territory west of the Mississippi, land that had been passed to Spain and then reverted to France over the previous twenty years. It ran from the Great Lakes and the Mississippi/Missouri basin west across the Great Plains to the Rocky Mountains, north to the Canadian border and south to the Gulf of Mexico. Its principal port was the fast-growing New Orleans. Napoleon's price was a modest $15 million, money the French emperor urgently needed to finance his planned invasion of England.

It was ironic that America was to pay for the conquest of their founders, the British, albeit that the venture was notably unsuccessful. To this end Napoleon was prepared to sacrifice the entirety of what had been France's imperial dream in America. The purchase was definitive in America's history. The eighteenth century had delivered to the new union a doubling of its land area. The Louisiana Purchase was a quantum leap, doubling it again and propelling the United States into territorial superiority over Spain.

Both acquisitions breached treaties and land rights granted over the years to Native tribes. The issue was not just legality – the rights having been unilaterally negated on independence. It was that, like most Europeans, Jefferson regarded the Native people as culturally inferior and without 'rights' of any sort. In this he could be both sympathetic and insulting, but in his opinion 'the ultimate point of rest and happiness for them is to let our settlements and theirs meet and blend together, to intermix and become one people'.

Jefferson took the view that the Native people should either merge or move west. To him the Purchase gave Americans 'possession of a chosen country with room enough for our descendants to the thousandth and thousandth generation'. Already the new land between the Appalachians and the Mississippi had come under federal supervision through a law that Jefferson had himself passed through the Continental Congress in 1785. It was an 'ordinance for ascertaining the mode of disposing of lands in the Western Territories'. It stipulated that the whole region belonged to the federal government, in effect to dispose of as it wished. It was probably the most breathtaking act of true 'nationalization' in the Western world, giving rise to stupendous corruption with the coming of the railway.

This land grab required a survey of everywhere beyond the Appalachians. A band of army cartographers under Thomas Hutchins set to work, dividing the new America into a grid pattern. They began on the Pennsylvania–Ohio border at an obelisk still standing, called appropriately the Point of Beginning. Usable territory became ten-mile-square ranges, reduced by Congress to six miles square, each covering a 'township' of thirty-six-square-miles. These squares became the universal pattern of American settlement, looking relentlessly uniform seen from above.

Specific plots were reserved for 'education' and for the use of the federal government. It is why most American roads are straight, unlike those in Europe, which tend to respect natural contours and vegetation, and why most American towns are laid out in rectangular 'blocks'. It was the ultimate geography of bureaucracy, a continent designed at an office desk, to create what Jefferson called America's 'empire of liberty'. The new America was to be in every sense of the word 'statist'.

As for the form of government that was to prevail in the new territories, Jefferson was meticulous. He decided that when a designated area reached a settler population of 5,000 it could have a governor appointed by Congress and an elected assembly. When it reached 60,000 it could apply for statehood, and its citizens could vote in federal elections. This top-down pattern proceeded slowly. Law and order had to be introduced. Land disputes had to be resolved and rudimentary infrastructure supplied. Washington was a long way away. Many settler communities protested that they were being treated as cursorily as British colonies.

With Louisiana in his pocket, Jefferson's chief concern was to press westwards, even to the Pacific, for fear of rival empires pre-empting him. Britain still held on to Canada to the north and Spain held greater Mexico or New Spain to the south. Jefferson duly sponsored his assistant, Meriwether Lewis, and a retired army officer, William Clark, to lead a Corps of Discovery across the newly acquired land, reaching the Rocky Mountains and beyond to the Pacific. The Lewis and Clark expedition, which took two years and did indeed reach the Pacific, passed through lands chiefly in the control of Native peoples who had held them since time immemorial. These Native peoples were not like the more passive tribes of the east coast. Lakota, Sioux, Apache and Comanche had acquired horses and guns and pride. Jefferson's concept of the new frontier lying empty and apparently eager for exploitation was fanciful. The reality was that it would require military conquest over the best part of a century to complete.

From the start, the acquisition of the new lands was also bedevilled by the issue of slavery. Since independence, north-eastern states had voted for abolition. In 1777 Vermont had stated that slavery offended 'natural, inherent and inalienable rights'. New England courts began granting freedom to escaped slaves and in 1787 an ordinance of the new Great Lakes territories abolished slavery in what became Illinois, Michigan and Wisconsin.

Jefferson himself frequently acknowledged that slavery would have to end. He wrote, 'I tremble for my country when I reflect that God is just' and might deliver the appropriate punishment. His solution was the slaves' eventual repatriation to Africa, including at least five born to him by one of his own, Sally Hemings. He even staffed his White House with slaves.

In 1808 Jefferson and Congress finally outlawed the international slave trade – technically an 'interstate' issue and therefore an issue for the federal government– the year after it was outlawed by Britain. Any future American slaves would now have to be born to old ones. The ban was to be postponed for two years, leading South Carolina to import some 70,000, though illegal importation continued to the 1860s. Prices soared and 'seasoned' – that is disease-free – slaves fetched $2,000, the equivalent of $60,000 at today's rates.

Black people were already being freed across the Caribbean, where slavery was in decline. In 1804 the first black Caribbean nation of Haiti became independent after a revolution. Jefferson had to concede the planters' pleas that he not recognize it lest American slaves be encouraged to revolt. He admitted to the 'moral outrage' of enslavement, but, like presidents before and after, he handed the poisoned chalice to his successors.

For the union, the issue was how the additional western states' presence in the Senate might affect the balance of slave states versus free. Initially the balance held. The three states in the Midwest, Illinois, Indiana and Ohio, were free and the other three, Louisiana, Alabama and Mississippi, were below the Mason–Dixon Line and became slave states. This line had been informally extended westwards from Pennsylvania and was the agreed northern limit of slavery. But when in 1820 slave-owning Missouri applied for statehood, the senatorial balance tipped and a crisis loomed, to be restored by the prompt arrival of slave-free Maine. None the less, Missouri was north of the informal Mason–Dixon Line. Congress shrugged and dubbed it the 'Missouri Compromise of 1820'. In truth it was a win for slavery.

Jefferson had honoured Washington's warning to steer clear of overseas conflicts, confining his intervention to commerce. He banned trade with both Britain and France in Europe's Napoleonic Wars. The consequence was a bout of tit-for-tat embargoes and counter-embargoes, disrupting business to a degree that neither he nor his successor, James Madison (1809–17), could handle. America's economy was heavily dependent on trade in cotton and tobacco with Britain. Conflict also arose over the British seizing American merchant ships and pressing their crews into the undermanned Royal Navy.

Relations with Britain swiftly deteriorated and in 1812 a British blockade of trade with America led to Madison declaring war on Britain. Countries that had been on good terms with each other since the Paris treaty were at war. American attacks at three points on the Canadian border were repulsed, most with support from Native tribes strongly opposed to the Americans. War continued for two years, culminating in 1814 in a British raid up the Potomac to attack Washington. British soldiers entered what was an undefended city and set fire to the vacant Capitol building, leaving it a smoking ruin. They then burned the White House to the ground, leaving Madison and his wife homeless until it could be rebuilt.

The War of 1812 and the desecration of Washington marked a nadir of the union's first quarter century under what critics dubbed the 'Virginian dynasty'. To northern federalists, the dynasty's neglect of America's physical and commercial security had led to ruin. A convention of federalists was called to Hartford, Connecticut, in December 1814. They proposed a constitutional amendment that would enable union members to control their own trade and restrict Congress's right to admit new ones – presumably slave states. There was even talk of expelling the new western states from the union, and of a northern secession.

This talk subsided in 1815 when an American army, led by the future president Andrew Jackson, confronted an ill-led British force outside New Orleans and defeated it. The Treaty of Ghent, being negotiated at the same time, had formalized the union's existing borders and was a clearing of the decks of a new America. Above all it ended America's treatment of Canada as the unfinished business of independence. The thirteen former colonies had assumed Canada would join them, if necessary by force. Jefferson said it would be 'merely a matter of marching'. As it was, America recognized Canada and took possession of the often ambiguously allotted state of Maine.

Canada went on to emerge in 1867 as a united dominion, loyal to the British Empire and with a future of its own. It was a future achieved even as Quebec continued as effectively a French outpost, bilingual to the present day. Relations between America and Canada became stable. In 1844 Canada even introduced America to cricket, an international match being played that year on a field in New York City between 30th Street and Broadway. The sport did not catch on, but the match continues as the Auty Cup to this day, claiming to be the longest-running international sporting fixture in the world.

The eastern United States was completed as a fast receding Spanish empire now ceded Florida to the union. Spain's retreat saw independence won from Chile (1818) to Colombia (1819), Peru (1821) and Mexico (1821). The US was now home to 7.7 million people, or 85 per cent of North America's European population. It had acquired a national hero, Uncle Sam, after Sam Wilson, supplier of beef to its army. It also acquired a future national anthem, 'The Star-Spangled Banner', celebrating the American defiance of the British at a fort in Baltimore in 1814, a fact of which I find few Americans are aware.

In 1823 a new president, James Monroe (1817–25), accepted the restored diplomatic relations with Britain. He added a bold declaration. Elaborating on what Washington and Jefferson had said in distancing America from Europe, he announced that 'the American continents . . . are henceforth not to be considered as subjects for future colonization by any European powers'. To Monroe, 'We could not view any interposition for the purpose of oppressing them or controlling in any other manner their destiny by any European power in any other light than as the manifestation of an unfriendly disposition towards the United States.' This laborious formulation became known as the Monroe Doctrine.

The doctrine was significant. It stated that what, for just half a century, had been a European settlement along the Atlantic seaboard now regarded itself as guardian angel not just of an entire continent but of an entire hemisphere. Indeed, it went further. It presented Central and South America and a still ill-defined British Canada as having a sovereign neighbour, the United States, assuming supremacy over them. It was an open question how future presidents might interpret such a doctrine, not least in regard to the newly independent Mexico's territory in North America's south-west.

10.

The Taming of America

1828–1850

The North–South divide that had briefly jeopardized the union at Hartford in 1814 did not subside. The carefully constructed constitutional balance was constantly at risk with the creation of new states advancing westwards. Nor was the divide confined to the issue of slavery. The future of the Native tribes under the union was also coming to the fore. They could not be offered Jefferson's 'solution' for the slaves. Native Americans had no notional homeland to which to return. That homeland was in the process of being stolen from them.

The remaining tribes of New England, such as the Iroquois, Mohican and Lenape, had been all but wiped out by disease and local conflict, the survivors being moved. Elsewhere some, such as those in formerly Spanish Florida, still occupied hundreds of square miles of territory. Unlike the slaves, they were subject to no laws controlling their movement or banning mixed marriages. Many were dwindling in population and their lifestyle was traditional. But many others were being assimilated as farmers and planters with their own settlements. By the nineteenth century the Five Civilized Tribes – the Cherokee, Choctaw, Chickasaw, Creek and Seminole – were occupying communities that compared with those of poorer Europeans. They lived in houses rather than wigwams and often had stable relations with neighbouring settlers.

In 1827 the mixed-race chief of the Tennessee Cherokee, John Ross, introduced a new constitution embracing an earlier bicameral assembly of his local people at Chattanooga. It had its own judiciary and what amounted to a state authority. Ross then went further and proposed independence from the United States. The state of Georgia, at the time embracing Cherokee territory, overruled any such declaration, leading to months and then years of legal argument.

The issue coincided with the presidential campaign of 1828 and the emergence of a new and dynamic figure on the American political scene. Andrew Jackson (1829–37) was a gaunt, red-haired orator with staring eyes and a wild manner, son of a passionately anti-British Ulster immigrant. Like all upwardly mobile Americans he had studied law, and he had then settled in Tennessee, rising to be a slave-owning planter and a soldier in the federal army. After commanding the victory at the Battle of New Orleans he went on to fight the Spanish in Florida. Though a national hero, Jackson had been defeated for the presidency in 1824 by a well-oiled campaign for John Quincy Adams (1825–29), son of the second president John Adams.

Four years later Jackson secured Adams's defeat, to become the first president from west of the Appalachians. He was a rough diamond with little sympathy for either Native people or the enslaved, or for that matter northerners. His victory was celebrated by a mob on Capitol Hill that cheered his ride to the White House. There it gatecrashed his welcome reception and wrecked it. The event was described as the 'arrival of King Mob' at the heart of American democracy. At the mere prospect of moving to the White House, Jackson's wife Rachel died of a heart attack.

A southerner to his roots, Jackson had no constitutional inhibitions in using his office to fight northern federalists, most of whom he detested. He hated Hamilton's 'monster' First Bank of the United States – now officially the Second Bank – which he saw as a tool to enrich the north-eastern patriarchy at the South's expense. He used more presidential vetoes against congressional measures than any of his predecessors. His refrain was that America's strength lay 'in leaving individuals and states as much as possible to themselves'. This his supporters declared to be a 'second declaration of independence'. Jackson was not the man to heal the splits now looming on the union's horizon.

Ross's 1828 bid for an independent Cherokee state received short shrift. It encouraged Jackson's proposal of a seismic moment in the history of America's domestic imperialism. This involved the mass relocation of Native tribes to lands west of the Mississippi. It meant the total expulsion of eighteen of the largest tribal groups, including all Five Civilized Tribes from the south-east. Southern tribes were allotted land in Oklahoma while the northern ones received land in Kansas. Jackson initially suggested that relocation be voluntary and even grant-aided, though the Native people would all have to become American citizens.

The eviction of Native people from their ancestral lands into what was largely wilderness provoked outrage among more liberal Americans. Many tribes had been guaranteed their territories by Britain and even subsequently by the colonists. Jackson's expulsions were breaches both of faith and of the Declaration of Independence. The Native people were being denied the freedoms and privileges that Americans had fought and recently won for themselves, often with Native help. Jackson did not give an inch; indeed, his supporters pointed out that his policy was no more than had been proposed by Jefferson for black people. In 1830 he duly signed the Indian Removal Act. It was a clear case of ethnic cleansing.

The Chickasaws, the Choctaws and the Creeks were the first to take up the offer, and great treks ensued west across the southern territories. The Florida Seminoles refused to move and the result was an eight-year conflict in which 1,500 American soldiers and unknown numbers of Native people were to die. The experience of Ross and his Cherokees was no less shocking. When in 1838 they also refused to move, the United States army drove some 15,500 of them at gunpoint from their homes onto a forced march to the west. A quarter died of disease and starvation along a route that became known as the Trail of Tears. In just fifteen years following Jackson's law, some 130,000 Native people living east of the Mississippi were reduced to 30,000, mostly in reservations. Their former lands were soon occupied by settlers and their slaves from Virginia, the Carolinas and Georgia.

These settlers now supplied Europe's markets with a deluge of sugar and cotton exported mostly down the Mississippi to New Orleans. Three thousand bales of cotton in 1790 rose to 3 million in 1850. The number of slaves in what became the state of Louisiana increased over the same period from 20,000 to 100,000. Meanwhile, 40 per cent of America's black population was now composed of freed people, most having migrated to northern states.

Jackson's persistent use of his presidential veto, which could be overridden only by a two-thirds majority of both houses of Congress, was seen by the northern federalists as monarchy if not dictatorship. He was depicted in cartoons wearing a crown and robes as King Andrew the First. But he and his newly formed Democratic Party won a second term in 1832. The party's primary cause was states' independence in conducting their internal affairs, notably the interests of southern slave-owning farmers. In the North, Jackson's formerly federalist opponents adopted the name of Whigs, after Britain's proto-Liberals.

The 1830s in America coincided with a burst of reformist zeal in Europe, with France seeing a resumed revolutionary upheaval and Britain passing its seminal 1832 Great Reform Act. In 1831 a twenty-six-year-old French aristocrat and political idealist, Alexis de Tocqueville (1805–59), was asked by his government to study American prisons. He came with a friend and spent nine months on a remarkable visit, along the east coast, west to Michigan and down the Mississippi to New Orleans. How far his observations, published in 1835–40 as *Democracy in America*, were conditioned by Jackson's turbulent presidency is a matter of debate. But his insights even today seem fresh and astute and were to influence all future studies of American politics.

What fascinated de Tocqueville above all was the capacity of democracy to balance liberty with equality. Though liberty was his 'foremost passion', and he believed excessive equality led to tyranny, the essence of a successful society was that neither should curb the other. He loved the openness of American debate, noting the lack of an aristocracy. Anyone could become 'a gentleman', though it

led to 'less refinement of manners'. He reached the intriguing per-
ception that 'the American is the Englishman left to himself'. This is
a foretaste of Jonathan Freedland's conclusion that England's radical upheaval may have taken place under the eighteenth-century
Enlightenment, but in truth 'the Founding Fathers took a revolution intended for [Britain] and shipped it across the Atlantic'.

De Tocqueville admired America's prisons, whose efficient 'despotism' he saw as rooted in equality and the need for rehabilitation.
But as for slavery, 'man's degradation by man', that it should 'tarnish
the glory' of a Christian nation appalled him. He longed for 'the
day when the law will grant equal civil liberty to all inhabitants of
the same empire . . . without distinction'. His parting thought was
ahead of his time, that one day America would share with Russia
'the destinies of half the world'.

In the 1830s and 40s the American far west became what history
later labelled it: the Wild West. Much of the land legally belonged to
now liberated Mexico, granted its independence by Spain in 1821, or
more appropriately to various Native tribes. This territory stretched
from the Gulf of Mexico north through what became Texas and
west up the long Pacific coast of California. Here lay Spanish settlements and missions as far as Oregon, where Britain claimed territory
as part of its Canadian colonies. Outside the missions, Spain had
had little effective control, any more than Mexico now did. Borders
were indistinct. The result was a random influx of newcomers, land-
hungry and often aggressive towards the Native people.

In Texas in 1835 a group of settlers in what had been a part of
post-Spanish Mexico declared themselves independent of the Mexican government and indeed an independent nation. A year later a
Mexican army reacted by overwhelming a settler fort, the Alamo in
San Antonio, killing all its occupants. Among them was one David
'Davy' Crockett (1786–1836), a soldier adventurer and archetype of
the American frontiersman. Crockett was the son of a struggling
Tennessee farmer. He had volunteered to serve with Andrew Jackson's army in Florida and then won election to Congress in 1827.

Crockett had become a fierce defender of Native rights, the

only Tennesseean in Congress to vote against Jackson's 1830 Indian Removal Act. For this he received fulsome thanks in a letter from the Cherokee chief, John Ross. Falling out of favour with his electors, he famously told them that if they were unsatisfied with him as their representative, 'They could go to hell and I would go to Texas.'

In 1836 Crockett did just that. He arrived with a troop of supporters in time to die defending the Alamo. For some reason he was reborn by Hollywood a century later as 'Davy Crockett, King of the Wild Frontier' with a signature racoon-skin cap. American history acquired a new genre, the frontiersman charging over the desert on horseback in search of Indians, justice and adventure, and not a woman in sight.

A month later a Texan army under Sam Houston avenged the Alamo. It defeated a Mexican force and won independence for Texas from Mexico in return for releasing its president, Antonio de Santa Anna, from captivity. Independence lasted for a decade from 1836 and was recognized by both France and Britain. The Texan embassy in London is still recalled in a plaque at the bottom of St James's Street. But the new nation was rejected by Congress and the state of Texas was annexed by the union in 1845. Its distinctive origins were recognized in its nickname, the Lone Star state. It was also given the right to pocket revenues from its natural resources, later overwhelmingly oil.

In 1845 a new president arrived in Washington, a follower of Jackson in the person of James Polk of Tennessee (1845–49). He was determined to complete Jefferson's ambition and carry the union beyond the Great Plains across the Rocky Mountains and down to the Pacific. He did this despite the opposition of northern states, who saw nothing but danger in such uncharted territory. They also saw the added risk of tilting the senatorial majority south of the Mason–Dixon Line and towards slavery.

Polk tried to purchase California and New Mexico from the Mexicans. He offered $40 million but this was rejected. He then turned to outright war and initiated a one-sided conflict that lasted two years from 1846. A series of battles leading to 15,000 American deaths culminated in American troops marching into Mexico City in 1847. A final settlement saw California and New Mexico purchased for just $15 million.

This meant that by 1848 Polk had assembled almost all of what was to be the United States, east to west, sea to sea. Half of America's land area had now been acquired from France, Spain and Mexico for less than three cents an acre. The seizure of much of what had been Mexico was straightforward military conquest. There was no reference to America's duty to bring higher values to the aid of lesser people, to Jefferson's 'empire of freedom' or Thomas Paine's 'birthday of a new world'. The Mexican war was one of naked imperialism. The future victor in the Civil War – and later president – General Ulysses S. Grant, was to say 'to this day I regard the [Mexican] war as one of the most unjust ever waged by a stronger against a weaker nation. It was an instance of a republic following the bad example of European monarchies.' Grant saw its intention as to expand slavery. Meanwhile the Oregon Territory, long disputed with British Canada, was also established and organized in 1848, eventually becoming the states of Washington, Oregon and Idaho.

Polk's initiatives were not without congressional controversy. There was now popular pressure to seek more distant lands to conquer. Attention moved to Cuba, Nicaragua and Honduras, with a vision of the entire Caribbean becoming a slave-owning American possession, 'the American Mediterranean'. The incorporation of the remaining half of Mexico into the union was championed by the 'All of Mexico' movement, encouraged by Polk's creation of Oregon. But in 1848 it was damned by the leading South Carolina senator, John Calhoun, who declared that American citizens had always been Caucasian. 'Ours, sir, is the government of a white race.' The Caribbean should be taboo. In the event the debate subsided and Congress finally agreed to rest its ambitions at the Rio Grande and the Texas border.

The 1840s were thus a time of much uncertainty over the nature and extent of the country now over half a century old. Northerners were full of foreboding at what expansion into the Caribbean might mean. The essayist Ralph Waldo Emerson saw America as home of a humanity at one with nature. 'I have taught one doctrine,' he wrote, 'namely, the infinitude of the private man.' This philosophy was well suited to America's newly acquired horizons. But to Emerson it also implied respecting the rights of the Native people, a people who seemed closer to nature. He allied what he regarded as the free spirit of America's original Dissenting religion to the Romanticism that he admired in Britain's Wordsworth, Coleridge and Carlyle.

Another prophet of the new frontier was Henry Thoreau (1817–62) with his belief that young America had an obligation to self-reliance and nature. Like Emerson he was a follower of the Transcendentalists and the related Unitarian movement. These were among the many religious sects to which the new American frontier offered psychological as well as geographical liberation. The most eccentric were the Amish Mennonites, who had migrated in the eighteenth century from Alsace and Switzerland to Pennsylvania, where they hoped to settle uncontaminated by worlds old and new. They split into Old Order and New Order, the Old Order speaking 'Pennsylvanian Dutch' (a dialect of German), wearing old-fashioned clothes and having nothing to do with machinery. They survive as such to the present day.

Most ambitious were the Mormons. Led by a charismatic preacher, Joseph Smith, they abandoned the east coast and headed west in search of a promised land. Their early practice of slavery, polygamy and other customs caused difficulties wherever they settled. Smith died, but in 1847 his successor, Brigham Young, arrived at what appeared to be a fertile valley deep in the Rocky Mountains. The land turned out to be barren and the apparent lake therein was composed of salt. But the Mormons were hard-working, the settlement prospered and Salt Lake City became capital of the future state of Utah.

The far west meanwhile erupted into a different kind of promised land. In 1848 two men found gold in the water of a mill race close to the northern border. Attempts to keep the discovery secret failed and, as word spread, prospectors arrived in their thousands.

Copious quantities of gold were found in northern California and east of Sacramento in the Sierra Nevada. The result was pandemonium, enhanced by President Polk announcing the discovery to Congress. Not just Americans but Mexicans, Chinese and even Europeans came in a frenzy.

California experienced what was the world's greatest gold rush. Shanty towns sprang up, and a crash economy emerged to sustain them. The population of San Francisco, just 1,000 in 1848, grew in two years to 25,000. The area's population soon became 300,000. The so-called 'forty-niners' were legendary. A few made fortunes, most left empty-handed. The wisest ran boarding houses and banks, selling the gold-seekers food, picks, shovels and whiskey.

The discovery of gold in California and its lurch from anarchy towards statehood – achieved in 1850 – reopened old wounds of the North–South division. The issue for Congress was, yet again, whether it should accept slavery in the new west or not. California had no slaves and was effectively a state founded afresh. The result was a series of confrontations in Congress. Northerners demanded that all states acquired from slave-free Mexico continue as such. The anti-slavery New York senator William Seward called for a welcome to the 'youthful Queen of the Pacific in her robes of freedom gorgeously inlaid with gold'. Southerners suggested that perhaps the 1820 Missouri Compromise might be extended across the entire continent to the Pacific.

Once again the heirs to Madison's mastery of arbitration won the day. This time the mediator was a senior senator, Stephen Douglas of Illinois. It was decided that California should be free of slavery but other western states could be considered at a later date. Meanwhile, slaves escaping from the South to the North could still be caught by licensed 'slave-catchers' and returned as their owners' property. This was declared to be the 'Compromise of 1850'. Douglas asserted that 'the South has not triumphed over the North nor has the North achieved a victory over the South. Each has preserved its honour.' Washington saw bonfires all night in celebration.

The can had been kicked yet further down the road, to end in the horrors of civil conflict. But later historians who deplored America's pile-up of compromises could see them as perhaps the necessary outcome of a clash of interests. It meant their resolution through debate and concession rather than violence and anarchy. It was compromise that in 1776 salvaged a union from discord. It was compromise that brought Massachusetts and Virginia – both with passionately held intolerances – to sign up to a constitutional coalition. If the American union was based on any principle, it was not liberty or equality, it was compromise.

Nothing more vividly illustrated America's westward expansion than its need for means of transport, long limited to the horse and cart or carriage. Mobility was to prove the great agency of federal power. Jefferson's federal government had assumed sovereignty over the new lands to the west, and taken responsibility for bonding them into the union. But these lands were still governed by the tyranny of distance, by the speed of a horse's hoof.

The answer as the nineteenth century progressed was the canal and eventually the railway. The first and most spectacular project was the Erie Canal, running from Buffalo on Lake Erie some 363 miles to the Hudson River at Albany in New York. Opened in 1825, it linked the Great Lakes to New York City and thus the Midwest to the Atlantic by a route faster than down the Mississippi. On the canal's final opening in New York City, a libation of Erie freshwater was poured into the sea at Manhattan in a ceremony dubbed the 'Wedding of the Waters'.

As in Europe, the American age of the canal did not last long before being overtaken by the age of the railway. In 1828, just three years after the Erie Canal opened, work began on the Baltimore and Ohio railway. It ran from Baltimore south to Washington and across the Appalachians to Ohio. Boston followed with a line up the coast to Maine. The way ahead was clear and construction became frantic. By 1840, America had twice as many miles of railway as had been laid in the whole of continental Europe.

With the track came the other great aid to industrialization: the electro-magnetic telegraph, invented by Samuel Morse (1791–1872) in the 1830s. He was an extraordinary character, typifying the openness of America to new talents and new technologies. Morse was for the first half of his career one of the nation's most distinguished artists. He travelled to London, met his fellow American Benjamin West and studied at the Royal Academy before returning to become professor of painting at New York University. He depicted classical and religious scenes and painted presidents and congressmen, including Adams and Monroe.

Morse was a stern Calvinist and a defender of slavery as 'God's will'. At the same time he became fascinated by electro-magnetic telegraphy. In the 1830s he was duly involved in a race to patent a 'single-wire' telegraph. This involved using relays of batteries to send messages over long distances. Morse also co-invented a code, patented in 1840, of short and long bursts to transmit letters of the alphabet, most famously S-O-S. Within ten years, telegraph wires extended alongside 12,000 miles of American railway line. The code remained in use into the twenty-first century, though Morse spent much of his life suing rival inventors. His art subsided into history.

By then railways were transforming movement up and down the east coast and across the Mississippi Basin. The Illinois Central turned Chicago, which had barely existed in 1830, into the capital of the Midwest. The city welcomed its first train in 1848 and within twelve years was served by eleven lines with a hundred trains a day. It serviced the Midwest's so-called 'Corn Belt' and initially became America's 'porkopolis'. By 1860 Chicago was home to the largest livestock market in the world. An estimated 80 per cent of Midwest farms were located within five miles of a railway.

How this boom was financed was a different matter. At root was the belief, or Jeffersonian claim, that the land 'belonged to America', interpreted as the federal government. There were as yet no local states in much of the west and the federal executive felt entitled to dispose of the land within the terms of the constitution as for 'inter-state commerce'. Washington incentivized railway builders by giving them land and even grants to lay tracks.

During the 1860s it is estimated that some 100 million acres of supposedly virgin America were handed to railway companies to speed their growth. This included a quarter of Minnesota and an eighth of the whole of California. American railway bonds were sold the world over, including an extraordinary $4 billion-worth in Britain. British investors could reasonably claim to have built America's railways. I have a *Punch* cartoon of Queen Victoria pleading with Albert not to buy American railway bonds.

The impact was transformational. West of the Mississippi, trains slashed transport times and sent farm profits soaring. The railway was to dominate the emergence of American corporate finance, operating largely from New York. It was unregulated and highly monopolistic, the creature of a small number of so-called 'robber barons'. But it fuelled the frontier myth. Over the Great Plains there now thundered huge engines charging towards an ever receding boundary. With their cow-catcher fenders and high funnels the engines came to embody the Wild West machismo. They were the mammoths of old returned to America, bringing in their wake progress, profit and corruption.

II

The Union in Disarray

1850–1860

As America charged forth into its new hinterland, its constitution – and its compromises – struggled to keep pace. They were now close to breaking point, and the bone of contention was still slavery. In the days before mass media, public opinion could only on rare occasions be assaulted by a writer and a book. It had happened with Tom Paine's *Common Sense* in 1776. It happened again in 1852 with the publication of *Uncle Tom's Cabin* by Harriet Beecher Stowe.

Stowe's novel was the work of a devout abolitionist from Connecticut who had spent time in Ohio's Cincinnati amid a turmoil of escaped slaves and racial violence. The story was set against the anarchic backdrop of the Mississippi River and told of an enslaved person whose family was broken by his being sold by his owner and thence dispersed into the maelstrom of mid-century southern America. The result was cruelty and kindness in equal measure, before a sort of redemption is found in emigration and the Christian faith.

The book revealed to northern Americans, often for the first time, the moral degradation of slavery as practised in the South. It was a publishing sensation. Three hundred thousand copies were sold in a year, and for the rest of the century it was outsold only by the Bible. *Uncle Tom's Cabin* was translated into twenty languages, with 1.5 million copies bought in Britain in the first year alone. These yielded Stowe not a penny, as there was as yet no copyright agreement with Britain. She later met Abraham Lincoln, who reportedly called her 'the little woman who made the book that made the [Civil] War'. This may be apocryphal, though the sentiment is accurate.

A measure of the completeness of America's racial oppression was the rarity with which any black personality emerged, North or South, to lead the anti-slavery cause. An exception was Frederick Douglass (1818–95), the son of a black mother and an unknown white father. He began life as a slave, taught himself to read and write and eventually escaped to New York. He arrived in 1838 'on a day of joyous excitement, as one might feel on escape from a den of hungry lions'.

Douglass soon began a career as an abolitionist writer and speaker across the North. He was no militant, but he lived in perpetual danger of arrest and return to his owner. In 1845 and still in his twenties Douglass travelled to Europe, where he spent twenty-one months delivering some three hundred speeches in England, Wales and Ireland. He delighted in being received everywhere 'as a man not a colour', and money was eventually raised to buy his freedom. He condemned his country as 'guilty of crimes that would disgrace a nation of savages'.

On returning home, Douglass's celebrity was such that in 1872 he was nominated as running mate for the first woman to stand for president, Victoria Woodhull. He was also America's first black ambassador, to liberated Haiti in the Caribbean. His three volumes of memoirs, begun in 1845 and finished in 1881, became a classic. Douglass was determined that America should never forget slavery's 'ghastly terror, the wails of millions that pierce my heart and chill my blood . . . the chain, the gag, the bloody whip, the deathlike gloom overshadowing the broken spirit of the fettered bondsman, the appalling liability of being torn away from wife and children and sold like a beast in the market'.

Over the course of the 1850s, the slavery issue moved swiftly to crisis. The international trade in slaves had long been banned in western countries, and slavery with it. Yet Virginia was thought to have exported 25,000 'home-grown' slaves a year across the American South. New western states were lining up for membership of Congress and in 1854 Kansas and Nebraska joined the queue. Yet again, the stalling issue was slavery. The maestro of constitutional compromise, Senator Stephen Douglas of Illinois, negotiated a

Kansas-Nebraska Act that left it to the new states to decide on slavery for themselves. In other words, though both applicants were north of the informal Mason–Dixon Line, they could still join as slave states. It was hardly a compromise.

Nebraska voted against slavery, though initially denying black people the vote. Kansas descended into chaos. It was invaded by northern activists able to register and vote against slavery, whereupon 'border ruffians' poured in from Missouri to vote for it. Riots ensued and the would-be state was dubbed 'Bleeding Kansas'. The pro-slavers won the vote, but the bid for statehood was turned down by the House of Representatives. Kansas now found itself with two 'duelling constitutions', for and against slavery. For months it had rival governments, rival assemblies and even rival capitals, in Lecompton and Lawrence. The Lecompton Constitution, written in 1857, was shamelessly pro-slavery. But by 1861 Kansas changed its mind, voted against and won admission to Congress.

Douglas's act traumatized American politics as no previous compromise had done. The South's new Democratic Party was pro-slavery and, for the time being, was disowned in the North, where it confronted a revitalized Republican Party. This was committed to 'free soil, free labour, free speech, free men'. In 1857 the Supreme Court added fuel to the flames. Throughout the pre-Civil War period, the court was dominated by Justice Roger Taney, a pro-slavery appointee of Andrew Jackson. Almost all its judges had been appointed by slave-owning Virginian presidents. As long as these judges lived – and they were appointed for life – the court would have no sympathy for abolition.

That year the Supreme Court went too far. In the case of a slave, Dred Scott, it upheld the owner's right to hold him in bondage even after migrating with him to a northern state. The judges reasoned that American 'rights' applied only to white people. Black people were 'beings of an inferior order and altogether unfit to associate with the white race, either in social or political relations; and so far inferior that they had no rights which the white man was bound to respect'. The matter was considered closed.

But closed it was not. In 1858 and 1859 Minnesota and Oregon were accepted into the union, both free of slavery. The result was unequivocal. The South could now be outvoted in both the Senate and the House of Representatives, in the latter by 147 votes to 90. Slavery appeared doomed. In 1859 a white Puritan evangelist named John Brown, who believed himself appointed by God to end slavery, took up the Beecher Stowe cause. He attempted to start a slave uprising in the South by seizing weapons stored at Harper's Ferry in Virginia. The mission was suicidal. Brown was arrested along with his accomplices and hanged, and became a martyr to abolition. Children round the world were later to sing the abolitionist chant, 'John Brown's body lies a-mouldering in the grave . . . But his soul goes marching on.'

An Illinois politician, Abraham Lincoln (1809–65), now took up the cause. He was a rugged Midwesterner and son of frontier toil, without a formal education and bred to the axe and the plough. He taught himself law and responded to the call of politics, being elected to Congress in 1847. He had a skill much lacking in public speakers, then and since: that of brevity.

Lincoln's first contact with slavery was seeing beneath his window on Capitol Hill 'a stable where gangs of negroes were sold, and sometimes kept in store for a time, pending transport to a southern market'. Shocked, he drafted a law to abolish slavery in the District of Columbia. In 1858 Lincoln ran for the Senate against Stephen Douglas and against any state's right formally to permit slavery. Addressing his Illinois convention, he summed up America's ills in a celebrated passage: '"A house divided against itself cannot stand." I believe this government cannot endure, permanently half slave and half free. I do not expect the Union to be dissolved – I do not expect the house to fall – but I do expect it will cease to be divided. It will become all one thing, or all the other.'

Lincoln lost to Douglas in 1858, but his widely reported oratory became so popular that in 1860 he ran for president and won. He and his wife had to sneak into the White House under cover of darkness after threats of assassination. Convinced that Lincoln would immediately find a way to free all its slaves, the state of South Carolina promptly seceded from the union and declared its independence. Mississippi followed two weeks later in January 1861. As other southern states prepared to follow their example, Lincoln understandably feared for the union's future.

In Washington's traditional spirit of compromise, Lincoln initially denied any wish to intervene in the internal affairs of southern states. He was not banning slavery and was only against its extension to the new states of the west. Expressing himself with characteristic fervour, he said, 'Though passion may have strained, it must not break our bonds of affection.' Lincoln appealed to the 'mystic chords of memory stretching from every battlefield and patriot grave to every living heart and hearthstone'. They must give way to 'the better angels of our nature'.

Even in Lincoln's hands the art of compromise had reached its limits. By February 1861 the states of the so-called Deep South – South Carolina, Georgia, Florida, Alabama, Mississippi and Louisiana – had seceded and formed the Confederate States of America. They were later joined by other slave states – Virginia, North Carolina, Tennessee and Arkansas. The North was now reduced to twenty 'free' states, while the border – and slave – states of Delaware, Maryland, Missouri and Kentucky were wavering in their loyalties. Though a slave state, Maryland remained narrowly Unionist.

The president chosen by the new southern Confederacy was a Mississippi senator, Jefferson Davis. He was a small-time planter who regarded the North's attitude to the South as, without irony, one of 'perfidious interference in the rights of other men'. Of secession he said, 'We should part peaceably and avoid staining the battlefields of the Revolution with the blood of civil war.' But Davis was no statesman and certainly no conciliator. Nor was he an aristocrat. When he and his wife moved from Mississippi to the South's patrician capital of Richmond in Virginia, the Virginians looked down on him and his wife as vulgar 'westerners'. It was said their dinner invitations were not accepted.

Initially for Lincoln, as for his opponents in the South, the argument remained one of states' rights. The mostly Virginian authors of the constitution had regarded those rights as the golden chain that bonded the thirteen divergent colonies together. The tenth amendment was explicit, that 'powers not delegated to the United States by the constitution nor prohibited by it to the states are reserved to the states'. Madison had elaborated on these words in a Federalist paper, no. 45. A state's power should extend to all its citizens 'all the objects which, in the ordinary course of affairs, concern the lives, liberties and properties of the people and the internal order, improvement and prosperity of the state'.

In other words, it was constitutional for the states to determine the definition of the rights of man. The union government was a mere treaty association, an alliance to be activated in limited circumstances for collective security and inter-state interest. Just as Massachusetts might define and regulate religion, citizenship and matrimony, so Virginia might define and regulate slavery. The terms of the Declaration of Independence, as Lincoln was to say, were those of pious intention rather than federal policy.

The reality was that by 1860 slavery in America was a 'right' too far. The trade had become illegal throughout the western world and enslavement was no longer practised in what was regarded by Europeans as civilized countries. Leaving it to individual states was no longer tolerable, nor was there scope for compromise. Abolition might not be acceptable to the South, but nor was secession acceptable to the North.

The two capitals prepared for war, Washington for the North and Richmond, just a hundred miles away, for the South. Lincoln offered command of the northern army to its most distinguished officer, Robert E. Lee (1807–70). But Lee was first and foremost a Virginian and put loyalty to his state before his country. He returned to his home in Arlington, offering himself as commander to the militia army of Virginia. That loyalty held to the end.

12.

Civil War

1861–1865

The outcome of a war between America's 'Union' North and 'Confederate' South was predictable but not certain. The North was in every sense bigger and better resourced than the South. It had twice the South's population, a third of the latter being slaves. The North had an industrial base out of all proportion to that of the mostly agricultural South. Of firearms manufactured in America, 97 per cent were made in the North. The South's only hope was that northern armies might be disinclined to fight over what was essentially a moral issue of no particular relevance to most of them.

A scene in America's most celebrated Civil War film, *Gone with the Wind*, depicts a southern sceptic, Rhett Butler, criticizing his colleagues for their reckless bravado. 'I'm saying very plainly,' he states, 'that the Yankees are better equipped than we are. They've got factories, shipyards, coalmines and a fleet to bottle our harbours and starve us to death. All we've got is cotton and slaves and arrogance.' Butler's colleagues turn on him and shout him down, accusing him of cowardice and treachery.

Certainly in terms of civilian morale, the South was ascendant. It was fighting for what it saw as its very existence. In April 1861 war formally began with the fall to Confederate forces of the Union's Fort Sumter in South Carolina, whose garrison surrendered and returned to New York. In July the Unionist general Irvin McDowell marched his army out of Washington in the direction of the Confederate army at Richmond. Spectators brought picnics to watch the battle and, they expected, to congratulate their soldiers on victory.

McDowell met Lee's army at Bull Run Creek, just twenty-five miles south-west of the northern capital.

In the event, the southerners defeated what was an ill-prepared and ill-trained Unionist force. In one assault the Unionists were rebuffed by the resistance of a Confederate officer, Colonel Thomas Jackson (1824–63), earning him the nickname 'Stonewall'. A veteran of the Mexican war, Jackson became one of the South's most famous soldiers. After two days of fighting at Bull Run, the undisciplined Unionists fled back to Washington in disarray, having suffered 481 fatalities against 387 Confederates. The South was elated and its morale boosted. Lincoln realized he had a serious fight on his hands.

The Union forces were now put under a more competent commander, George McClellan. He built a new army, though it was one that proved battle-averse. McClellan ordered his soldiers to show restraint, to avoid violence against fellow Americans and to respect property. They had lived together at peace and would have to do so again. This dignified civility was widely ridiculed. As McClellan moved his army slowly through Virginia – his nickname became the 'Virginia creeper' – an exasperated Lincoln lost patience. He asked sarcastically if he could borrow McClellan's army to fight a war.

A general of sterner pedigree was fighting for the North in Tennessee. While McClellan had promised to fight 'like a gentleman', Ulysses S. Grant (1822–85) did not. First at Fort Donelson and then at Shiloh in April 1862, this veteran of the Mexican war met Confederate armies in pitched battles. Though some 3,500 soldiers died in equal numbers on each side, Grant was the eventual victor. His first two initials were said to stand for unconditional surrender.

Lincoln did now try conciliation. He wanted to avoid the war degenerating into a 'violent and remorseless revolutionary struggle'. His intention, he told Congress at the end of 1861, was not to eradicate slavery but possibly to resettle the slaves somewhere 'in a climate congenial to them', for which the state might pay. Thus far he was happy to keep America white. This merely divided northern opinion. Some were happy to stop fighting so long as secession ended. Others thought the whole point of the war was to end slavery and achieve freedom for its victims.

By 1862 the war had become one of attrition. In September the South's Lee decided to force the pace by marching into Maryland. At the Battle of Antietam, though the Unionists lost 12,400 dead to the Confederates 10,300, the uncertain outcome led Lee to return to Virginia. McClellan's failure to pursue him to Richmond, which might have ended the war, enraged Lincoln and he was sacked. Lincoln now abandoned all interest in compromise and made abolition his goal.

Reinforced by Antietam, Lincoln proceeded, on 1 January 1863, to publish his Emancipation Proclamation. It announced that, as of the following year, all black people held as slaves in the rebel states should be 'thenceforward and forever free'. It did not free slaves in states not taking part in the war. Black soldiers serving in the Union army – there were eventually more than 100,000, or 10 per cent of the total – served in separate corps, often under white officers. Those defecting from the South were made American citizens and paid similar wages.

The proclamation delighted many in the North, but in many of the slave-owning parts of the Midwest and the western states it served to harden the South's resistance. Lincoln's own Illinois assembly protested that he had personally converted a battle to rescue the Union into a 'sudden, unconditional and violent liberation of three million negro slaves'. To one congressman this meant the most 'dismal foreboding of horror and dismay'. Border states such as Missouri and Kansas were split. The Mississippi remained a river of slaves.

As the war dragged on through 1863, Grant showed ever greater ruthlessness, with little respect for lives or property. A campaign began at Vicksburg on the Mississippi River, where a Union force besieged the town and forced the Confederate General John C. Pemberton to surrender. On the Confederate side in Virginia Lee fought and won a series of smaller battles, though to little advantage. He now attempted a mass advance northwards with an army of some 80,000 into Pennsylvania. His intention was to defeat the main Union force and reach Philadelphia, where he would demand that Lincoln call a ceasefire.

At the start of July he met a Union army around 100,000 strong under General George Meade outside the town of Gettysburg. In three days of fierce fighting Lee failed to penetrate the Union lines. On 3 July a final Confederate advance known as Pickett's Charge was launched against massed rifle and artillery fire. It was suicidal and led to the worst carnage of the war. Gettysburg saw over 18,000 American soldiers dead or missing in three days, evenly divided between the two sides. Finally, the Confederates admitted defeat and retreated south.

Though Lee's forces never again confronted the enemy in a pitched battle, the Confederacy still refused to surrender. Four months later, on 19 November 1863, a cemetery was opened at Gettysburg to commemorate the battle. At the ceremony Lincoln addressed a gathering that had already endured a two-hour speech from an orator, Edward Everett. His learned references to Athenians and ancient Greece passed over the heads of most of those present, who fled to feed and relieve themselves. They therefore missed Lincoln's ensuing speech, which lasted just two minutes.

The Gettysburg Address is like the Declaration of Independence, a treasured icon of American history. The ever concise Lincoln needed just 267 words (in his signed version) to make his point:

Four score and seven years ago our fathers brought forth on this continent a new nation, conceived in Liberty and dedicated to the proposition that all men are created equal.

Now we are engaged in a great civil war, testing whether that nation, or any nation so conceived and so dedicated, can long endure. We are met on a great battle-field of that war. We have come to dedicate a portion of that field, as a final resting place for those who here gave their lives that that nation might live. It is altogether fitting and proper that we should do this.

But, in a larger sense, *we* cannot dedicate – *we* cannot consecrate – *we* cannot hallow – this ground. The brave men living and dead who struggled here have consecrated it, far above our poor power to add or detract. The world will little note, nor long remember, what we say here but it can never forget what they did here. It is for us the living rather to be dedicated here, to the unfinished work which they who fought here have thus far so nobly advanced.

It is rather for us to be here dedicated to the great task remaining before us – that from these honoured dead we take increased devotion to that cause for which they gave the last full measure of devotion – that we here highly resolve that these dead shall not have died in vain – that this nation, under God, shall have a new birth of freedom – and that government of the people, by the people, for the people, shall not perish from the earth.

Few speeches in history have enjoyed more scrutiny than the Gettysburg Address. Lincoln primarily intended a tribute to the fallen in battle, so often the recipients of clichéd tributes. On a more subtle level the speech served as a redefinition of America and Americanism in the light of a conflict approaching its end. Nowhere did Lincoln refer to the individual states of the Union, let alone to their rights. He made no reference to North or South, nor east or west. Without referring to slavery, he talked of the 'new birth of freedom' in a land that he nowhere called the United States, singular or plural, but simply the nation.

With the South still refusing to surrender, the North grew increasingly exhausted. Its generals grew ever more ruthless. In September 1864 the western commander, William Sherman, laid siege to Atlanta. He ordered its population to evacuate and burned it to the ground. The flames of Atlanta became the most dramatic symbol of the war's ruthlessness.

Sherman then cut a swathe of destruction sixty miles wide through Georgia before advancing to Savannah on the coast, effectively cutting the Confederacy in two. The South's president Jefferson Davis was losing his sanity. He said he would never surrender unless the South became totally independent. He promised that his generals would 'bring the North to its knees by summer'. His vice-president resigned in despair and went home.

The South was afflicted with rampant inflation, starvation and the prospect of massacres. Its desperate army debated recruiting black people to its ranks. On this Lee was unequivocal. Did the South want abolition imposed on them by the North or was it prepared to incorporate black people somehow into their society? His conclusion was the latter: 'We should employ them without delay . . . with a well-digested plan of gradual and general emancipation.' As a result, in March 1865 the Confederacy admitted black people into the army's ranks. It was as if five years of war had been in vain.

In January 1865 Congress, with no southern delegates present, passed the thirteenth amendment to the American constitution, the first to be added for half a century. It stated in bald terms that 'neither slavery nor involuntary servitude, except as a punishment for crime whereof the party shall have been duly convicted, shall exist within the United States, or in any place subject to their jurisdiction. Congress shall have power to enforce this article by appropriate legislation.' The act was written and done. The South would have to accept it as a condition of eventually rejoining the Union.

In April the war approached its climax in the destruction of much of the Confederate capital of Richmond. Lincoln arrived in the city soon afterwards, to be greeted by crowds of now emancipated black people. West of Richmond at the town of Appomattox, Lee's troops came to a standstill and he finally met Grant to surrender. The two generals knew each other, having fought together in Mexico. Though the terms had been negotiated beforehand, the ceremony conducted in a modest private house was one of courteous emotion.

The southern army laid down its weapons, though the officers were allowed to keep their swords. Lee asked that his horses be left with the soldiers to whom they belonged, most of them being farmers desperate to plant that year's crops. Grant conceded. Lee then pleaded that his army was near starvation, and Grant offered rations to feed 25,000. As the two men left the house, their staff descended on the room and stripped it of souvenirs. The desk went to a certain General Custer, who was later to achieve celebrity in another domestic conflict. A lone Confederate warship, CSS *Shenandoah*, could not be informed. It went on to capture much of the Unionist whaling fleet in the Pacific Arctic after the ceasefire.

In five years of civil war it is estimated that 700,000 American soldiers died, about 60 per cent of them on the Unionist side. But it was the South that suffered worse proportionally, losing what was a fifth of its adult male population. Eleven of its principal cities were partially or wholly destroyed. There had been 237 named battles. In the out-turn more northern combatants died, of wounds and disease, than southern ones, largely because there were more of them. The northern poet and essayist Walt Whitman (1819–92) was one of many who visited hospitals during the war and was shocked at their conditions – echoing those found by England's Florence Nightingale a decade earlier in the Crimea. Three-quarters of field operations were amputations.

Whitman's brother served in the Union army and spent five months in a Confederate prison. In such prisons some 26,000 Union soldiers died of wounds and starvation. Whitman estimated that he had attended more than 100,000 soldiers in the course of about six hundred visits. It doubtless helped him become one of the great chroniclers of nineteenth-century America. Another writer turned hospital visitor was Louisa May Alcott, whose eternally popular novel *Little Women* (1868) was set during the Civil War.

On 14 April, Lincoln welcomed his principal general, Grant, to the White House in a state of relief and joy. Afterwards he and his wife Mary went to Ford's Theatre to see an English comedy, *Our American Cousin*. Amid a scene of much laughter, there was suddenly the sound of a pistol shot, which many in the audience thought part of the plot. Shouting the Virginia slogan, *Sic semper tyrannis*, 'Thus always for tyrants', a man called John Wilkes Booth leaped down from the president's box onto the stage. Lincoln's wife screamed, 'They have shot the president!' Lincoln was carried to a nearby house, where he later died. Booth evaded capture, but with a bounty of $100,000 on his head he was arrested and shot twelve days later.

Lincoln's assassination turned a partisan politician into a national hero. He had only recently been re-elected and remained a controversial figure, still regarded by many easterners as a vulgar newcomer out of the Midwest. Many also felt the war had gone on too long. The city of New York voted two to one against him. Others were averse to the speed and even the extent of black emancipation. All this appeared forgotten in the wake of his assassination. Lincoln and his cause came close to sanctification. His hearse was carried by train to his home in Springfield, Illinois, through cities deep in mourning. A quarter of a million turned out to see it pass through Philadelphia and through New York. The tragedy was an eerie postscript to the Civil War.

The union of states survived. It was perhaps relevant that at the time Spain's empire in South America, liberated in the early 1800s, was in the process of disintegrating. Simón Bolívar's war for independence across Colombia and Venezuela and similar movements in Peru, Chile and Argentina saw no Founding Fathers or congressional compromises. They fell into a morass of military coups, caudillos and juntas which showed scant respect for democracy and produced permanent instability. At no point did the Spanish-speaking countries achieve any sort of lasting union. Nor did the islands of the Caribbean or the statelets of Central America.

As it was, the battered coalition that was the post-war United States remained in working order. The Union had made its point and asserted its supremacy. But the mere fact of war had shown a weakness in the constitution at a terrible cost. Something needed repair. As for the South, it had been forced to surrender slavery, but it had made few concessions to the equality of mankind, so few that some historians have denied it really lost the war. Certainly slavery's legacy lived on to fight another century.

Reconstruction or Not

1865–1877

If the Civil War left America traumatized, it was a trauma that largely affected the eleven states of the Confederate South. The ensuing decade had been envisaged by Lincoln as a time of healing and recovery. The South's economy lay in ruins, its leaders initially banned from office and all but powerless. Davis was arrested and narrowly escaped execution before disappearing to Canada. Lincoln had wanted to forgive and to create an updated union to embrace all Americans. It was surely time for reconstruction, and so it was called.

Many northerners none the less felt that the South should be punished for the agony it had inflicted on the nation. At the very least the North should dictate the basis on which the South be readmitted to the union. Others wanted to know what was to become of those in whose cause so many had fought and died, 4 million emancipated black people. Others still, mainly in the South, wanted to do all they could to stop any such emancipation. They simply refused to accept the fact of their defeat.

In this they were assisted by the new president, Lincoln's vice-president, Andrew Johnson. He was a Tennessee senator and slave-owner, and the last person suited to completing Lincoln's legacy. The South was still in secession. Its economy was reliant on cotton and therefore on what had been slaves, albeit liberated by federal order, free from bondage and free to move. If the black people rose up and seized their master's property, no one was sure how the states should react. If there were compromises to be sought, there were no Jeffersons, Madisons or Lincolns to negotiate them, only a politics toxic with the bitterness of war.

The Congress was now overwhelmingly northern and Republican in composition, since the southern states had yet to achieve readmission. On one matter it knew it should act with speed. It should enforce emancipation and set the slaves free. This was simpler said than done. As president, Johnson did all he could to aid his southern colleagues in their resistance. He formally pardoned southern leaders for causing the war and turned a blind eye to the re-establishment of southern assemblies. As for the slaves, he felt the southern states should be left to decide the meaning of Lincoln's emancipation order as they saw fit.

In 1866 both houses of Congress followed the thirteenth amendment with a new Civil Rights Act, overriding a veto by Johnson. This was followed by a fourteenth amendment to the constitution. This stated unequivocally that 'all persons born or naturalized in the United States . . . are citizens of the United States and of the state wherein they reside'. In addition, 'nor shall any state deny to any person within its jurisdiction the equal protection of the laws'. Next came a fifteenth amendment which prohibited the denial of the vote on grounds of 'race, colour or previous condition of servitude'. The words of the three 'reconstruction' amendments were emphatic and unambiguous.

Then came the Reconstruction Act of 1867, which formally suspended the southern states' governments that had been operating under what amounted to martial law. Order in the South was reliant on Unionist officers and troops, with the South divided into five military districts each under a general. An army of teachers and missionaries arrived in their stead, as did another army of entrepreneurs and speculators after money. A southern politician, Andrew Fletcher, deplored 'the office-seeker who comes among us with one dirty shirt and a pair of dirty socks, in an old rusty carpet bag, and before his washing is done becomes a candidate for office'. These 'Yankees' – the word deriving from New York Dutch for John and confined to the north-east – were thus despised as 'carpetbaggers'. Any southerners, white or black, who aided them were 'scalawags'.

Much of the ruined South descended into lawlessness and money-grubbing. No fewer than 430 Republican-backing news-papers sprang up, sponsored by northerners to promote reform and supported by purloined state funds. Corruption was everywhere, most of the installed governors being northern carpetbaggers giving their friends contracts for rebuilding towns and railways. North Carolina's Milton Littlefield became known as the Prince of Carpetbaggers, buying votes and selling railway bonds without regulation or legal constraint. His bond sales raised a wildly exces-sive $28 million, much of which went into bribing state legislators to pass whatever measures Littlefield wanted.

The governor of Louisiana, Henry Warmoth, also ran his state as a business, through bond sales, scalawag votes and a newspaper. The state's politics were a travesty of democracy and frequently degenerated into anarchy. In 1873 a massacre was carried out in the Louisiana town of Colfax of a militia of freed slaves by a gang of white paramilitaries. It left more than a hundred black people murdered after they had surrendered. There were some signs of change. Some freedmen did vote and for a while were elected to state legislatures. There was a brief black majority in South Caro-lina's assembly, but one state after another conspired to curb the franchise with voter literacy tests, poll taxes, new state constitutions and bogus qualifications.

The war had, like all wars, expanded the responsibilities of the central state. A federal veterans' and war widows' pension scheme was established and by 1890 a million veterans were in receipt of assistance. It was soon to consume over 40 per cent of the federal budget. In addition, a 'Freedmen's Bureau' was created to offer food, clothing and support to vagrant slaves who had left their masters' estates. President Johnson tried to abolish the bureau and indeed to suspend Reconstruction as infringing states' rights, but he was again overruled by Congress. In particular, black schools with northern teachers were extensively funded by the federal government.

These measures were the nearest nineteenth-century America came to state welfare. They and the settlement after the Civil War led historians to call Reconstruction the 'Second Republic'. It was dubbed by the distinguished black historian W. E. B. Du Bois the 'brief moment in the sun'. He went on to found the National Association for the Advancement of Colored People in 1909 and formulate a revisionist view of this period as one of great hope and then failure, a view that has persisted since.

The intended redistribution to slaves of confiscated Confederate land just did not happen. Johnson persistently ordered that such land be restored to its former owners. Nor did fragmentary attempts at black advancement survive. Two black politicians went on to serve in Congress in 1870, Hiram Revels of Mississippi in the Senate and Joseph Rainey of South Carolina in the House of Representatives, but neither survived Reconstruction. Twenty years after the war, just fifteen southern black people had made their way to either house of Congress. Southern capitals took time to reassert their control of local politics, but reassert it they did. Self-government was ingrained in the South's political landscape, conditioned by an agrarian culture and a lingering English deference to a landed class. There was little of the social mobility then galvanizing the industrialized North.

The reality was that the North could not rule the South against its determined will, with states' rights as still the South's not so secret weapon. The result was to achieve by war what the constitution had previously done by compromise. The South accepted the end of enslavement but rewrote the former slave laws as 'Black Codes', dictating the living and working conditions of the black people. The meaning of 'freedom' mostly took the form of sharecropping. This involved freed people continuing to work as before but donating a share of their surplus crops to the owner. In effect, the enslaved person was to pay rent to work.

As for the freedom to move, this was made subject to meticulous laws on 'vagrancy'. These put all black people who tried to leave their place of work at the mercy of the white police. Former slaves required labour contracts from their plantation owners which, if lost, rendered them vagrants. The law was then fierce. In the absence of prisons, a black person could be returned to his original plantation as a convict labourer. So-called 'convict-leasing' was slavery by another name, permitted under the thirteenth amendment. In most though not all states, black people were also denied the right to own property or conduct a business.

In support of Black Codes there developed informal vigilante movements, such as the White Brotherhood, the Red Shirts and the White League. They became the guerrillas of resistance to Reconstruction. In Tennessee a Ku Klux Klan of Civil War veterans was formed in 1865 and soon led by a southern soldier, Nathan Bedford Forrest. Its name was supposedly based on the Greek word for a circle, *kyklos*. The Klan was never a mass organization in this period, though it proliferated as a white supremacist freemasonry, with Jewish people, Catholics, as well as black people, as its victims. It was often suppressed but re-emerged in various guises over the succeeding century. These groups took it upon themselves to enforce the codes, utilizing violence including ritualized lynching for transgression.

How long 20,000 northern troops, white and black, could maintain order even while stationed in the South was doubtful. The old Democrat and Republican parties – once simply representing South and North – now fragmented and developed factions, much like New England's religious sects. There were Redeemers, Whigs, Stalwarts, Readjusters, Exodusters, Mugwumps and Bourbons. Congress was overwhelmingly reformist, but forcing reform upon the South bordered on the impossible. Its impoverished states lacked competent administrations and hovered between bankruptcy and anarchy.

In short, Johnson's opposition to Reconstruction and a general exhaustion with the drive to refashion a post-slavery South was a major test of the constitution's concept of checks and balances. Johnson was impeached in 1868, though not removed from office. By the end of his presidency in 1869, the constitution's laborious structure of votes, vetoes and overrules had won enough victories to prevent the president from negating the Civil War. But it was a close-run thing.

Johnson was succeeded by the former Unionist commander Ulysses Grant (1869–77), who restored efforts to enfranchise southern black people. He prosecuted the Ku Klux Klan and set up a Department of Justice to enforce federal law. But his fate was to oversee America's first plunge into economic recession, following a stock-market collapse and financial panic in 1873. The South was devastated by a halving in the world price of cotton. Hamstrung by the corruption of Washington's still-embryonic institutions, Grant resorted to the solutions of compromise. He softened the imposition of Reconstruction on the South and conceded a widespread withdrawal of federal troops.

Grant was succeeded by an Ohio Republican, Rutherford Hayes, who went a step further. In a deadlocked electoral college in 1876 he won the support of southern Democrats by what was widely seen as a pact with the Devil. In a move dubbed the 'Compromise of 1877', Hayes won southern support for agreeing formally to end Reconstruction in the South and 'bring the blessings of honest and capable local self-government' to its states. In other words, there would be no more federal interference, as the South saw it, in the process of emancipation. Hesitant black advances made since the Civil War went into reverse. In 1877 Reconstruction unofficially but effectively came to an end.

The South now mutated the Black Codes into what became a new form of black oppression, segregation. While black and white communities could live separately from each other in the country, this was more difficult in towns and cities. The result were so-called Jim Crow laws. Places of public resort, from cafés and shops to parks and buses, were separately designated for the two races. It was a crime for a black person to enter a white facility. Most problematic was public transport. In 1896 in Louisiana a black man refused to move from a whites-only part of a train and was arrested and jailed. With the support of activists and campaigners, the case of *Plessy* v. *Ferguson* found its way to the Supreme Court, which issued a blanket judgment. The court's still-lingering southern majority declared that the constitution's definition of black 'equality' related to America's political and not its social life. The latter fell within the realm assigned to the states. It was for them to decide their laws 'with reference to the established usages, customs and traditions of the people . . . and the comfort and the preservation of the public peace and good order'. States could thus outlaw 'the enforced com-mingling of the two races' so long as it could be shown that services were 'equal in quality'. The motto for race relations became embed-ded as 'separate but equal'.

The long-term impact of Reconstruction has been much debated, with opinions having shifted back and forth. It certainly eased the path back to union. But historians have seen it as failing in its primary ambi-tion, which was to liberate black Americans from racial discrimination. Heather Cox Richardson in her *How the South Won the Civil War*, con-cludes that its true victors were the South, not the North. Slavery's wounds were too deep and their resurfacing as segregation did not heal them. The South's resentment also continued at the arrogance with which Reconstruction was being imposed. As for the old South, American cinemagoers viewing *Gone with the Wind* were advised in the title sequence to 'Look for it only in books, for it is no more than a dream remembered. A Civilization gone with the wind . . .'

My own in-laws in the 1980s were a southern family who had emigrated from Mississippi to Texas. They could not bring them-selves to discuss the Civil War for its 'unfairness'. Their sense of the dignity of the Old South was intense – Texas was an upstart state in comparison – and their one relief was that at least their daughter had not married a northern 'Yankee'.

For others the war passed into a shared history. The fiftieth anni-versary of the Battle of Gettysburg was celebrated in 1913 on the original battle-site. It was attended by some 50,000 people, including veterans from both sides. At its climax, survivors of the two armies lined up opposite each other to re-enact Pickett's Charge, most of them armed with sticks and crutches. Onlookers were openly alarmed at how it might end. A signal was given and the southerners charged, hobbling across the field towards the northern lines. As they met, the sight was of hundreds of men falling on each other in a thousand embraces and tears.

Those seeking centres of energy in the mid-century South could at least visit the port of New Orleans, already known as the Queen of the Caribbean. In the 1840s it had been second only to New York as the port of entry for European immigrants, and America's third-largest city after New York and Baltimore. In one sense it was all that the North had hoped the war might deliver. It was occupied by Union forces and received thousands of freed black people coming to work in its docks and shipyards. They mixed freely with descendants of its creole Spanish and French empires. The city's language was still mostly French, though this went into decline with the arrival of thousands of Irish, German and Italian immigrants.

At times after the war New Orleans teetered on the edge of anarchy. In 1874 the Reconstruction authorities and police were confronted by armed White League vigilantes. The state governor was even forced to flee the city. Yet by 1884 it was doing well enough to host the World's Cotton Fair, and even survive the state treasurer disappearing abroad with $1.7 million of its budget. Meanwhile the bars and brothels of its lurid red-light zone had become notorious. The district was named Storyville after a councillor, Sidney Story, who had attempted to regulate the city's most infamous service industry: prostitution. Such was the diversity of its population that New Orleans saw little formal segregation and even had black policemen.

Key to New Orleans' prosperity was its location at the outlet of the Mississippi Basin. Until the coming of the railway, the great river with its tributaries the Missouri and the Ohio, was the artery of the American interior, from the Appalachians to the Rockies. Its plains and its port were supplying ever more of the world's food markets. As such the river attracted contrasting comments. To the visiting Charles Dickens, the Mississippi was reminiscent of the murky Thames. It was 'a slimy monster, hideous to behold; a hotbed of disease, an ugly sepulchre, a grave'.

Another writer, Samuel Langhorne Clemens, began his career as a pilot on the river before volunteering for the Confederate cause and then escaping to become a miner in Nevada. To him, the Mississippi could do no wrong. He saw it as a paradise, 'majestic, magnificent . . . rolling its mile-wide tide along, shining in the sun'. He even chose his pen-name, Mark Twain, from the sailor's call to the helmsman when the depth was two fathoms.

Most exciting to Twain was the way the magnificent riverboats raced each other daily upstream from New Orleans. At their peak in mid-century there were some 6,000 of them, competing in capacity, luxury, gambling and women. Twain described their departure at four o'clock in the afternoon when their boilers built up a cloud of smoke that hovered over the town: 'Then the bells rang and they all slid out into the river, an amazing sight . . . Races between the two fastest steamers were advertised weeks in advance and were watched all along the river.'

The racing became reckless and the cost in burst boilers was shocking. It sank a third of all Mississippi's steamers in the early part of the nineteenth century, killing up to a hundred people a year. In 1850 business on the river topped $650 million annually. Then the railway came and the profits abruptly collapsed. The river lost much of its traffic, but Twain ensured that it never lost its magic.

14.

The Gilded Age

What became known as the Gilded Age ran from the aftermath of the Civil War – with former colonies struggling for their identity – to an America rising to global prominence just a quarter-century later. The rise was sensational. It witnessed the growth of a manufacturing industry ready to overtake that of Britain and the rest of Europe. America experienced an astonishing burst of technological innovation. At the same time it saw capitalist excesses in a reckless railway boom and in not one but two stock-market crashes. The epithet 'Gilded Age' was taken from a novel by Mark Twain and Charles Dudley Warner, subtitled *A Tale of Today* (1873). It satirized the graft, greed and corruption of Washington and the eastern establishment, the word 'gilded' indicating the thinness of its respectability.

By the 1870s the Civil War had long ceased being of concern to the North. The South might still be in ruins, but that was the South's fault. If anything, the war had benefited the North's economy. It had supplied the Union army with equipment and munitions. The revolver created by Samuel Colt – slogan: 'God created man; Colt made them equal' – sold in its thousands to both sides. Meanwhile new citizens were crossing the Atlantic in ever greater numbers in an unending economic blood transfusion. Twelve million people arrived in America in the half-century after Reconstruction. It was an advertisement for the economic gold of immigration.

The period also saw the birth of the modern city. At the time of the Civil War just a sixth of the North's population lived in cities, with the rest mostly devoted to the land. By the end of the century a third of the population was urbanized. New York in particular was phenomenal. Its population in 1880 was 1.8 million or twice the size of Philadelphia. Twenty years later it was 3.4 million. New York was now bigger than Paris or Berlin and was second only to London among world cities. Its factories, warehouses and counting houses made it the foundation stone of a new American prosperity.

The nation's growth had initially been supercharged by the railway. The trains that opened up the west rarely made large profits, but building them did, notably from steel for their rails and engine-building for their traction. The profit derived largely from government grants and other incentives. By the late 1860s rail building had become excessive and its planning and federal subsidizing corrupt. No less than 33,000 miles of track were laid in just five years before the crash of 1873. That year the onset of recession caused first railway construction and then the wider economy to plummet. Railway bonds evaporated in value and millions of dollars were lost. In New York City unemployment soared to 20 per cent.

What was dramatic was America's capacity for recovery. This was in part thanks to immigration and an openness to innovation. At root was a transition from ancient sources of power such as wood and coal, to gas, oil and electricity. Electric urban transport enabled streetcars and elevated railways to replace horses in moving city-dwellers to and from suburbs in ever larger numbers. Lighting no longer depended on naked flames.

Then arrived the car. The first commercial petrol-driven vehicle was created by the Duryea brothers in 1893, to be followed by the Oldsmobile designed by Ransom Olds in 1897. Next came Henry Ford, who never went to secondary school and was brought up on a Michigan farm. He was fascinated by simple steam engines and then by petrol ones, migrating to work in a factory in Detroit. After a number of false starts in business his celebrated Model T appeared in 1908, selling 10,000 in its first year. Ford went on to become the richest man in the world and for a while the most successful car maker.

Other creations of the period that saw either their invention or their successful exploitation in America were equally remarkable. They included Thomas Edison's light bulb and phonograph, Alexander Bell's telephone, Orville and Wilbur Wright's aeroplane, the typewriter, the sewing machine and the safety razor. America was a textbook case of economic growth generated by a seemingly unlimited supply of ingenuity, investment, immigration and raw materials, all impelled forward by a soaring demand.

One consequence of this bonanza was the monopolistic behaviour Adam Smith had predicted. The industrialists on whom this technological progress was founded became rich beyond precedent. They were largely free of tax and untouched by regulation. Many of the so-called robber barons behaved without constraint. The business of petroleum came under the control of one man, John D. Rockefeller (1839–1937), creator of Standard Oil (later Esso). There was nothing and no one to stop him consuming every rival. Rockefeller was called by his biographer 'an amalgam of godliness and greed, compassion and fiendish cunning'. He justified his wealth on the grounds that 'God gave me my money'.

Alongside him was Andrew Carnegie (1835–1919), a Scotsman who migrated to America at the age of twelve and began life as a boiler-worker in a Pennsylvania slum. He ended by producing a third of all America's steel, not least its rails. As a capitalist he was ruthless, but he was also a philosopher of business. His maxims published in his *Gospel of Wealth* became management-school texts: 'Put all your good eggs in one basket, then watch the basket' and 'Pioneering don't pay: let others take the risk'.

Carnegie rewarded his managers well and called his factories 'slave-driving with willing slaves'. Some workers in his rolling mills were working at peak for twelve hours a day, seven days a week. The Carnegie steelworks in Pittsburgh were the most productive in the world. Its 4,000 employees made three times as much steel as Krupp in Germany with 15,000. That said, in 1892 a breakdown in negotiations at Carnegie's Homestead works led to a 143-day strike and the toughest labour dispute in American history. It culminated in a battle with the state militia, leading to ten deaths and the works reopening with non-union labour.

An America that was a welfare desert resorted to self-reliance. Carnegie developed a social conscience. He saw his profits as 'trust funds to produce the most beneficial results for the community', believing that 'the man of wealth becomes the agent and trustee for his poorer brethren'. He famously declared that 'the man who dies rich dies disgraced'. Over his lifetime Carnegie gave away a third of a billion dollars, leaving a mere $50 million unspent. His best known monuments were the Carnegie concert hall in New York and research institutes and libraries across America and in his native Scotland. His only failure was in joining George Bernard Shaw in a campaign to reform English spelling. This worthy cause proved a challenge too far even for Carnegie.

The late-nineteenth-century tycoons were as celebrated as presidents, largely through their legacies. Carnegie's business partner, Henry Clay Frick, developed a company turning coal to coke for the steelworks, but became a fierce rival for control of the firm. He is better known for bequeathing one of the world's finest art galleries to New York. The banker George Peabody (1795–1869) formed a partnership with J. S. Morgan and eventually moved to London. He left a fortune for the promotion of education in America and working-class housing in London, where Peabody estates survive to this day. Cornelius Vanderbilt (1794–1877) was a railway and shipping magnate remembered for Vanderbilt University in Nashville, Tennessee. Others recalled for their university foundations included Leland Stanford of California, Ezra Cornell of New York and James Duke of North Carolina.

The king of bankers was the financier, J. P. Morgan (1837–1913), son of J. S., who built an empire through merging America's grossly overextended railway companies. A titan of a man, his presence was described as 'like a gale blowing through the house'. His deformed nose was habitually concealed behind a massive cigar. Morgan's collection of European art, books and antiquities was extensive. Much of it was collected by his personal librarian, Belle da Costa Greene, the Virginian daughter of black parents. In Europe she befriended the art dealer Bernard Berenson and operated out of Claridge's in London and the Ritz in Paris. Her well-judged purchases formed much of the Morgan Library and the Metropolitan Museum in New York, of which Morgan was chairman.

Not all tycoons died blessed. The creator of luxury sleeping carriages for the railway, George Pullman (1831–97), was fiercely unpopular with Chicago's labour unions. When he died his family buried him in lead and concrete for fear of his tomb being desecrated. Yet his name brought slumber to overnight travellers throughout the world. In 1890 Carnegie wrote a letter to Gladstone in London boasting that he was in one of Pullman's carriages. He described his 'meals fresh-cooked, a ladies' maid, men servants, the latest daily papers . . . a barber shop, excellent library and special telegrams to be received as we proceed'. Whether this was available to ordinary passengers was not clear, but by the twenty-first century such service would be a mere memory.

The most conspicuous gift to the American people at this time was, surprisingly, from France. In 1865 a statue was offered by a French abolitionist, Édouard de Laboulaye, to celebrate victory in the Civil War and the centenary of America's independence. The interior was designed by two distinguished French architects, Eugène Viollet-le-Duc and Gustave Eiffel, while sculptor Frédéric Auguste Bartholdi's exterior design depicted the Roman goddess of freedom welcoming immigrants to New York harbour, with Liberty stamping on her chains. The statue was inscribed with a sonnet by Emma Lazarus, including the celebrated line, 'Give me your tired, your poor, your huddled masses yearning to breathe free.' It was finally unveiled in 1886, accompanied by New York's first ticker-tape procession.

The reference to huddled masses might have seemed double-edged. The America to which immigrants were being welcomed saw little of the philanthropic housing and early health care that was coming to cities in Britain and Germany. There was certainly none of the welcome offered to New England's seventeenth-century newcomers. There were few shelters for the hundreds of thousands of arrivals other than the anarchy of the street. New York's living quarters were primitive tenements being rushed up almost overnight.

Most immigrants gravitated towards neighbourhoods already colonized by their countrymen, notably Italians, Germans, Poles and other east Europeans. There were no rules or regulations and public order was rudimentary. As the numbers rose yet faster at the turn of the twentieth century, opposition began to be shown by established communities. Whereas earlier immigrants had been treated as enterprising and God-fearing workers, now a newspaper could refer to 'every foul and stagnant pool of population in Europe . . . beaten men from beaten races representing the worst failures in the struggle for existence . . . spewing forth from a pipeline across the ocean'.

To one group there was a specific aversion: migrants from China and Japan were 'the yellow peril', living in slum conditions and undercutting white labourers. Across the country in California a workers' party stated in 1876 that 'to an American, death is preferable to life on a par with a Chinaman'. In 1882 came the Chinese Exclusion Act, the first American law banning a particular group of immigrants other than professionals. The ban lasted until 1943.

Two other groups of immigrants, the Irish and the Italians, were to remain a fixture in many of America's inner cities. Desperate Irish flooded into Boston from the time of the potato famine of the 1840s and took over civic leadership from the former Puritan hierarchy. Such was the inflow that 'No Irish need apply' signs went up in Boston shops. In New York an Irish-American society called Tammany Hall, founded in the eighteenth century, became a force in Manhattan politics. It would care for newly arrived Irish immigrants, finding them work and somewhere to live. With local government steeped in corruption, Irish societies exercised a discipline without which many cities would have descended into chaos.

If the Irish took control of much of local government, the Italians brought a more introverted form of control. It was that of communal tradition, offering security in return for family loyalty. The so-called mafia linked migrant groups in many north-eastern cities back to their originating towns in Italy. It fostered comradeship and rivalry in equal proportion. But the discipline was that of medieval Europe, a world of feuds, vendettas and violence. Once the mafia took hold in America's cities, it would prove hard to remove.

The self-confidence of the north-eastern states was reflected in the planning of their cities. Given the American aversion to state regulation, this planning was remarkably *dirigiste*. Unlike in Europe, its cities had never needed surrounding walls or other forms of security. The rectangular city block – dating back to Jefferson – became the developmental norm, often stretching for miles into the surrounding country, with never a bend in sight. Distances that were once defined by horse-drawn vehicles were rendered limitless by petrol traction.

Civic leisure was not forgotten. In 1858 Frederick Olmsted laid out the spacious Central Park in New York at the considerable cost of $14 million. It remains one of the world's largest and most variegated urban parks. It was followed by Olmsted parks and gardens in Brooklyn, Boston, Chicago, Milwaukee and Louisville. His designs were described as paintings using 'lakes and wooded slopes, with lawns and banks and forest-covered hills, with mountainsides and ocean views'. One of Olmsted's finest settings was for viewing Niagara Falls. He also invented the American college campus as modelled on a southern plantation estate, set with Palladian mansions in spacious lawns. The plan was copied across America.

In style, America's civic buildings were firmly revivalist. At the turn of the nineteenth century, Washington had been fashioned as the new Athens, birthplace of democracy. State capitals copied it. Their assemblies, however modest, emerged resplendent in columns, colonnades, porticos and domes. Classical was to be the language of American government in perpetuity. New York's Federal Hall of 1842 was an imitation of the Parthenon. Doric, Ionic and Corinthian were the orders of the age.

If America imitated Greece in civic buildings, religious architecture took after England, even imitating the early Victorian 'battle of the styles'. Throughout the eighteenth century, American churches had mimicked London's St Martin-in-the-Fields, with almost tedious precision. Every street in town or suburb seemed incomplete without a copy of James Gibbs's church in Trafalgar Square. Whether Protestant or Catholic, Episcopal or Congregational, in Connecticut or in California, the model was a Georgian box fronted with a portico topped by a steeple.

Earlier, in the 1830s, ecclesiastical taste had switched as it did in England to Gothic Revival. New York's Trinity Church in downtown Wall Street was designed by the British architect Richard Upjohn in 1846. It might have been imported from a Cotswold wool town. America's new cathedrals also looked for inspiration to Salisbury or Wells. James Renwick's St Patrick's in midtown Manhattan, one of the finest Gothic Revival structures in America, was begun in 1858. When in 1891 a need was felt for a 'national' cathedral in Washington, it seemed natural to choose as architect England's most distinguished Gothic Revivalist, George Frederick Bodley.

As for domestic architecture, the ubiquitous American suburb displayed an ambivalence common also in England. In more confined cities such as Boston, Philadelphia and Baltimore, the point of departure was the English Georgian terrace. In New York the urban 'brownstone' and its lesser companion the brick townhouse echoed Italianate west London. Brooklyn Heights was a supercharged Pimlico. The exaggerated porch steps or 'stoops' – Dutch for veranda – were analysed by the urbanist Jane Jacobs in her classic work *The Life and Death of American Cities*. She saw them as extensions of the sidewalks, aids to self-policing and the good neighbourliness of a city street.

After a catastrophic earthquake in 1906, San Francisco became the epitome of this English revivalism. It even described itself as 'Queen Anne Victorian'. Here in one of the world's most innovative cities, residents wanted to live surrounded by colonial loggias and porches, bay windows and mansard roofs. In no area of American culture was the bond with its mother country as strong as in architecture.

By the turn of the twentieth century, the new America was making its dynamism felt overseas. Europe's marketplaces were being invaded by American businesses and products. The epithet 'American' conveyed novelty and success, from Woolworths and Selfridges to Heinz beans and Quaker oats. A hard-driving rail developer turned fraudster, Charles Yerkes, driven out of Philadelphia and Chicago, found a ready welcome in a London still completing its underground rail network.

Encouraged by Yerkes, who in 1902 set up a business to build electrified underground lines in London, a group of speculators built sixty miles of Piccadilly, Northern and Bakerloo lines in just four years (1903–7). The achievement was extraordinary, even as opponents of the Hampstead line accused it of causing earthquakes and 'desertifying' Hampstead Heath. The result left London, like America's Great Plains, with an oversupply of railways. Some lines almost went bankrupt and London Transport became the first British industry to be nationalized between the wars. London had no need to extend its Underground until the 1960s.

Tunnels were not the only magnets that drew Americans back to Europe. The shadowy wealth of the Gilded Age yearned for respectability and status. This took the bizarre form of creating an 'aristocracy' from New York's wealthier families, their ancestry traced back to the Knickerbockers of Dutch New York. One of their number, Caroline 'Lina' Schermerhorn, married into the family of America's first millionaire, John Jacob Astor. Lina Astor formed a 'Patriarchy' and a list of four hundred families who were considered sufficiently rich and reputable to attend regular balls in Newport and New York, where they could introduce their offspring to each other.

This led in turn to a craze for titles for daughters in what became a market for aristocratic English sons-in-law. Back in Europe, the British upper classes were going into decline. Great houses were falling derelict in the 1880s recession and estates were no longer able to support them. The cry went up for transatlantic rescue and the answer came in dowries on offer to any titled English bachelor.

The result was often bizarre. Already in 1874 the proposed alliance of Jeanette 'Jennie' Jerome, daughter of a New York financier, to Lord Randolph Churchill, involved desperate efforts to make Jennie's family acceptable to Churchill's snobbish father. It even required the intercession of the Prince of Wales, himself an admirer of Jerome. The most sensational case was that of Consuelo Vanderbilt, a beauty whose godmother had married the prospective Duke of Manchester and whose parents had already received five offers for her hand. In 1895 the prize went to the heavily indebted Duke of Marlborough in return for a total of $2.5 million and $200,000 a year for both man and wife.

So statuesque was Consuelo that James Barrie, creator of Peter Pan, said he would 'stand in the street all day to see her get out of her carriage'. Both young people at the time were engaged to someone else and the duke admitted that the loveless marriage was 'to save Blenheim', his rural palace. At the wedding in Manhattan, Consuelo was seen to be weeping behind her veil, her face puffy with tears. She and the duke were soon living apart but the unhappy marriage endured for twenty-five years before its annulment. Consuelo went on to wed a French hydroplane pioneer.

Between 1870 and 1914 no fewer than 174 American young women were listed as having crossed the Atlantic to marry English peers. The Gilded Age saw a roughly calculated billion dollars pass into the coffers of the British aristocracy. For America's rich it was a social supertax, a doffing of the hat to the old country. For Britain's least deserving poor it was a lifeline.

Nothing so vividly conveyed this attraction of Europe to America's moneyed class as the worlds of art and letters. Many American painters of the period left for Britain as if in pursuit of the wealthy ladies they painted. John Singer Sargent and James McNeill Whistler became leading members of London's artistic community. William Merritt Chase visited Europe extensively before returning his flamboyant style of portraiture to New York. Mary Cassatt settled in Paris, befriended Edgar Degas and became a distinguished Impressionist artist.

As for the novel, gone was the frontier spirit of Mark Twain and Herman Melville, the spartan naturalism of Henry Thoreau and the

17. Assiniboine Native Americans at Fort Union, Missouri, 1833. The trade in bison robes, beaver pelts and other furs in exchange for imported manufactures such as cloth and guns transformed the culture of the indigenous peoples of the Great Plains. Print after a painting by Karl Bodmer, c.1840–45.

18. Andrew Jackson, seventh president of the United States from 1829 to 1837. Portrait by Thomas Sully, 1845.

19. Miles Holmes, a 'forty-niner' in the California gold rush of 1848–9. Daguerreotype, 1853.

20. Harriet Beecher Stowe, abolitionist and author of *Uncle Tom's Cabin*. Portrait by Alanson Fisher, 1853.

21. Frederick Douglass, the pre-eminent African-American voice of the nineteenth century. Daguerreotype, *c.*1858.

22. General Winfield S. Hancock riding along the Union lines during the Confederate bombardment in the Battle of Gettysburg, 1863. Painting by Thure de Thulstrup, *c.*1877.

23. A locomotive on the Baltimore and Ohio Railroad, near Oakland, Maryland, c.1860. Men and women appear to have come from the passenger car to the front of the train for this special occasion. The railroad was founded to serve merchants from Baltimore doing business with settlers crossing the Appalachian Mountains. Throughout the Civil War a total of 143 raids, skirmishes, and battles directly involved the B&O Railroad.

24. Abraham Lincoln, photographed by Alexander Gardener on 8 November 1863, eleven days before his Gettysburg Address.

25. General Robert E. Lee, leader of the Confederate Army, photographed in 1864.

26. Night-time steamboat race between the *Baltic* and *Diana* on the Mississippi River, 1858. The paddle-wheelers were within sight of each other for most of the 1,382 miles from New Orleans to Louisville.

27. *Picking Cotton* by William Aiken Walker, 1880s. Although no longer enslaved, the sharecroppers lived in a poverty that was slow to change, even as the rest of the nation became industrialized. Walker's pictures were nostalgic souvenirs, made popular by Currier & Ives prints.

28. Bird's-eye view of New York City *c.*1880, with the Hudson River and New Jersey waterfront. On the left is New York Harbor and in the right foreground, Battery Park, with Brooklyn Bridge behind.

29. Keokuk was the chief of a tribe officially recognized by the government as the Sac and Fox band of the Mississippi. At the time, the tribe lived on the Nemaha Reservation, south of the Missouri River, moved there from Iowa just months before he visited the studio of the photographer, Thomas Easterly, in St Louis, 1847.

30. The Land Run of 1893, also known as the Cherokee Strip Land Run, marked the opening to settlement of the Oklahoma Territory. The Land Run saw an estimated 100,000 participants racing to create 40,000 homesteads on what had formerly been Cherokee grazing land.

31. Programme for a performance of *Buffalo Bill's Wild West and Congress of Rough Riders of the World*. The show drew 3 million attendees to the World's Columbian Exposition in Chicago in 1893; it later travelled to New York and eventually to Britain, to be enjoyed by Queen Victoria.

32. Consuelo Vanderbilt, 1900.

33. J. P. Morgan, 1900.

34. *Touchdown*, by Frederic Remington, depicts a Yale football player scoring a touchdown against Princeton during the Thanksgiving Day game in 1890.

35. Performance politics: Theodore Roosevelt during an election speech in New Castle, Wyoming, 1903.

domestic realism of Louisa May Alcott. The novels of Henry James and Edith Wharton (née Jones) were self-consciously Gilded Age and mid-Atlantic. Wharton's parents were so status conscious that 'keeping up with the Joneses' later became a well-known maxim. The two writers were perhaps the shrewdest observers of Twain's Gilded Age. Both observed its participants in the streets and drawing rooms of New York and Europe, and the tensions between the two. When Wharton's Europeanized Fanny Frisbee meets some compatriots in Paris, she bursts with delight at the 'dear, good, sweet, simple, real Americans'. James's Isabel Archer is a construct of every rich American girl amorously involved with grasping European suitors. James and Wharton enjoyed comparing their respective incomes. Wharton once met James in her American limousine, boasting, 'I bought it with the money from my new novel.' James later met her in a horse-drawn trap, 'which I bought with mine'.

One aspect of the Gilded Age that became emphatically American was the adaptation in the 1870s of the English sports of football and rugby, amalgamated into the more violent world of American football. Its rules included the freedom to attack physically players off the ball. It became so violent, with nineteen deaths in 1904–5, that it was close to being banned. Regulation intervened and ordered extensive protective clothing. American football became immensely popular across the nation, like its summer sibling baseball, but it never caught on abroad, other than in a Canadian version.

15

The Last Frontier

1860–1900

While the Knickerbockers were moving between New York's Park Avenue and London's Park Lane, America's 'Wild West' could hardly have seemed more distant. It had been largely untroubled by civil wars, gold rushes and robber barons. Its settlements were little more than dusty streets, filled with bars and boarding houses, horses and carts, where struggling traders eked a living from struggling farmers. Indeed, in a sense the West was experiencing a facsimile of America's colonial beginnings, a wrestling with soil, poverty and Native hostility, and with only their determination to rely on.

The difference was that these western landscapes were not the richly watered contours of America's north-east or south. There was rarely a welcome committee, let alone a pastor or doctor, a mayor or policeman. The further America pushed beyond the Mississippi Basin, the rougher became the terrain. It was a land more suited to grazing than sowing, to cattle than to crops. And beyond lay an arid country of mountain, plateau and desert, including some of the most barren land on earth.

The Native occupants of the west had once depended on the bison and the buffalo. Its newest arrival was the cow. It proved able to prosper in both hot and cold climes, and met the booming demand of America's cities for beef. Ever larger ranches spread from Texas in the south to Kansas, Nebraska and Wyoming The invention of barbed wire in the 1870s obviated the need for large numbers of cattlemen – or cowboys – as security, leading to 'enclosure' as a major term. The scale of cattle rearing soon became immense, with droves of livestock pouring east into the markets of St Louis and Chicago.

For many Native people this region had been their last redoubt. It was the land into which, since President Jackson in 1830, settlers had driven them from their ancestral territories. Sometimes deals were done and guarantees given, but they were seldom honoured. Researchers have identified some five hundred treaties with Native people over the previous century that were violated. In 1851 at Fort Laramie in Wyoming a grand treaty was reached between incoming settlers and a coalition of Cheyenne, Sioux, Crow and others. The Native people were given money and promised secure possession of their hunting grounds in return for safe passage for the northern Oregon stagecoach trail. It was estimated that 250,000 pioneers duly passed along the trail to the Pacific coast over the next two decades.

Like most such deals, the one made at Fort Laramie did not stand the test of time. It was violated by settlers and redrawn in 1868, with the Sioux agreeing to receive half of the Black Hills of the Dakota territory as a reservation together with various hunting rights. This too was not honoured. The culture of the west was not that of the lawyer or the politician. It was literally wild.

In the 1860s a new phenomenon arrived to render the Oregon Trail obsolete. The railway had already saturated the Midwest and the Great Plains. The federal government now saw trains as conferring the final blessing on the new America as they penetrated the Rocky Mountains and reached the west coast. Accordingly in 1863 the laying of a Union Pacific track was begun west from Omaha in Nebraska, while a Central Pacific track set out to meet it eastwards from Sacramento in California. The mammoth task of excavation took six years and was undertaken by a migratory army of Chinese labourers.

The eventual meeting of the two lines took place in May 1869 on Promontory Summit in Utah, the first transcontinental railroad. The ceremony was delayed by a strike. The workers, claiming they had not been paid, chained the company's train to its track. A photograph taken two days later depicts the driving in of the last 'golden spike', its significance captured in a plaque stating, 'The rail-road that unites the two great oceans of the world.'

The moment was filled with symbolism. The frontier spirit of the west had long been embodied as the archaic and unreliable stagecoach, usually surrounded by 'cowboys and Indians'. Now a Currier and Ives print depicted *The Stride of the Century*. A youthful Uncle Sam stretches his legs from the Atlantic to the Pacific, the land beneath crossed by a continuous rail track. It had previously taken six weeks to traverse America. Now a passenger could get from New York to San Francisco in six days, sleeping and eating in Pullman comfort en route. The idea of a single 'united' states of America at last had a certificate of reality.

In 1883 this reality was formalized by an agreement to replace a chaos of local chronometry with four time zones across the continent. By 1890 the federal government had also put its geographical house in order. All of America north of Mexico and south of Canada was now fashioned into forty-five states and four territories. The Star-Spangled Banner's night sky was crowded. The 1890 census declared that there was no longer a 'frontier' on the American continent.

The statement reflected an event the previous year in what was still known as the Oklahoma Territory. This was land that had been set aside under the 1830 Indian Removal Act to receive Native people evicted from points east. Since 1830, 17,000 Cherokee had arrived with 2,000 slaves along the Trail of Tears. Some fifty tribes were listed as having been allocated land there, including the Choctaw, Cherokee and Seminole of the Five Civilized Tribes of Florida. 'Oklahoma' was Choctaw for 'red people'. There was even talk of Oklahoma becoming an 'Indian state'.

In the 1880s such was settler pressure for land that the territory was divided and much of the Native peoples' territory was declared 'unassigned' under the 1887 Dawes Act. Plots of 160 acres were put up for sale to new settlers, thousands of whom flocked to Oklahoma by train, horse and carriage. Plots were claimed by staging gigantic horse races started by the firing of a gun. On one day in April 1889 a 'land rush' town called Guthrie went from near empty to 10,000 people between mid-morning and sundown. The federal authorities issued titles, marked out streets, licensed shops, even erected schools. Within a month Oklahoma 'city' had five banks and six newspapers. In nine months the state had 62,000 new residents, a truly phenomenal migration.

That said, most of the west of America was still a land of few settlers and scant government. Attempts were made to bring law and order to small dispersed communities, a pressing issue in areas of rapid enclosure and rudimentary land tenure. The commonest crime was horse-stealing, with conflict rife between farmers eking a living from the soil and cattle-driving cowmen. This conflict was later reflected in the 1943 'frontier' musical *Oklahoma!* and its admonitory theme song, 'The Farmer and the Cowman Should Be Friends'. There was no mention of Native people in the whole show.

One consequence of ingrained tension was the free rein given to vigilantes and guns. A number of state judges did not accept the common-law maxim that a man should not retaliate if threatened with violence. He was entitled to kill in what he considered self-defence. This was seen as an interpretation of the constitutional right to own weapons. The 1957 film *Gunfight at the OK Corral* glamorized a real event in 1881, featuring outlaws, gunslingers, gamblers and lawmen. It became the defining memoir of the Wild West.

Trouble persisted elsewhere between settlers and Natives, and between tribes that had been forced to share one or the other's territory. The Sioux and their related Cheyenne and Lakota were driven west into buffalo country, leading to a long conflict with the federal government over the second half of the nineteenth century. The fiercest battles erupted in 1876, when the Lakota/Sioux occupied land that had been assigned to the Crow. The Crow in turn asked for federal assistance in reclaiming it.

In the resulting operation a unit of US cavalry under the Civil War veteran George Custer found itself surrounded by armed Lakota at the Little Bighorn River in Montana. The result was a massacre of 278 soldiers, including Custer and all his officers. Fourteen years later in 1890, Custer's regiment exacted a savage revenge on the Lakota, killing up to three hundred of their civilians in what became the Wounded Knee Massacre.

Wounded Knee entered the hall of shame as the final atrocity of the Indian Wars of the 1870s and 80s, also known as the Sioux Wars. They were the last sustained attempt by the Native tribes of the west to resist American colonization. The Lakota to the north and the Comanche and Apache to the south had become well-armed fighting bands. A series of battles saw a last generation of Native chiefs such as Red Cloud, Sitting Bull and Crazy Horse fighting to the end. The Apache leader Geronimo (1829–1909) led raids and breakouts from his Native reservations in Arizona and New Mexico from 1850 to 1886.

To the resident US army commander, General Philip Sheridan, this was no straightforward imperial clean-up operation. He complained that 'no other army in the world has such a difficult line to keep in order'. He claimed that the reduction of 'these wild tribes and the occupation of their country' would anywhere else have required up to 70,000 men, yet he had just 14,000. Besides, by the end of the nineteenth century the treatment of conquered tribes was starting to nag at the conscience of liberal America. It was being accepted that the once-enslaved black population should sooner or later receive equality of treatment. But Native people were beyond the pale, locked out of sight in reservations. This occasionally evoked shocking responses. Frank Baum, author of *The Wonderful Wizard of Oz*, had in 1891 suggested of the Native people that America, 'having wronged them for centuries, had better, in order to protect [its] civilization, follow it up by one more wrong and wipe these untamed and untameable creatures from the face of the earth'. Though explained as semi-satirical, Baum's remark was not unusual.

The handling of America's Native population was never resolved into one of partnership, partition or even purchase. From the 1890s onwards they were officially confined to reservations, and their cause to history. Barely a word was written of them until 1920, when a 'first history' was published by William Bagley and Charles Beard. Only in 1970 did Dee Brown's *Bury My Heart at Wounded Knee* start to do for the Native people what *Uncle Tom's Cabin* had done for the enslaved.

As for the concept of a western frontier rolling forward into the future, it buried itself in the romance of America's founding narrative. The frontiersman was in line of descent from the explorer, the pilgrim and the intrepid settler. The frontier myth was now transformed and elevated in the hands of writers, artists and entertainers. Twain's personal memoir recalling his youth did not dwell on his attachment to the Mississippi River. It told of the drama of his time spent mining in the far west. It was of a land 'at once awful and sublime . . . a level, great prairie covered in wild strawberry plants, vividly starred with prairie pinks and walled in on all sides by forests'. This was the nature sought by Emerson and Thoreau, the authentic country to be adopted as their birth soil by all true Americans, not the plantation estate or Wharton's Rhode Island weekend.

In 1872 an Iowan soldier turned railway scout named William Cody (1846–1917) appeared in a theatrical show depicting prairie life. It was based on his job supplying buffalo meat to rail workers, hence his nickname 'Buffalo Bill'. The show evolved into an outdoor as well as indoor entertainment, embracing a series of frontier vignettes. There were cowboys and Indians, skilled horsemanship, Custer's Last Stand, Pony Express, Calamity Jane and the sharpshooting Annie Oakley. Native people were recruited to appear in tribal costumes. Each show ended with Cody riding on stage to rescue a brave frontier family from aggressive Native people.

What was called the Wild West Show was immensely popular. After touring the Midwest it took to the stage at New York's Madison Square Garden, where it was seen by a million people. It then crossed the Atlantic and toured Europe four times. When it came to London's Earls Court in 1883 it so entranced Queen Victoria that she asked for a second performance. Her diary declared her delight at the 'horses tearing around at full speed, shrieking and screaming'. The twenty-six-year-old Annie Oakley amazed the Queen by shooting at her husband over her shoulder after aiming through a mirror. The Queen was enthralled by Oakley and shook hands with a cast of Sioux Indians. She called Cody 'a real gentleman'.

The show stimulated an outpouring of writing. It lent drama and excitement to the often sordid reality of the 'opening up' of the west. It had its heroes, however unreal, and their names and antics became extraordinarily renowned. Thus Jesse James was a small-time bandit, but his train hold-ups delighted Karl Marx, who hailed him as a champion of the revolution. William 'Billy the Kid' Bonney was an outlaw who killed twenty-one men before being shot when barely twenty. James 'Wild Bill' Hickok was a gun-slinging soldier, gambler and lawman. As good as his name, he died during a poker game. As for Wyatt Earp, he was another gambling lawman serving in the appropriately named Dodge City, Deadwood and Tomb-stone. He killed three outlaws at the OK Corral and lived to the age of eighty. The celebrated Apache chief Geronimo ended his life as an exhibit in army displays.

American entertainment at the end of the nineteenth century thus served to sanitize the final suppression of Native resistance to settlement. It was portrayed as civilization triumphing over savagery. It legitimized ethnic cleansing, depicting Native people as primitive and dangerous, if loveable when tamed. Who could not admire Sitting Bull's wives' names, Light Hair, Four Robes, Snow-on-Her and Scarlet Woman? His children were Many Horses, Standing Holy, Lodge in Sight and Runs-away-from-Him.

To children growing up in 1950s and 60s Britain, the American frontier exerted a powerful hold. Thanks largely to Hollywood and comics, games of 'cowboys and Indians' dominated the playgrounds of the world. A toy 'six-shooter' was a standard Christmas present, along with a ten-gallon hat. I shall not forget my father returning from America with my first cap gun, a huge silver-coloured pistol. Cody illustrated the power of entertainment to rewrite history as myth and pass it down the generations.

The Wild West was also depicted by a generation of artists, attracted to a theme that America could call its own. It was glamorized by the artist and illustrator Frederic Remington (1861–1909), who had experienced the frontier at first hand. He brought it to life in drawings for *Harper's Weekly* and then in vigorous watercolours and oils. His westerners were cowboys, settlers and Native people, frenetically riding, fighting, parading and dying. With his western costumes, Remington became a New York celebrity, even adopting a pseudo-cowboy accent. A contrasting artist of the period was emphatically devoted to America's eastern frontier rather than the west. This was the landscapist Winslow Homer (1836–1910). His depiction of maritime New England was every bit as romantic as Remington's, portraying a timeless world of ships, sailors, sea and weather, an America in perpetual contest with nature and not always winning.

In 1892–5 New York was visited for three years by the composer Antonín Dvořák (1841–1904) to research, teach and compose. He brought to Carnegie Hall exhilarating tunes inspired by music he had heard in his American travels, including from both black and Native sources. In his 9th Symphony, 'From the New World', he claimed to compose 'only in the spirit of those American melodies'. The work became almost a national anthem.

16

Roosevelt and the Progressive Dawn

1892–1912

As the nineteenth century drew to a close, the accelerating economy of the Gilded Age exploded. Demand from an ever-rising
population led to the number of American farms tripling between
1870 and 1900. The result was an overproduction of food and other
resources and an economic downturn. Markets over-expanded and
supply chains collapsed. Families spilled into cities where buildings
were overcrowded and property prices spiked. Official unemployment in New York at one point topped 35 per cent. Soup kitchens
appeared everywhere.

The result was that the recession of 1873 was repeated in 1893, aggra-
vated by a speculative boom in world bonds tied to the price of gold. An
archaic constitutional ban on inter-state banking had prevented banks
from combining across state boundaries and from building reserves
against credit collapses. As the overheated stock market crashed, some
five hundred state banks shut their doors. Railway contractors laid off
thousands of workers, who were often stranded miles from home,
without employment or any other means of support.

A phenomenon arose that was new to America, an outburst of
industrial unrest that turned political. As prices fell and businesses
failed, farmers formed into associations and workers into labour
unions. An early sign of dissatisfaction had occurred in 1873, when
Pennsylvania miners had come out on strike. They were protesting
their working conditions and the rents they had to pay for company
houses. Parallels were made with slaves' post-emancipation conditions in the South.

A centre of militancy was Chicago. In 1886 its stockyard workers staged a riot in Haymarket Square with calls to take up arms. Mobs took control of districts of the city and there was a breakdown of order. At the Pullman railway works a leading figure in the union movement, Eugene Debs, described George Pullman as 'a slave holder with his human chattels. [We] are striking to avert slavery and degradation.' In 1894, a few months after the closing of Chicago's World's Fair, its fake European palaces went up in arsonists' flames.

Debs was a rare American who actually referred to socialism and Marxism. Karl Marx himself was watching developments in America. Despairing of revolution in Europe, he in 1852 became London correspondent of the *New-York Tribune*, holding the job for ten years. He wrote to Lincoln in 1864 congratulating him on the Civil War and on his re-election. He told him that, just as the War of Independence had 'initiated a new era of ascendancy of the middle class, so the American anti-slavery war will do for the working class'. In 1872 he even moved his International Workingmen's Association headquarters to New York, though he did not himself cross the Atlantic.

Given America's harsh treatment of industrial workers, the relative lack of interest in socialist activism on that side of the Atlantic was curious. One explanation was that real wages were rising strongly while working-class militancy was undermined by immigration. Another factor was that Europe's left-wing parties relied on support from an entrenched and cohesive working class. America's equivalent – it came to call itself 'middle class' – was composed of first- and second-generation immigrants who had come to America as individuals. They moved frequently and faced fewer social or geographical barriers than in Europe. Meanwhile, America's political parties were strongly controlled by financial interests.

Even so, trade unionism did bed down. In 1881 a new federation of skilled craft unions was formed in Ohio by a British immigrant cigar-maker, Samuel Gompers. Later named the American Federation of Labor (AFL), it was headed by Gompers until 1924. He was firmly anti-socialist and proclaimed capitalism to be 'the spirit that embodies our broadest and our highest principles'. But the language of socialism often reared its head. In 1893 the AFL was demanding 'the collective ownership by the people of all means of production and distribution'.

In this turbulent climate new political forces did emerge. A People's Party, later renamed 'Populist', was founded in 1892. It was initially composed of western farmers to campaign against the ideology of laissez-faire that had bred corporate corruption and recession. An early star was a militant feminist, Mary Elizabeth Lease, who demanded farmers 'raise less corn and more hell'. Their particular enemies were the railway's robber barons, rich on federal and state incentives and sustained by monopolies and price fixing. Trade unions blamed easterners, banks and the rich. At root lay America's attachment to the gold standard monetary system, which they claimed with some justice starved the economy of liquidity, especially at times of stock-market collapse.

A leader of the Populist movement was a charismatic young Nebraskan named William Jennings Bryan (1860–1925). To him the gold standard was 'a crown of thorns pressed down upon the brow of labour'. Bryan's speech to the 1892 Congress in favour of bimetallism, which meant adding silver to the dollar's gold standard, held the house spellbound. He spoke without notes for three hours and was received with roars of applause. Like Debs, Bryan said America was embarked on a new civil war, that between 'the idle holders of capital and the struggling masses'. It needed a national income tax and a nationalized railway network. Dorothy's magic silver slippers in Baum's *The Wonderful Wizard of Oz* were widely taken as a populist metaphor for Bryan's silver standard. The point was rather lost when the Technicolor film replaced them with a red pair for better effect on the Yellow Brick Road.

Bryan was the nearest America came to a truly left-wing leader. He invented the practice of going 'on the stump', travelling the country and addressing crowds of voters who had never seen or heard a national politician before. In 1896 he pulled off a coup in securing the Democratic nomination for the presidential election that year. As a result of his youth, cartoonists portrayed him in a cradle while his Republican opponent, William McKinley, was a Civil War veteran and congressman, chiefly known for the McKinley Tariff Act of 1900. The tariffs, of up to 50 per cent, caused inflation, conspicuously failed to ease recession and were withdrawn as a failure after four years.

Though McKinley won the election, the year was seen as a turning point in America's political history. The Democratic Party was still regarded as the party of the South and therefore deeply conservative, while the Republicans were the party of the more forward-looking progressives of the north-east. Coming from the west, Bryan's dynamic charisma established a new image for Democrats outside the South against the Republicans' northern establishment. He was the Democratic candidate again in 1900 and in 1908, though he lost each time.

The reason was in large part that the Republican who beat him, though from a patrician background, was in many ways as populist as Bryan. Theodore 'Teddy' Roosevelt (1858–1919) was America's most distinguished politician since Lincoln. Born in New York to wealthy parents, he was home schooled, went to Harvard and entered the legal profession, which instantly bored him. Possessed of an intense intellectual energy, Roosevelt was a dilettante, in turn zoologist, naturalist and naval historian. He plunged into local politics and in 1881, at the age of twenty-three, he secured election to the New York state assembly for Manhattan's wealthy 'silk stocking' district.

Here Roosevelt acquired a reputation for speaking out against the corruption endemic in many of America's state legislatures. He was on his way up the Republican party ladder when, in 1884, he experienced the death in one week of both his young wife and his mother. He was shattered and decided to become a rancher and cowboy, exiling himself to Dakota. Briefly steeped in the frontier spirit, Roosevelt deplored the 'milk-and-water moralities admired by the pseudo-philanthropists', preferring the western cowboy's 'stern, manly qualities that are invaluable to a nation'.

This did not last. After two years Roosevelt was bored and returned to New York, standing for but failing to win the city's mayoralty while still under thirty. Instead, his patrician friend Henry

Cabot Lodge secured for him the headship of Washington's civil service commission. He struggled to transform what was a notorious source of patronage into a federal service recruited on merit. Then in 1894 he won appointment as New York's police commissioner, where he again fought against the maladministration rife in the force, walking the city beats at night to check that officers were doing their duty. He inevitably ran up against the Tammany Hall Irish, but protected himself through his close relations with the press. Throughout his life Roosevelt was a master of publicity, forming friendships and alliances with journalists whom most politicians dismissed as mere 'muck-rakers'.

McKinley's 1896 presidency saw yet another break for Roosevelt through his friendship with Henry Cabot Lodge, who persuaded the president to make him assistant secretary of the navy, a job the one-time naval historian seized upon with enthusiasm. Despite the modesty of the post, a new Roosevelt emerged. He turned his attention from the streets of New York to the place that he felt America should assume on the world stage. It needed to show a new self-confidence in its foreign policy. That meant nothing less than a new navy.

An opportunity was soon at hand. Cuba at the time was still a listless Spanish colony sunk into near anarchy. In 1898 the blowing-up by an unknown hand in Havana harbour of an American warship, the USS *Maine*, led to pro-war hysteria. There was no evidence that Spain was responsible, but Roosevelt used the incident to accuse Spain of 'dirty treachery'. War fever was fuelled by fabricated reports of Cuban concentration camps published in the popular Hearst and Pulitzer newspapers. This was a period of outrageous misreporting by what was called the yellow press. When Frederic Remington was sent by Hearst to illustrate Cuba's horrors and protested he could find none, Hearst replied, 'You furnish the pictures. I'll furnish a war.'

Global imperialism was now at its climax. The British, the French, the Germans, the Belgians, the Dutch were all feeling their way to a global presence. The so-called manifest destiny of America's founders to be the 'light of the world', whatever it had meant, seemed to call Americans to join the enterprise, almost the adventure. Columbia University's leading political theorist at the time, John Burgess, wrote that most of the world was occupied by peoples with 'no capacity to establish national states'; indeed he described them as 'barbaric'. Civilized nations such as America were therefore 'authorized to force organization on them by any means necessary in their honest judgement . . . There is no human right to the status of barbarism.' This tendentious thesis, regularly re-expressed, became America's self-granted licence to overseas intervention throughout the twentieth century.

Roosevelt duly put the American fleet on standby to invade Cuba, as well as Spain's colony of the Philippines. This appears to have been without his president's permission. McKinley throughout was eager to avoid war, while Roosevelt sought 'one more step towards the complete freeing of America from European dominion'. Echoing Burgess, he felt the federal government should acquire some higher purpose beyond mere 'material gain'.

The pressure of public opinion on Congress became irresistible. It wanted nothing less than war with Spain, validated by the terms of the Monroe Doctrine against outside involvement in the Americas, in this case by imperial Spain. McKinley eventually capitulated and agreed 'to secure in [Cuba] a stable government . . . and to use the military and naval forces of the United States as may be necessary for these purposes'. But he was carefully instructed by Congress, once pacification had been achieved, 'to leave the government and control of the island to its people'.

So intense was Roosevelt's enthusiasm for the war that, even though he was a senior official, he vacated Washington in early 1898 to form a volunteer regiment to fight in Cuba. This was against the protests of his new wife and family. The regiment advertised in the press for recruits and was inundated. Harvard graduates, athletes, cowboys, frontier farmers, miners, sheriffs, even Native Americans, rallied to the flag. They adopted the title the Rough Riders, taken from Buffalo Bill's Wild West Show.

In what might have served as a frontier scene from Cody's

spectacle, Roosevelt landed in Cuba and led his men on horseback in a successful attack on a Spanish position, subsequently dubbed the Battle of San Juan Heights. Spain soon capitulated and America took over Cuba within four months. From then on Roosevelt insisted on being addressed as Colonel – he disliked the nickname Teddy. The army denied him a Cuban Medal of Honor on the grounds of his shameless publicity seeking.

At the same time as hostilities were launched in Cuba, America's Pacific Fleet was sent to the Philippines – in effect by Roosevelt – to attack a Spanish fleet in Manila harbour. As in Cuba, the islands were subject to a popular rebellion against its rulers that America claimed to be supporting. Again there was no question of Washington simply achieving its goal and leaving. America was clearly pushing out a new frontier and reviving the days of Polk in the 1840s. Jefferson's empire of freedom was now to extend across both the Caribbean and the Pacific.

A subsequent Treaty of Paris saw Spain conceding degrees of American authority over the Philippines, Guam, Puerto Rico and Cuba. The last was to remain under American control until the revolution of Fidel Castro in 1959. Also in 1898, the islands of Hawaii in the Pacific were formally annexed by America following the toppling of their monarchy by a group of American businessmen five years earlier. Hawaii became the fiftieth state of the union in 1959, though it kept Britain's Union Jack in its flag as a token of long-standing ties with that other empire. As for the extension of sovereignty to the far side of the Pacific, the abuse of the Monroe Doctrine was flagrant. If America could interfere in the affairs of Asia, why should Asia – or anyone – not interfere in America's?

In 1898 Roosevelt returned in a blaze of publicity to New York, where he stood for and won the governorship of the state. He held the job for two years, during which he resumed his fight against corruption and in particular the role of monopolistic trusts in state commerce. In this he was in accord with a widespread body of public opinion at last coming to the view that American corporate power was in need of control. Anti-trust became his watchword.

His exploitation of the press was exhaustive. Every working day began and ended with press conferences.

In the run-up to the 1900 presidential election, New York Republicans opposed to Roosevelt's progressivism persuaded McKinley, then seeking re-election, to nominate him as vice-president. Roosevelt felt he could not refuse, though he disliked the vacuous post. He moved to Washington as vice-president in March 1901 and was thoroughly bored. Six months later he experienced his last and greatest turn of fortune. The president was the third in half a century to be assassinated in office. Roosevelt found himself in the White House.

In retrospect there were two Teddy Roosevelts. One was a passionate believer that America should catch up with the progressive reforms now being seen in much of Europe. The other was almost fanatically imperialist. Both roles indicated a president supremely confident of taking America forward into a new age. He sought a capitalist democracy worthy of worldwide admiration and came to regard the presidency not as part of a constitutional triumvirate, more as the nation's plenipotentiary chief executive.

Roosevelt's domestic programme was based on reversing what he called its 'riot of individualistic materialism'. Its much-vaunted freedom had come to mean only 'a perfect freedom for the strong to wrong the weak'. He detested big business and made the monopolists Rockefeller and Morgan explicit targets for his criticism. 'The power of the mighty industrial overlords of the country has increased with giant strides,' he said, yet the federal government's means of curbing them 'on behalf of the people . . . remains archaic and therefore practically impotent'.

What would today be termed a distinctly radical creed sought to bring America up to date with the Declaration of Independence. All American citizens should be equal not just in law but also in the opportunities open to them and in their treatment by the state. Roosevelt dubbed this his 'square deal'. He intervened in respects inconceivable under his predecessors. He initiated a federal anti-trust lawsuit against a monopolistic takeover of railways by J. P. Morgan.

He involved himself in a miners' strike in Pennsylvania, summoning the parties to the White House for a settlement. He created and forced through Congress a new Department of Commerce to champion the disciplines of the marketplace.

As if this were not ambition enough, Roosevelt turned to his fascination with the natural world in terms way ahead of his time. America's natural resources were 'not inexhaustible', he said, but finite. In particular he was concerned at the felling of trees in the western forests. Though the president's power to intervene was constitutionally limited, he wielded executive orders – supposedly 'emergency' measures – to declare the Grand Canyon as well as Yosemite and Yellowstone among five new national parks. To these were added 150 national forests, totalling 16 million acres, and fifty bird reserves. An Antiquities Act was secured in 1906 'to declare historic landmarks and pre-historic structures' as national monuments. Roosevelt reputedly used as many emergency executive orders in the cause of conservation as all his predecessors combined. He taunted his opponents, most of whom had logging interests, as 'the land-grabbers'.

Overseas, Roosevelt was no less ambitious. The Spanish–American War of 1898 had stirred imperial ambitions in many American breasts. With the fighting barely over, in 1899 Rudyard Kipling wrote a poem published in the *New York Sun* newspaper. Titled 'The White Man's Burden', its intention was to encourage America to intervene in the Pacific. The time had come for it to take on similar responsibilities to those that were now weighing down the British, the global obligations of a nation that thought itself superior in both power and race. It should understand that this burden could be heavy.

Kipling invited Americans to 'take up the white man's burden . . . the savage wars of peace'. But they must be ready to 'watch sloth and heathen folly/ Bring all your hopes to nought'. They would earn 'the blame of those ye better,/ The hate of those ye guard', and would have to suffer 'through all the thankless years . . . The judgment of your peers.' Kipling knew what he meant. He had spent much of his youth in India and was imbued with its culture and contradictions. His poem was hardly a sales pitch for empire.

To many Americans the prospect was exhilarating. There was delight at taking on a world role similar to Britain's. The *Washington Post* was exultant. 'The policy of isolation is dead,' it said. 'The taste of empire is in the mouth of the people, even as the taste of blood in the jungle.' America was experiencing a new national ambition, a yearning to show its strength in the imperial ranks. There was no reference to Kipling's note of warning, though it was to echo through the isolationist subplot to the nation's politics over the next century.

Roosevelt's ambitions were brazen. In 1904 he advanced what became the 'Roosevelt Corollary' to the Monroe Doctrine. It asserted that any overseas 'wrong-doing or impotence which results in a general loosening of the ties of a civilized society . . . may force the United States, however reluctantly, in flagrant cases to the exercise of an international police power'. The fell phrase was born, that of the big stick.

The big stick was to enter the lexicon of American interventionism. Roosevelt celebrated it in his autobiography with the claim that 'no men's actions are fraught with greater mischief to their country and to mankind than those who exalt unrighteous peace as better than righteous war'. There was no mention of righteous peace and unrighteous war. The Roosevelt Corollary was a blank cheque for the outreach of American power.

This was not to every taste. Not only was the adamantly isolationist George Washington turning in his grave; in Congress a number of living senators and representatives also could see the risks. They agreed a resolution that American troops should drive the Spanish out of Cuba and the Philippines in order to establish 'pacification', but they should then 'disclaim any disposition or intention to exercise sovereignty, jurisdiction or control over the said islands'. In the case of Cuba, America should simply 'leave the government and control of the island to its people'. Congress was clearly seeking to check the executive. It was an argument that would not go away.

For the time being, the glory of empire reigned supreme. America in effect colonized Cuba and some 7,000 Philippine islands. It regarded the Caribbean, the Gulf of Mexico and all of Central America as within its purview. Most spectacular was Roosevelt's blatant backing for Panama's seizure of its canal-building project from Colombian control in 1903. Roosevelt endured severe criticism even from a normally supportive press. The *New York Times* called it 'an act of sordid conquest' and a cabinet colleague called it rape. Panama remained an American 'protectorate' until 1939 and the canal under US control until 1999.

Roosevelt did honour the more benign intentions of his imperialism. When the five Central American republics of Nicaragua, El Salvador, Guatemala, Honduras and Costa Rica seemed in unresolvable conflict, he persuaded them to set up a joint court of justice to adjudicate their disputes. He also brought an end to the Russo-Japanese war in 1905 by forceful mediation. In all these interventions he understood the importance of power behind the policy projection. He built the world's second largest number of battleships after the British.

One of Roosevelt's last actions as president was an extravagant gesture of egotism. At the end of 1907 he sent an American 'Great White Fleet' – sixteen new battleships plus an armada of supporting vessels – on a fourteen-month world tour as a display of the nation's new global role. Congress and the press were furious at the cost. Roosevelt was ecstatic on its triumphant return after he had left office. He then went on safari in Africa, returning to stage a fourteen-carriage parade from New York docks, this time displaying 13,000 specimens of elephant, rhino, antelope and other victims of his adventure.

By the time of the 1908 election, Roosevelt had established himself as an extraordinary character, both progressive and popular. This was not to the taste of important sections of conservative Republicanism. He had served almost two terms and it was felt he could not realistically stand again. He secured the nomination for a favoured follower, William Howard Taft. The choice was eccentric. A 300-pound giant of a man, Taft was everything Roosevelt was not. He was retiring, unenergetic and content to defer to Congress whenever controversy occurred. But he stuck to his patron's anti-trust programme and obtained two constitutional amendments, one permitting a federal income tax and the other selecting senators by election rather than by often corrupt party choice.

By the end of Taft's first term in 1912, Roosevelt was on his own, crossing the country making speeches and being received as if still in office. He then decided he would stand against Taft as an independent in that year's presidential election. The effect was to divide the still substantial Republican vote and let in a Democrat, Woodrow Wilson, on a minority vote.

Roosevelt went on to campaign against isolationists seeking to keep America out of the First World War, dying still in his early sixties in 1919. Though he was to be overshadowed by his namesake and distant cousin, Franklin Delano Roosevelt, he ranked among America's most activist and reforming presidents. He rightly secured inclusion in the quartet of holders of the office carved from 1927 on the face of Mount Rushmore in South Dakota. He shared this distinction with Washington, Jefferson and Lincoln.

The America that Roosevelt left behind had demonstrably matured from that of the Gilded Age and the new frontier. Its manifest destiny was coming of age. Its physical character was adjusting to fit this role. Three of America's cities, New York, Chicago and Philadelphia, ranked among the ten biggest on earth. Washington was a metropolis of white classical palaces. New York was emerging as a wonder of the world. Some sixty skyscrapers of twenty storeys or more were under construction, like nowhere else on earth. The tallest, the Woolworth building, completed in 1913, was an effusion of technological ingenuity and Gothic adornment.

Chicago, always 'the second city', was following suit. In half a century it had been transformed from a provincial market town into the authentic gateway to the frontier. It lacked the elitist veneer of New York and Philadelphia. Its mayors were populist, its mafia ruthless, its colleges hard-edged. In her essay on the city, Jan Morris recalled a train conductor announcing, 'You are approaching the boss city of the Universe.' The architecture of the more traditional Louis Sullivan and the Modernist Ludwig Mies van der Rohe was emphatically Chicagoan. The city's Magnificent Mile vied with New York in its skyscrapers.

When traditionalists protested that the modern American sky-scraper was dangerous and ugly, Sullivan scoffed. He claimed his buildings afforded 'the most magnificent of opportunities that the lord of nature in his beneficence has ever offered the proud spirit of man'. To him the skyscraper was the very symbol of America as a city on a hill, soaring over land, sea and now into the sky overhead.

17.
Wilson's Great War

1912–1923

Woodrow Wilson (1913–21) brought to the White House a rarity, a man of serious intellectual calibre. He brought the same progressive outlook as Teddy Roosevelt and the same belief in an executive presidency. Otherwise they could hardly have been less alike. Where Roosevelt was extrovert, energetic and given to flights of rhetorical exaggeration, Wilson was cautious and dry. He was born in the South but migrated north to New Jersey, there to become a political scientist and president of Princeton University. He wrote extensively on American politics and was moved to participate more actively. He was elected governor of New Jersey, where he struggled to cleanse the Augean stables of corruption, winning the support of a then ailing Democratic Party. It selected him as its candidate for president in 1912.

On winning the White House thanks to Roosevelt's splitting of the Republican vote, Wilson employed a grandiloquence suited to his opponent's new imperial age. 'Here muster the forces not of a party but of humanity,' he announced. 'Men's hopes await us, men's lives hang in the balance . . . I summon all honest men, all patriotic, all forward-looking men. Who dares fail to try?'

Wilson did not depart from the progressive impulse that was now part of the national conversation. He continued Roosevelt's 'trust-busting' creed, forming a Federal Trade Commission to protect and promote competition. In 1913 he founded a Federal Reserve Board as a critical arm of government, tasked to intervene to avert the banking 'panics' that had twice afflicted Wall Street.

·By now all eyes were straying across the Atlantic. Europe in 1913 was displaying the violent instability to which George Washington had told his successors to shut their eyes. Wilson honoured that warning, emphasizing, 'We are at peace with the world.' Any impending conflict in Europe was one 'with which we have nothing to do, whose causes cannot touch us'. He was adamant that America would remain detached.

Wilson was aware that many Americans originated in nations that might soon be at war with each other. Most had British origins, but 8 million had German ancestry. With the outbreak of hostilities in 1914 he pleaded with his fellow Americans 'to be impartial in thought as well as in action'. He had studied the Civil War and knew how easily reason surrendered to violence. Lead people towards war, he said, 'and they'll forget there was ever such a thing as tolerance'. Again, America had to remain neutral.

The opening of hostilities in 1914 showed how hard such detachment would be to sustain. In 1915 a German U-boat torpedoed the British liner *Lusitania* off the coast of Ireland, killing 128 Americans among 1,000 others. Germany warned it would also attack American cargo ships heading for Europe. While Wilson had this threat rescinded, domestic sentiment increasingly sided with the Allies. Britain received US war loans that grew steadily larger until they covered half its military spending. American exporters followed with a boom in supplies to the Allies.

Wilson himself initially intervened to seek to avoid war. He offered to negotiate after the murder of the Austrian archduke Franz Ferdinand, remarking that America was 'the one people holding itself ready to play a part of impartial mediation and to speak the counsels of peace and accommodation'. He was rebuffed, and watched as Europe went to war in 1914. In his 1916 re-election convention he was cheered to the rafters as 'the man who has kept us out of the war'. He again offered to bring the antagonists together, but was again ignored. The German response was to resume indiscriminate U-boat warfare and begin sinking American vessels supplying the Allies, including three in March 1917.

At this point Wilson felt he had no option but to ask Congress to take sides against Germany. This was agreed and extensive war powers were bestowed on the president, including a limited military draft. Yet Wilson remained emphatic that 'We desire no conquest, no dominion.' But he added what became a motto of American interventionism: 'The world must be made safe for democracy.' At home the state was galvanized. Washington took control of the railways. The draft was even hailed by Congress as 'a melting pot which will mould us into a new nation and bring forth new Americans'.

Throughout 1917 confusion surrounded America's intentions. It was formally 'at war' with Germany but not strictly an 'ally' of France and Britain. Recruitment, supplies and training continued throughout the year but with no sign of troops travelling to Europe. One reason was that America had never sent an army out of its continent, other than briefly to the Philippines, and lacked the appropriate transport. A more bizarre difficulty was that, when the first soldiers disembarked in France in June 1917, America's General Pershing wished to fight a battle with Germany on his own, not as subordinate to some other army. Britain's Field Marshal Douglas Haig was furious. What the exhausted Allied forces most needed was reinforcements for its trenches on the front line.

The American army was to rise from a strength of 200,000 to an extraordinary 4 million men by the war's end, though only half were serving in France. They did not encounter the Germans in strength until May 1918, and then not until September was Pershing ready to lead an army of 500,000 men into battle alongside the French, a full year after his arrival. The battle followed the defeat of Germany's Spring Offensive towards Paris at the River Meuse. The Battle of Amiens began the war's final Hundred Days Offensive. In its first three hours the American army used more artillery firepower than had been used in the entire four years of the Civil War.

Fighting was fierce and American soldiers were not yet equipped like the other Allies with tanks and planes. They were inexperienced when confronting a battle-hardened enemy. But the weight of American numbers was critical, pushing back the Germans and contributing to the Allied victory along the entire Franco-Belgian frontier. Two months later an armistice was called and the war was over. The American arrival was crucial, its death toll, half in action and half from a devastating influenza epidemic, rose to 112,000.

The terms of the armistice and the establishment of peace in Europe offered Wilson his moment. On entering the war he had established in New York an inquiry of 150 strategists to explore a possible settlement. In January 1918 this group delivered the president a manifesto of fourteen points for a 'new world order'. With America as their implied guarantor, the points embraced open treaties, freedom of the seas, free trade, arms control and a string of boundary changes. It was unimaginably far from the isolationism of four years earlier.

As for Europe's imperial powers, Wilson could hardly have been more opinionated. He expected 'an absolutely impartial adjustment of all colonial claims . . . The interests of the populations concerned [must have] equal weight with the equitable claims of the governments whose title is to be determined.' The fourteen points were mostly platitudinous and suffered from not being discussed with the other armistice nations. Wilson was in effect telling everyone to go home and do what he said. His reference to colonialism failed to refer to America's recent acquisitions.

Wilson's decision to go in person to the 1919 Versailles peace conference was a mistake. He took no political allies, let alone opponents, with him. He was not practised in diplomacy and shocked those who met him with how little he knew of Europe. His public activities were memorable – at a London banquet the former prime minister's wife, Margot Asquith, said he made 'one of the greatest speeches I have ever heard in my life'. But as a negotiator he was out of his depth. His bid for Allied leadership was upstaged by French and British eagerness for a display of revenge. Their imposition of crippling reparations on Germany ended all hope of the emergence of a secure and moderate German leadership. The economist John Maynard Keynes resigned from the British team in disgust, remarking that if he were German he would die rather than sign. The path was duly laid for the rise of Hitler.

One additional proposal put forward by Wilson was for a 'general association of nations'. The ambition was grandiose, with 'mutual guarantees of political independence and territorial integrity to great and small states alike'. In addition the League would be committed to 'collective security'. Its members would be empowered to defend militarily each other's sovereignty, which meant coming to the defence of any member that was a victim of aggression. The League was claiming authority to declare war.

Throughout the negotiations Wilson was touchy and inflexible. He made a serious error in insisting that the League be included in the Versailles treaty, since treaties had to be approved by Congress. This meant he would have to convince Washington of the wisdom of a complete about turn in America's foreign policy. One former secretary of state, Elihu Root, pointed out that Americans might now be obligated 'to enter into foreign wars in faraway places where they would almost certainly not want to fight'.

On his return from Versailles in July 1919 an exhausted Wilson announced that America was now 'the great idealistic force of history . . . with a spiritual energy in her which no other nation can contribute to the liberation of mankind . . . with the infinite privilege of fulfilling her destiny and saving the world'. If America did not support his League, 'I can predict with absolute certainty that within another generation there will be another world war.'

Selling this to Congress might have suited the flair of a Roosevelt, but Wilson suffered a series of strokes from October 1919 and became bedridden. Access to him was in the hands of his wife Edith for the remaining year of his office. She was termed the first woman president. Ratification of the treaty became chaotic and America's membership of Wilson's League did not survive congressional opposition. One senator accused Wilson of 'entering into a covenant of death to become the policeman of the world'. He would 'plunge our people forever into the maelstrom of European and

Asian slaughter'. The sick Wilson was humiliated. The League was agreed in Europe, but without the power of America behind it.

One result of the war was to loosen the constitutional barriers to reform. In 1919 an amendment was passed by an alcohol-prohibition movement in its ascendancy. It claimed that the mostly German brewing industry had used its product to weaken the fighting spirit of American soldiers. The manufacture and sale of 'intoxicating liquors' was banned and, in their publicity, they declared 'a new nation is born. John Barleycorn makes his last will and testament.' The mafia rubbed its hands with glee.

In a more progressive spirit the campaign for women to vote was galvanized. When women were answering pleas to join the war effort on farms and in factories, it was hard to maintain that their place should remain in the home. Already a number of states had granted women the franchise, starting with Wyoming and other western states in the nineteenth century. California and New York had followed in the 1900s. Resistance came from the South, fearing that such votes would encourage black people to exercise their voting rights. But the relevant nineteenth constitutional amendment was enacted in 1920. What did not pass was another amendment proposing equal rights for women.

At the same time America was seized by a bout of political hysteria. With communism having triumphed in Russia and surging across Europe, 1919 in America saw the so-called 'Red Scare'. A series of letter bombs addressed to Congress gave rise to police overreaction against anyone with supposedly socialist leanings. Over 6,000 people were arrested, including a large number of foreigners. The veteran trade unionist Eugene Debs was imprisoned for 'espionage'. Twenty-four states outlawed the 'criminal anarchism of syndicalism'. California criminalized advocacy of 'a change in industrial ownership'. Constitutional freedom of speech was flagrantly disregarded.

In the circumstances, the 1920 presidential election seemed a welcome opportunity to stop rocking the boat. The election was a classic reversion in America's political cycles, from a period of progressiveness to one of retrenchment. The Republicans chose a homespun Ohio senator named Warren Harding (1921–23), a small town newspaperman who emphasized simplicity. He believed in answering his own front door, even (at times) at the White House, and in riding a horse to church.

Harding promised 'not heroics but healing, not nostrums but normalcy, not revolution but restoration', and won one of the biggest popular majorities in American history. He brought with him to Washington a bevy of Midwesterners with a reputation for corruption. This reputation was fully vindicated in the monumental Teapot Dome scandal of 1923, in which areas of federal land found themselves in the pockets of Harding's friends. He died of a heart attack the same year.

The years of Roosevelt and Wilson were followed by an amiable stability. They indicated how far the personality of an American president could affect the nation's political debate. In his study of the twentieth-century presidency, the historian Stephen Graubard remarked on how easily the office transformed by 'learned and ambitious men' such as Roosevelt and Wilson could revert to the live-and-let-live of what had gone before. It was 'a throwback to an older America, less interested in the world outside and less commit-ted to establishing its credentials as a great power led by a powerful chief executive'.

The 'normalcy' of Harding, who died in office, was continued by his vice-president and successor, Calvin Coolidge (1923–29), who was even more a presidential minimalist. On being summoned to the White House he was working on his family's Vermont farm. He had to take the oath of office in the farm kitchen by the light of a kerosene lamp, a scene beloved of American romantics. Coolidge was a president of whom little was expected, though he did oversee the grant of citizenship to all Native Americans. His chief claim to fame was his belief in saying as little as possible. 'If you don't say anything, you won't be called upon to repeat it' was his motto. His inaugural speech was short and ended with, 'Be brief – above all things be brief.' He took no interest in foreign affairs and his biographer praised him for having 'the genius of the average'. His nickname was Silent Cal.

These men ruled America at a time when Joseph Stalin, Benito Mussolini, Kemal Atatürk and Chiang Kai-shek were bestriding the globe. In Britain the Tories and Labour were advancing the power of the state to intervene ever more in the lives of citizens. Yet in 1924 Coolidge, like Harding, stood for election with no declared programme beyond the enigmatic statement that 'the chief business of the American people is business'. Like Harding, he won a popular landslide.

18

Roaring Twenties

The 1920s were known as 'America's decade'. While the Gilded Age saw a moneyed elite searching for pseudo-European status, the next generation sought something different, an America that was American. Impelled forward by prosperity and the presidencies of Roosevelt and Wilson, a nation long formed of other empires, colonies and frontiers, of slave-owners, immigrants and tycoons, had come of age. America was now a world power with a national culture of its own.

The defining object of the age was the motor car. In 1913, Ford had switched his eight-year-old factory in Detroit to an automated production line, reducing the time taken to assemble a vehicle from twelve hours to ninety minutes. Like Carnegie before him, he rewarded his workers handsomely. His lowest paid were on five dollars a day, or twice the industrial worker's average. Ford wanted his cars to be 'so low in price that no man making a good salary will be unable to own one'. Families could then enjoy 'the blessing of hours of pleasure in God's great open spaces'. As for the car's colour, Ford said his customers could have any they wanted 'as long as it's black'.

In 1914 America produced 461,000 cars. By the end of the 1920s car production was 5 million a year, or five times that in the entire rest of the world. In 1927, 85 per cent of tractors were imported from America, even to the Soviet Union. The pace of technological innovation in the previous three decades was now delivering breathtaking results. In 1903 the Wright brothers had flown a plane for fifty-nine seconds. Twenty years later America enjoyed transcontinental air mail, and in 1927 Charles Lindbergh flew from New York to Paris. In 1912 just 16 per cent of American homes had electricity. Fifteen years later the figure was 63 per cent. By 1930 a third of American homes had radios, served by more than six hundred stations. Equally remarkable was that all states, however politically conservative, were looking after their own, with spending on schools doubling in just six years from 1920.

A similar dramatic advance was in the status of American women, or at least the better-off. The war and the franchise freed them to enter the workforce and politics, and this was followed by a revolution in lifestyle. The under-thirties seized on the 'flapper' fashion for bobbed hair and body-hugging garments. Full-length skirts were discarded. Ankles and legs became visible, sported in new dances at 'night clubs'. As numbers going to college doubled, the student surge fed a youth culture largely unknown before the war. All contributed to the dubbing of the decade the 'Roaring Twenties'.

America's creative hub had moved over the century from Boston to Philadelphia to New York. It now travelled west and touched down in California. San Francisco matured from a gold-rush frontier town to the capital of the west. Its Nob Hill district – named after its resident 'nabob' rail tycoons – boasted the finest town mansions in the country. William Randolph Hearst's *Examiner* newspaper became so powerful it was regarded as an alternative state assembly. San Francisco's Barbary Coast was its answer to New Orleans' Storyville, where prostitutes indulged in nightly shouting matches with evangelical preachers.

Most dramatic was the transformation of the ancient Spanish settlement of Los Angeles. It had become open house to Mexicans and Chinese and then to booming oil and aviation companies. Its population of half a million tripled in the 1920s, liberated by access to fresh water, demand for which was met by the giant Hoover Dam on the Colorado River in Nevada. Authorized in 1928 and completed in 1936, it was the biggest concrete structure in the world. Los Angeles was ready for a rebirth, hosting the 1932 Olympic Games.

From 1905 America's first moving pictures were shown in so-called nickelodeons, scruffy booths charging five cents for short silent films. They were especially popular among immigrants who did not speak English. In the mid-1900s the movie-makers, largely Jewish, migrated en masse to Los Angeles, where the weather was fine and the light ideal for filming. Land for sets was plentiful and labour was cheap. Universal City in Hollywood was founded in 1915 and was soon producing a picture a day. By 1930, 80 per cent of Americans regularly visited a movie theatre and Hollywood's profits were enormous.

The 1920s film industry came to influence the American way of life much as did the motor car. Producers such as Samuel Goldwyn, Louis B. Mayer, Cecil B. DeMille, D. W. Griffith and Darryl F. Zanuck became national celebrities. The first was famous for his Goldwynisms, such as 'I'll give you a definite maybe', and 'When I want your opinion, I'll give it to you.' On a visit to Britain he invited the playwright George Bernard Shaw to try his hand in Hollywood. After an hour, Shaw said, 'Mr Goldwyn, there is not much use our going on. I can see you're only interested in art and I'm only interested in money.'

Within a decade Los Angeles had become a citadel of extravagance. Griffith's epic *Intolerance* – arguably the greatest film of the silent era – cost $2 million to make. It contrived to employ 3,000 extras and its sets became a tourist attraction. Actors such as Douglas Fairbanks, Charlie Chaplin, Lillian Gish, Mary Pickford and Gloria Swanson outshone presidents and sportsmen in fame. Swanson built herself a palace in Beverly Hills of twenty-two rooms and a bathroom with gold fittings. The Canadian Pickford was a phenomenon. Born in 1892, she was reputedly the highest paid woman in the world and with the best-known face, undaunted by being under five feet tall. At one point she was making a film a week for $10,000 each. In 1919 Pickford and fellow stars, including Chaplin and Fairbanks, were able to form their own company, United Artists, exercising total control over their output. Pickford's *Pollyanna* (1920) was the first film to gross over a million dollars.

Pickford and Fairbanks married in 1920 and became 'king and queen of Hollywood'. As a couple they enjoyed fame on a scale unequalled before or probably since. Heads of state visiting the White House would beg for an introduction to them. Though the marriage lasted sixteen years until they divorced in 1936, Pickford became a Hollywood recluse, receiving visitors only over the phone from her bedroom. Her sweet girl-next-door image was dated and her Hollywood era ended with the birth of the talkies at the end of the decade. Feminine sweetness gave way to the sex goddesses of the 1930s, to Claudette Colbert, Jean Harlow, Greta Garbo and Katharine Hepburn. The talkies were rivalled by the arrival of a phenomenal talent in the cartoonist Walt Disney (1901–66). His hero Mickey Mouse was launched on the world in 1928 in the film *Steamboat Willie* and was to star in 130 films. His creator branched out to become the leading impresario of American popular entertainment and leisure.

Along with the movies came the other cultural innovation of interwar America: jazz. Its origins in the South, and particularly New Orleans, have long puzzled scholars. The word itself has been traced to the African-American slang 'jasm', meaning spirit or energy, or possibly the French *jaser*, to chat. The music originated in a mix of slave-plantation songs and the folk traditions of the Franco-Spanish Caribbean. Both its slow, sad 'blues' and the vigorous tempos of ragtime were characterized by originality and intensity. It was said that a jazz band would play blues on the way to a funeral and ragtime on the way to the wake. 'Rag' was itself a borrowing from the English 'to rag' or defy convention.

As the New Orleans red light district of Storyville grew in musical fame, its artists migrated north to Chicago. It yielded an enduring legacy of players, including Louis Armstrong, Sidney Bechet, Jelly Roll Morton, Joseph 'King' Oliver and Buddy Bolden. Its slang entered the language and its style was adopted by white as well as black musicians. In the North the gangster name for a machine gun was a Chicago Piano, while black pianists stressed the five black keys – they called them 'n—— keys'. An irony of the film business was that it took a Lithuanian Jew, Al Jolson, to black up as *The Jazz Singer* (1927) and introduce the music to white audiences. Many black performers were to become as famous as their white counterparts, notably Armstrong, Duke Ellington, Dizzy Gillespie and Charlie Parker.

A measure of the popularity of jazz was the reaction to it of conservative America. To many it was prime evidence of the Roaring Twenties' decadence. The General Federation of Women's Clubs declared jazz a music from 'the hands of infidel foreigners' and 'black slum-dwellers'. Feminists persuaded the American Federation of Musicians to promise never to play jazz. In 1921 the *Ladies' Home Journal* suggested it had 'put the sin in syncopation'.

A more concerted resistance to the influence of movies and jazz came from the churches. Films were regarded as being morally degenerate to a degree that books or other media never were, largely because everyone watched them. Hollywood presented the Jazz Age, a term popularized by F. Scott Fitzgerald in 1922, as if it was the new normal. The typical American family was encouraged to imitate the promiscuous materialism of a California tycoon. Religious opinion demanded that states uphold traditional values through censorship. It was states' rights in a new guise.

By 1921 thirty-seven states had already passed 'decency' laws censoring which films might be shown within their borders. Hollywood producers faced the prospect of a torrent of controls over what could be shown and where. To avoid a bureaucracy of censorship, the film industry commissioned the president of the producers' association, William Hays, to draw up a voluntary code of practice. Published in 1930 and co-authored by a Jesuit priest, this sought to dictate what actors and directors could and could not put on the screen.

Hays's edicts had the meddlesome hilarity of twenty-first-century health-and-safety commands. They covered religion, swearing, violence, sexual intimacy, homosexuality, crime and punishment, anything to which anyone might object. Kisses could not last for more than three seconds of film. There should be no suggestion of 'perverted sex'. In all romantic scenes, 'one and preferably both [actors] should have one foot on the ground'. Hayes stipulated overall that 'The audience must feel sure that evil is wrong and good is right.' One critic described the code as 'Jewish film-makers imposing Catholic values on Protestant Americans.'

There were few signs that the Hays code damaged the film industry or its profits. Indeed, it probably attuned films more correctly to the values of most audiences. Goldwyn made a practice of watching his own films from the front of the cinema, with his back to the screen to see how viewers were reacting. The rules were eroded only in 1968, following a court ruling in support of film-makers' freedom of speech and the growth of imported foreign films.

Meanwhile alcohol prohibition was illustrating the futility of allowing prejudice to dictate policy. The 1919 ban applied to the manufacture and sale of liquor but not to its consumption. It took the liquor industry a matter of six months to switch production from legitimate to illegitimate sources of supply. Bars duly became 'speakeasies' where customers pretended to buy non-alcoholic drinks. Washington was said to have had three hundred bars before prohibition and seven hundred speakeasies after it. The 1920 Democratic convention in San Francisco had whiskey supplied free by the mayor. The alcohol monopoly run by Chicago's mafia boss, Al Capone, was said to be turning over $65 million at its peak. He was driven round town in an armour-plated Cadillac, until finally convicted of tax evasion.

Prohibition did little to stifle New York's twenties taste, not least the craze for the Dry Martini cocktail, invented in 1906. The drink was described by the columnist H. L. Mencken as 'the only American invention as perfect as the sonnet'. President Harding was said not to drink martinis solely on the grounds that he preferred whiskey. It was much admired by members of the New York Algonquin Circle, mostly writers and actors, who defined the frenetic style of the period. One of its number, the sharp-edged humorist Dorothy Parker, summed up the risqué libertarianism of the period with her salute to the great drink: 'I like to have a martini,/ Two at the very most./ After three I'm under the table,/ After four I'm under my host.'

Not content with alcohol, reactionary politics turned to immigration. In 1921 Congress passed the first of two measures to curb what had been the greatest contributor to American growth over three centuries, access to regular supplies of able-bodied labour. A 1921 act cut immigration to 357,000 and another in 1924 cut it to 150,000. Only Mexico was excepted, its labour still essential to the South's post-slave economy. In the words of Sam Gompers of the AFL union, it was time to end America's status as asylum to the world's oppressed. The nation had become 'honeycombed with foreign groups living a foreign life'. The inflows seen in the 1880s and 90s fell in the 1920s by 90 per cent.

Instead there began a new migration on a scale unprecedented in American history. It was not of immigrants from abroad but of black people from the South to the smokestack industries of the north-east and Midwest. Four million made this move between the wars. Many were fleeing continued racial discrimination and violence. In 1920 a group of whites in Ocoee, Florida attacked black people seeking to vote, killing more than thirty of them. Hundreds fled the town. An appalling massacre took place in a black suburb of Tulsa, Oklahoma in May 1921, when thirty-five blocks were reduced to ashes and the death toll ranged from an official thirty-nine to possibly hundreds.

Large parts of Chicago, St Louis, Baltimore and Washington now acquired all-black neighbourhoods. Racial segregation became a running issue in these cities as never before. A Chicago massacre in 1919 led to thirty-eight deaths. In New York one result was seen in the transformation of the prosperous mostly German/Jewish suburb of Harlem. Property developers in a downturn in the market in the first decade of the new century began marketing it to wealthier black people. As they arrived, the whites moved out, a trickle becoming a torrent. It is estimated that some 100,000 Harlem residents changed home during the 1920s. A major force in this transformation was the leading black property entrepreneur Philip Payton of the Afro-American Realty Company, who came to be known as the Father of Harlem.

At first the middle-class black people formed a sedate suburb, giving rise to the Harlem Renaissance school of artists, promoted by the black writer Langston Hughes. It portrayed local figures and their families as the epitome of respectable middle-class America with a strong emphasis on churchgoing. The district also became home to a booming night-life and part of the New York jazz scene, celebrated in Duke Ellington's Harlem Cotton Club. By the late 1930s its character had begun to change. Landlords found they could gain more rent through multi-occupation. As with many of America's inner cities, the Harlem terraces and tenements became less a melting pot, more a segregated enclave.

The most extreme reaction to 1920s modernity came in a different realm, that of education. Here the subject was creationism. In 1925 Church pressure forced Tennessee to pass a law insisting on biblical creationism in schools. It banned teaching that humans were 'descended from a lower order of animals'. Mississippi and Arkansas passed similar laws. The state duly prosecuted a local teacher, John Scopes, for instructing his pupils in Darwinian evolution. The state turned the case into the 'trial of the century', held partly in the open air, broadcast on radio and attended by two hundred reporters. The nation's most celebrated lawyer, Clarence Darrow, appeared for Scopes, supported by the American Civil Liberties Union.

What came to be called the 'Monkey Trial' ended in the conviction of Scopes, a modest fine and a reversal on appeal. The state's law was allowed to stand, though it was eventually repealed. The creationist prosecution was led by none other than the ageing ex-Populist leader William Jennings Bryan, rooting his case in the tradition of states' rights. Bryan was appealing to a wider constituency than just creationists. He claimed to speak for 'Middle America', for the right of democratic citizens to preserve their own values, in this case those of religion, against others who disagreed with them.

Bryan's message was that Tennessee 'has been the centre of active social philanthropy and political progressivism . . . folk who express the spirit of kindly goodwill towards classes which are at an economic disadvantage'. It was the classic Populist response to what sections of provincial America saw as an east-coast, liberal, college-led establishment, a response that was frequently to reassert itself in American politics.

This was an America whose devout conservatism was satirized in Sinclair Lewis's popular novel *Main Street* (1920), about a young woman who tries and fails to reform a small Minnesota town. One such town, sensing it might be Lewis's model, even banned the book from its library. A converse commentary was offered by Scott Fitzgerald's depiction of east coast wealth, arrogance and insecurity in *The Great Gatsby* (1925). Both books described a more fractured society than that of Wharton and James and the Gilded Age.

A conservative reaction to the new ethos was also seen in painting. Now, as Europe flirted with cubism and abstraction, artists turned to home for inspiration. Edward Hopper (1882–1967) depicted a community of individuals seemingly lonely and alienated in rooms, streets and cafés. Hopper's new America was anything but a happy place. A solemnity was also echoed in the most celebrated image of conservatism, Grant Wood's portrait, finished in 1930, of a farmer and his wife or his daughter in Iowa. They stand with plain, stern faces in front of a gabled farmhouse, the man holding a pitchfork. Grant titled it *American Gothic*.

The most lasting assertion of American culture in the interwar period came in the field of architecture. Frank Lloyd Wright (1867–1959) flirted with the abstract modernism of the European Bauhaus school, notably in his much-publicized Fallingwater in Pennsylvania. But it was the open spaces and ground-hugging contours of the south-west that inspired the low-pitched roofs of Wright's Arizona settlement. He was a topographical architect, the true stylist of the frontier. In the Wright room at New York's Metropolitan Museum there is not a whisper of a European motif.

Yet the Roaring Twenties could still hit back. Over 1930s Manhattan there rose William Van Alen's Chrysler Building, asserting itself as the tallest building in the world. Festooned with gargoyles, eagles, car radiator caps and arches, it showed that Art Deco ostentation could embrace sculptural beauty. America was still the land of superlatives. No sooner was Chrysler's skyscraper completed than the Empire State Building rose even higher across town. The monster building remained largely empty before being taken over by government offices during the war, becoming colloquially known as the 'empty state building'. In 1945 a USAF bomber crashed into it in a fog and fourteen people died, though the steel and stone building remained structurally intact. A curiosity of American architecture between the wars was that, apart from these skyscrapers and the New York Rockefeller Center, European Art Deco was not widely adopted.

19.
Depression and New Deal

1929–1941

'A chicken for every pot and a car for every garage' was the slogan of the Republican president Herbert Hoover, inaugurated in March 1929. Unlike Harding and Coolidge, he had had a distinguished career in diplomacy in the aftermath of the Great War and was very much the apostle of business. Brimming with confidence, he boasted that the America that emerged from the Roaring Twenties was rich beyond the dreams of even its wealthiest rivals. With an average of one motor vehicle per household, it enjoyed 'a higher degree of comfort and security than ever existed before in the history of the world'. Hoover concluded, 'I have no fears for the future of our country. It is bright with hope.'

He spoke too soon. That same month of March 1929, the New York Stock Exchange experienced a minor dip, which was corrected by a cash injection from a leading bank, the National City. Companies in steel, construction, cars and retail were still reporting a phenomenal 36 per cent rise in profits on the previous year. Some commentators noted a fall-off in demand and possibly a market oversupply. But such scepticism did nothing to prevent a speculative burst on the stock market in September, when it soared 20 per cent in four months. This climax to an extraordinary ten-fold rise over the previous nine years was out of all proportion to the surges prior to the 1873 and 1893 crashes.

In London on 20 September a leading financier, Clarence Hatry, confessed to a multi-million-pound stock fraud, sending a shudder through the also-inflated London market. Five weeks later, on

24 October, New York suffered Black Thursday, when the market followed London, losing 11 per cent on opening. The rush led to a panic so severe that the ticker-tape machines failed to register deals. A group of financiers gathered to stabilize prices by buying heavily, but without success. Buyers had wildly overborrowed and banks overlent. There was no mechanism for suspending trade; no market underpinning; no lender of last resort.

Through the following Black Monday and Black Tuesday selling continued. The three-day cumulative fall of 23 per cent was unprecedented in the exchange's history. No one was buying and the market continued a long slide, falling from 381 points to 198 in two months. There was a pause and recovery in early 1930, but by then the entire economy was in decline.

No fewer than 9,000 banks now failed, with no system of credit insurance. Thirty-eight states had no working banks at all. American citizens were stripped of an estimated $7 billion in wealth, with no insurance cover. An economy devoid of statutory rescue measures floundered. The stock market continued down throughout 1931 into early 1932, when the Dow Jones Industrial Average hit a bottom at just over 41, down from a high approaching 400 in September 1929. The American private sector economy had lost almost 90 per cent of its value. The central institution of American capitalism had effectively collapsed.

The role of the stock-market crash in what became known as the Great Depression is much debated. Only 12 per cent of Americans invested in shares and there was no reason for such a collapse in underlying confidence. But an economy built on forecasts of rising demand – in overseas trade as well as in domestic consumption – found business stalled. Buyers stopped buying, prices fell, factories lost business, laid off staff and went bankrupt. Farm prices collapsed and the rural economy with them. It was indeed a great depression.

Hoover was not idle. He immediately summoned industry leaders and pleaded with them not to cut wages. He advanced $500 million to farmers and then millions more through a Reconstruction Finance Corporation, eventually advancing $5.4 billion. To pay for at least some of it he drastically increased top-rate income tax from 25 per cent to 63 per cent. Public spending soared, including on the Bay Bridge in San Francisco and the Hoover Dam in Nevada. In three years of his presidency, Hoover was unceasing in his efforts to rescue the ailing American economy, though he won little credit for it. He was in many ways the true initiator of the New Deal programme of his successor, Franklin Delano Roosevelt. The one thing he did not propose was direct unemployment relief. He felt it a progressive step too far and un-American.

So identified was Hoover with the Great Depression that his actions went unrewarded. The reality is that his available tools were limited, given the country's aversion to federal intervention. America had no central bank as lender of last resort. It had Wilson's Federal Reserve Board, which could fix interest rates and advance limited credit, but nothing on the scale clearly required.

Matters were not helped by Congress reacting as it had under McKinley in 1890, supposedly to defend home production with prohibitive tariffs. The Smoot-Hawley Act of 1933 increased average taxes on dutiable imports from what had been up to 40 per cent to a new high of 60 per cent. Retaliation was instant, not least from America's oldest trading partner, Canada. Roosevelt began to cut them two years later and they were considered among the great mistakes of American economic policy.

As the Depression deepened it spread across Europe and round the world, with countries everywhere protecting their markets by restricting trade and banning imports. This merely added to the recession. By 1933 world trade was down by two-thirds. US Steel's shares plummeted from $262 to $22, General Motors from $73 to $8. The latter's plants closed, leaving its 225,000 employees jobless. Usually hard-working citizens in respectable jobs found themselves without an income.

Across the country local taxes went uncollected and schools could not pay their teachers. American unemployment, 3 per cent in 1929, rose within three years to 25 per cent. Over a quarter of the population was thought to have no income at all. Mortgage payments became unaffordable. Evicted residents squatted in parking lots and queued outside hotel kitchen doors. In this climate, Hoover's reputation disintegrated.

Satirists were cruel. A 'Hoover blanket' was a newspaper. A Hoover wagon a motor truck drawn by a horse. The outskirts of towns developed shanty communities in which the homeless took shelter, becoming known as Hoovervilles. When in 1932 the president needed a campaign song, the nearest he got to an answer was the anthem of the Great Depression, Rudy Vallee's 'Brother, Can You Spare a Dime?' That same year a demonstration of war veterans 20,000 strong marched on Washington demanding payment of a future bonus. Hoover foolishly ordered the army to disperse them. The result was tear gas, violence and dire publicity.

The subsequent election saw Hoover fighting against the odds. The Democrats were now emphatically the party of progressivism, the Republicans of conservatism. Nothing better illustrates this ideological alignment than that Hoover's Democratic opponent was Franklin Delano Roosevelt (1933–45). He was a distant cousin of Teddy, though he called himself 'Rose-velt' against Teddy's 'Rooz-velt'. To be known as FDR, he shared Teddy's progressivism and belief in the power of the presidency, but it was implausible to hold such views as a Republican, even though, like Teddy, he came from a patrician New England background. Since 1921 he had been severely handicapped by polio and wheelchair bound. Though he still managed to stand and walk, it caused him acute pain.

FDR's campaign song, though hardly appropriate, was 'Happy Days Are Here Again' and he secured a convincing victory. Hoover departed the scene, exhausted and humiliated, a shadow of the self-confident showman of four years earlier. FDR made sure he was always photographed smiling and was a master of platitude. His 1933 inaugural speech declared his 'firm belief that the only thing we have to fear is fear itself'. As for the recession, he could do little that Hoover had not already tried, but he was adept at doing it with conviction and at galvanizing Congress to follow.

One change was the necessity for federal intervention. Something had to be done, and three years of Depression meant the central government should do it. The time for regarding individual states as responsible for the lives and laws of American citizens was past. The nation was united in distress more than it ever had been in days of plenty. The year 1933 saw collaboration between president and legislature as never before or since in peacetime.

FDR's initial version of his much-vaunted New Deal was a rebranding of Hooverism. He was aided by a sharp Texan tycoon, Jesse Jones, who detested bankers and especially east-coast ones. Jones put the federal government on virtually a war footing, devoted day and night to the task of getting America's banks back to work. FDR passed through Congress an emergency banking act involving the creation of a host of bodies supplying loans, guarantees and insurance. A 300,000-strong Civilian Conservation Corps was formed to employ the unemployed.

Hoover's construction projects were extended to include a Tennessee Valley Authority, supplying cheap electricity to that state's consumers. Such public enterprise was bitterly opposed by monopolists, who had long profited at the consumers' expense. It made FDR the toast of America's few socialists for years to come. To cheer the nation, the president also engineered an end to Prohibition. A constitutional amendment was passed legalizing the sale of alcohol and removing what had become a boon to the mafia and criminal syndicates. The first drink was celebrated on 5 December 1933. FDR also began a practice of press conferences and radio broadcasts, known as 'fireside chats'. These became regular events that determined much of the president's lasting public appeal.

By the end of 1933 America had experienced four years of unprecedented hardship. Most European states had brought their economies out of the 1929 crash and were embarked on recovery. Despite the efforts of Hoover and FDR, America still seemed trapped in a downturn from which no amount of New Deal had been able to rescue it. While in cities charities could organize soup kitchens and keep starvation at bay, rural areas could not revert to a subsistence economy. Attempts at migration westwards were impeded by a severe drought afflicting the prairie states, turning them into a dustbowl throughout the late 1930s. Hundreds of thousands facing starvation left the land and sought a future further west, mostly in California.

Their plight was vividly captured in the novel art of documentary photography. Portraits of down-and-outs on the streets of New York deeply moved a country so recently told it was the richest on earth. So too did Dorothea Lange's pictures of depression-hit refugees trekking west. John Steinbeck's novel *The Grapes of Wrath* (1939) told of an Oklahoma family dispossessed and forced to seek work in California. It vilified America's laissez-faire economy, of individuals as pawns of money and power. The book helped Steinbeck to a Nobel prize for literature, but it also faced bans from public libraries, notably in California's farming districts. A film version starring Henry Fonda followed in 1940.

A different west was being revealed by the artist Georgia O'Keeffe (1887–1986). She found escape from the frenetic culture of 1920s New York in the recession year of 1929 by visiting the deserts of New Mexico, where she eventually settled in the 1940s. She dramatized the wildness of the landscape and the intensity of its flowers and nature, bringing an emotional depth to a part of America still chiefly associated with Buffalo Bill. Hers is an older America, unchanged.

In 1935, with the economy still struggling to recover, FDR introduced a New Deal Mark II. This tried tardily to catch up with welfare programmes such as public housing and sickness and unemployment relief, which were being introduced by Liberal and Conservative governments in Britain, and by governments between the wars across Europe. The New Deal's language sounded remarkably left wing. In his 1935 message to the people FDR complained that America was 'still suffering from the old inequalities . . . We have not weeded out the overprivileged and not lifted up the underprivileged.' America had not yet secured for its citizens 'a proper security, a reasonable leisure and a decent living'.

A Works Progress Administration now sought nothing less than the federal employment of three and a half million people, from street cleaners and building workers to artists, actors and writers. Though much of this was satirized as hardly work, it was better than a dole. FDR's Social Security Act (1935) finally brought to America a contributory unemployment and old-age pension scheme. There were also to be forms of federal insurance for bank deposits. In 1939 food stamps were introduced. Federal aid went from zero at the start of the 1930s to roughly a third of citizens receiving some assistance. For the first time this included large numbers of black people.

In 1936 FDR was overwhelmingly re-elected president on his New Deal ticket. His Republican opponent, Alfred Landon, won just eight electoral college votes. Federal policy was now firmly progressive. Agriculture was protected with loans and subsidies. Union power was also protected. The central government was accepted as a national executive, much as in Europe. For all that, it was not until 1941 that America's national product returned to the level it had been at in 1929. By then it was not so much the New Deal that won through, though it relieved the suffering of millions. Economic recovery lay elsewhere. The Second World War was to see an outburst of public spending beyond anything Hoover or FDR had dared contemplate.

The prospect of another European conflict initially shocked Americans. There was a widespread feeling that such a cost should not be inflicted on a nation still struggling out of depression. A conservative isolationism had been in the ascendant since the end of the First World War. America had failed to support the hesitant League of Nations in Geneva. In 1938 a majority of the public, though not a sufficient two-thirds majority in Congress, wanted a constitutional amendment insisting on a national referendum before a declaration of any future war.

FDR understood this. In public he firmly asserted America's neutrality, as Wilson had done in 1914. America, he said, had its own war to fight, 'a great and successful war against want, destitution and economic demoralization'. He then added Wilson's phrase, that this economic war was 'for the survival of democracy'. The implication was that democracy would depend on American prosperity at home, not intervention abroad. In Congress Senator Robert Taft, a staunchly conservative Republican, spoke for a majority in his aversion to intervention. He warned in particular against any involvement in 'undeclared wars all over the world in which America would do everything except actually put soldiers in the front-line trenches'. This, he implied, was unrealistic if not immoral. America should let the rest of the world sort itself out.

Congress was clearly of like mind. It passed four so-called neutrality acts in 1935–39, banning Americans from assisting or associating with belligerents in any foreign conflict. America was to have nothing to do with the rising tension in Europe. There was to be no question of another 1917–18, of America being inveigled into assembling a great army and suffering enormous casualties. All that FDR did persuade Congress to do was authorize a strictly selective conscription, confined to the purpose of 'national defence'.

Public opinion in America, as in Europe in the months before the outbreak of war, was still dominated by the horror of 'the war to end all wars' in 1914–18. It made any effort for peace welcome. My own parents, students at the time, would point out the overwhelming support for what came to be deplored as 'appeasement'. When the British prime minister, Neville Chamberlain, returned from Munich in 1938 with promises of 'peace for our time' from Adolf Hitler, virtually the whole nation gave a sigh of relief. FDR cabled Chamberlain two words: 'Good man.' But a furious rearmament commenced throughout Europe.

When war against Hitler was finally declared by Britain in 1939, many urged FDR to breach convention and stand for a third term in 1940 – the first president ever to do so. He publicly declined, but he privately encouraged his team to lobby within the Democratic Party for this continuation. This they successfully did. In his election speech, FDR felt compelled to address events in Europe. He duly promised in the most direct terms, 'I am talking to you mothers and fathers. I give one more assurance. I have said this before, but I shall say it again and again and again: Your boys are not going to be sent into any foreign wars.' They would fight in defence of their nation 'only on US soil'.

Roosevelt's private position was not always his public one. As Hitler's conquests became more outrageous, the president's statements became more ambivalent. He told Congress that countries such as America 'cannot let pass without effective protest acts of aggression against sister nations, acts which undermine all of us . . . even if they are thousands of miles away'. He did not explain the word 'undermine'. He agreed that America 'will remain a neutral nation, but I cannot ask that every American remain neutral in thought as well'. At the start of the war he had sent a message to all belligerents not to commit the 'inhuman barbarities' of bombing civilians. But in a speech at the end of 1940 he talked of assembling an 'arsenal of democracy' should conflict make it necessary.

News from Europe became a daily barrage. Not only had France fallen but the bombing of British cities had begun. There was even talk of a possible German invasion across the North Sea. Then in the summer of 1941 the Molotov–Ribbentrop non-aggression pact between Germany and the USSR collapsed and Hitler invaded Russia. All of Europe seemed at the mercy of the Führer's dictatorship. FDR asked if it was for this that thousands of Americans had died defeating Germany in 1918. Yet his pledge to America's mothers and fathers could not have been more emphatic.

20.

The World at War

The outbreak of the Second World War, like that of the first, forced Americans back to their roots. Germany had embarked on a project to enslave Europe and that was Europe's affair. Throughout the 1930s Gallup and other polls showed that 70–80 per cent of Americans were firmly against any intervention. Ernest Hemingway wrote that 'of the hell broth that is brewing in Europe we have no need to drink'. Congress expressly forbade Roosevelt even to aid the Allies in distress.

The question was how long this detachment would hold. In 1916 it had proved barely skin deep. Would the drums of war and the claims of justice again rouse Americans from their beds and draw them to arms? Old tensions re-emerged. Republicans in Congress feared they could not trust the president. Refugees were already fleeing across the Atlantic from Hitler's tyranny. Americans still had close relations with Britain, whose newly appointed prime minister, Winston Churchill, was himself half-American. Like FDR, he was a larger-than-life character. The difference between them was that FDR was still fighting a domestic recession, Churchill was fighting a war of survival.

Throughout 1940, Churchill pleaded with Roosevelt for help. At first this was out of the question. Roosevelt was conscious of Woodrow Wilson's broken promise of 1914 and of his own highly explicit election pledge. He did succeed in persuading Congress to send Britain military equipment, but Congress insisted it be merely 'lent'. It should be leased and later returned or replaced. FDR argued that it was no more than lending a hose to a neighbour whose house was on fire. The first piece of equipment lent in 1941 was, symbolically, a hosepipe. The Lend-Lease arrangement was to grow until it covered half Britain's wartime trade deficit.

FDR remained hesitant throughout 1940–41. He set the navy patrolling the Atlantic for U-boats that might harass American merchant shipping. He told Churchill when they met secretly in Newfoundland that Congress would quietly allow him to 'wage war but not declare it'. A solid phalanx mostly of Republicans in Congress were adamantly opposed to war. Their prime concern was getting over the Depression, and in that most Americans agreed with them. Polls still showed that 80 per cent of Americans wanted neutrality.

Then in December 1941 an event occurred that put this hesitancy into reverse. Japan's emperor had made a reckless decision to establish an empire across the entirety of south-east Asia, to the borders of Australia and India. Tokyo had a modern navy but it had neither the economy nor the government structure to sustain a scattered empire. The Japanese military was sceptical, but the nation's rulers were adamant.

This might seem of no matter to America and there was certainly no American expectation of war with Japan. But America had imposed an oil and steel embargo on Japan as a way of impeding its expansion. The Japanese decided to pre-empt any further intervention. They sent assault carriers across the Pacific to attack America's Pacific Fleet in Hawaii's Pearl Harbor. The operation killed 2,400 American servicemen and destroyed or damaged eight battleships, though it missed carriers and submarines.

Pearl Harbor overwhelmed American opinion. The attack wounded the nation's pride and its sense of security. FDR limped painfully into Congress, witnessed by the English journalist Alistair Cooke, who told of him as a crippled giant: 'We saw him walk and we thought of the wounded battleship over in Pearl Harbor.' The president described the event 'as a date that will live in infamy'. America promptly declared war on Japan. This activated the

Tripartite Pact between Germany, Italy and Japan, which meant that three days later Hitler declared war on America. The termination of American neutrality could hardly have been more dramatic or more explicit.

In the resulting about-turn, 120,000 American residents of Japanese origin, two-thirds of them full US citizens, were rounded up and interned in prison camps. No such discrimination was instituted against German or Italian Americans. Three million tons of American supplies to Britain were sunk by German U-boats in the first seven months of 1942. By June, America's naval strength in the Pacific was reinforced sufficiently to avenge Pearl Harbor at the Battle of Midway. But this was merely a prelude to a war in the Far East that took longer to win than the war in Europe, and at a higher cost to America.

The Second World War in America was a vivid demonstration of Keynesian economics. It saw probably the biggest and fastest military mobilization in history. Seven million American men and women were in uniform within two years, rising to 12 million at the war's peak. The economy was given an injection of public spending that achieved in two years what a decade of state intervention had failed to achieve. Within a year growth surpassed its 1929 level with no formal planning, just vast amounts of public borrowing.

Most extraordinary was the capacity of America's industry to show what it could achieve given unlimited resources. Despite losing manpower to enlistment, American factories in three years produced 100,000 tanks, 300,000 planes and a phenomenal 88,000 ships. Car factories were converted to making Jeeps. So-called Liberty cargo ships were mass produced on a giant assembly belt. Unemployment fell from 9 million in 1940 to 700,000 at the wartime peak. General Electric's output soared from $1 million's worth of marine engines to $300 million's worth. It usually took three months to repair and service an American aircraft carrier. It now took forty-eight hours. By the war's end America was producing 40 per cent of the armaments used by all combatants worldwide.

The war gave a battered nation a new purpose and a new unity.

The population was exhorted to Let America be America Again. Whatever it had so recently protested, it now took comfort in fighting the freedom trail, in honouring its manifest destiny. The nation's military commander, George Marshall, could declare without fear of contradiction, 'Before the sun sets on this terrible struggle, our flag will be recognized throughout the world as a symbol of freedom on the one hand and of overwhelming force on the other.' As new B-17 bombers thundered down their runways, the Hollywood star Betty Grable lent her bathing-suited image to its nosecone, bringing literal meaning to the blonde bombshell.

In place of a fierce isolationism, a new mood of patriotism was on display. The conservative artist Norman Rockwell (1894–1978) lived in rural Massachusetts and portrayed its landscape as if unchanged from America's earliest days. A Boy Scout standing to attention under the ghosts of Washington and Lincoln, a symbol of loyalty. Rockwell depicted America's Four Freedoms: freedom of speech and worship and freedom from want and fear. They were reproduced and displayed on posters everywhere, the quartet of American values now to be defended.

That said, unity was not everywhere on display. There remained the argument, and the hypocrisy, over race. Segregation was unrelenting. Black soldiers were recruited into black regiments, often with white officers commanding them. Their accommodation was everywhere inferior, a fact that shocked other Allied forces who shared them. An incident in Kansas late in the war saw a black soldier, Lloyd Brown, turned away from a cafeteria that had just served a group of German prisoners-of-war. He might have wondered who was America's real enemy. Even the supply of blood to the army's medical corps was segregated.

For America the war in Europe was progressing at a snail's pace. Americans were frustrated with a British leadership that had been driven out of France at Dunkirk and still had memories of First World War stalemates. Britain was reluctant to invade mainland Europe and wished first to clear North Africa and then advance up Italy. America disagreed but was not in a position to make the decision. US troops arrived in Morocco at the end of 1942, but fighting proved slow both in Africa and then in Italy in 1943. As yet, Britain was leading Allied strategy, while the Soviet Union was conducting the fiercest – and initially crucial – battles with Hitler on the eastern front.

Not until D-Day in June 1944 did an Allied force of British, Commonwealth and American troops finally embark on the reoccupation of western Europe. In deference to the Americans, overall command was given to an American general, Dwight Eisenhower. The advance across France into Germany was again slow, impeded by a desperate German breakout on the Belgian border in the Battle of the Bulge over the winter of 1944–45. The battle cost 8,500 American lives lost and 20,900 missing.

Despite a ferocious bombing campaign, it would still require an invasion of Germany and almost a year of ground fighting for the Red Army to reach Berlin. With the war nearing its end in February 1945, a meeting took place at Yalta in Crimea between the three principal Allied leaders, Roosevelt, Churchill and Stalin. It was to discuss Germany's impending defeat and decide the future borders of Europe. General Charles de Gaulle, head of the exiled French government in London, was furious at being excluded. The meeting was clearly critical in determining the shape of the post-war world and the relationship between its prevailing great powers.

Opinion differs as to how far the personal chemistry of the Yalta participants was critical to its outcome. FDR, who had been re-elected at the end of 1944 for a fourth term, was now seriously ill. He remained firmly well disposed towards Stalin. The conflict had cost the Soviet Union 24 million lives, military and civilian, and subjected the citizens of Leningrad and Stalingrad to two of history's most harrowing sieges. The president understood Stalin's wish for a buffer zone of 'free and democratic states' round his borders and within his sphere of influence. FDR said, 'I think that if I give him everything I possibly can . . . he won't try to annex anything and will work with me for a world of democracy and peace.'

It was a naïve expectation. FDR firmly rejected Churchill's

contrasting view that Stalin was 'a devil-like tyrant who led a vile system'. He even told the British prime minister that Stalin 'hates the guts of all your top people. He likes me better, and I hope he will continue to do so.' As for the future of Europe, FDR just wanted to shake hands and go home. He showed little interest in the fate of Hitler's captured territories in eastern Europe, even as Stalin was moving swiftly to establish 'people's republics' in all his frontline neighbours except Finland.

On one matter all were agreed. As far as Germany was concerned there must be no repeat of the disaster of Versailles in 1919. The Allied governments therefore decided they would share the administration of four separate German sectors, Britain the north, France the west, America the south and the Soviet Union the east. That far at least America would have to remain present.

The formal end to the war in Europe came with Hitler's suicide and the subsequent surrender of the German army in May 1945. Not long before the signing FDR died, to be succeeded by his vice-president, Harry Truman, a former serving officer and Missouri senator. Though well versed in Washington administration, he had little experience of foreign affairs, but he most firmly disagreed with FDR over Stalin, telling his wife in a letter that the Russian leader was 'as untrustworthy as Hitler or Al Capone'. But Truman's chief task was to bring America's war in the Pacific to a swift conclusion, and to decide on the appropriate means.

In the course of 1944–45 intensive investigation had taken place into what seemed a shortcut to victory. While initial research into an atomic bomb had been conducted in Britain, its manufacture required resources that only America could supply. The initial incentive was a fear that Germany might be developing a similar weapon at the same time. An astronomical $2 billion was accordingly poured into mining and processing the necessary uranium and lithium. A prototype was finally tested by a team under the scientist Robert Oppenheimer at Los Alamos in New Mexico in July 1945. Where and when it might be deployed was another question.

The Japanese army was now retreating across the Pacific towards home, but even as it did so its high command demanded it fight to the end as a matter of honour, even on the Japanese mainland. As the summer of 1945 drew towards autumn, the prospect was of continued slaughter. In July the Japanese rejected an American ultimatum to surrender. It declared that every inch of Japan would be defended to the last drop of blood. As a result, in August, just a month after the first test, two atomic bombs were dropped on the cities of Hiroshima and Nagasaki. No one knows how many died, possibly 150,000–250,000.

The slaughter compared with similar conventional bombings of Japanese and German cities. But such was the destructive horror that for once a bomb spoke. Within three weeks Japan surrendered. The ethics of the bombs and the targeting of civilians remain subject to debate. Estimates of how many American soldiers – and Japanese civilians – might have died in a conventional 'fight-to-the-finish' suggest that the two bombs probably saved more lives than they cost. We shall never know. We do know that no one was to use such a weapon again in living memory, and the most devastating conflict in human history was at an end.

America had survived the war with its cities unscathed and its economic growth rate doubled. But it had paid a heavy human price. By the end, 418,000 American soldiers had died, more than were lost by France, Italy or Britain. Roosevelt's pledge to America's mothers that 'your boys are not going to be sent into any foreign wars' had been shredded. There was pride that America had been party to victory over a great evil, but that was that. As in 1919, it seemed likely that most Americans would revert to avoiding intervention.

That was not to be. The basis for a post-war settlement was a bid to revive Wilson's new world order, essentially to repeat the order that had failed under the League of Nations. In June 1945 delegates from around the world met in San Francisco to debate the formation of a wider league, a United Nations of fifty states. (Poland, the fifty-first original member, would sign up in October.) Its declared purpose was the maintenance of 'international peace and security' and the 'observance of human rights and fundamental freedoms for all'. As with the old League of Nations, collective security was the watchword. The territorial integrity of members had to be respected. The charter would be binding on all signatories and supersede all other treaties.

A permanent United Nations Security Council was set up to enforce its ambitions, composed of America, the USSR, Britain, France and China. It was accepted by Stalin strictly on the basis of every Security Council member having a veto on its decisions. The repetition of the issues raised after the First World War was inevitable, notably in the realm of collective defence. Again, much would depend on how the 'enforcement of security' was interpreted, but at least this time America was on board. The Senate approved the charter at once.

The world was at peace and had in place a mechanism supposedly to avoid or resolve further conflict. It was a moment of optimism and promise. Though it was not clear who was to be the guarantor of that optimism, the assumption was clearly that it would be America, richest and most powerful of the member nations. It was also plain that a new chapter in the United States' relations with the outside world had dawned. The question was how that chapter would read – and how long it would last.

This was debated in 1944 in a remarkably explicit British Foreign Office document on the prospective post-war world. Given FDR's favouring of Stalin's Russia and given Churchill's (and soon Truman's) opposite view, Britain's objective should be 'to help steer this great unwieldy barge, the United States of America, into the right harbour. If we don't, it is likely to continue to wallow in the ocean, an isolated menace to navigation.' It was an archaic British arrogance but with more than a touch of truth.

The trouble was that, as the British historian Kathleen Burk has written of Anglo-American relations at the time, Britain persisted in its traditional hands-off approach to Europe's future. It played no part in post-war discussions on a future union of west European states. It preferred to concentrate its attention and resources on its overseas empire and on the transatlantic relationship, soon to be reborn as the North Atlantic Treaty Organization (NATO).

America in reply treated Britain as a broken reed, claiming a world status that its power no longer justified. In resisting a British plea for more post-war aid, one congressman said it would be used 'to promote too much damned socialism at home and too much damned imperialism abroad'. The result, said Burk, was an Anglo-American bond that was affectionate in person but, in policy, was 'a swirl of resentment, contempt and apprehension'. America now had to 'balance her wish to remain the cat who walks by herself with the need for a dependable ally in the jungle of international relations'.

21.

Pax Americana

America emerged from the war with its leaders seized by the same globalist urge as had overcome Wilson in 1918. As before, public opinion had performed an about-turn, driven first by an aggression against its forces in the Pacific and then by success in the resulting conflict, a success that honoured the oft-mentioned values of the Founding Fathers. Fascism in Europe and east Asia had been defeated. The power first projected by Theodore Roosevelt had risen to the challenge. There was now a new challenge, that of global communism. The question was how imperialist that challenge would prove. Would it seek global supremacy or, more realistically, a stronger Soviet border in Europe. America needed to decide if it was to resolve the contradiction of isolation versus continued intervention.

With eastern Europe solidly in Stalin's hands, communist factions were rising against the governments of both Greece and Turkey. Italy was similarly vulnerable, as indeed was Germany itself. There was a period in 1945–46 when the victorious Allies faced what seemed a real possibility of nations falling to Marxist regimes across western as well as eastern Europe. The American ambassador in London in 1946, Averell Harriman, told a colleague that 'half and maybe all of Europe may be communist by the end of next winter'. As for any hope that Britain might be the great power to counter this threat, that country was crippled by debt and disinclined to start yet another war. *Time* magazine was dismissive. It declared of Britain that 'great empires never die, they fade away . . . The sceptre has passed to other hands.'

Students of counter-factual history are left dazed by the question of how America might have reacted to Stalin's new empire had his admirer, Roosevelt, remained in the White House through the 1940s. As it was, Truman was alert to the danger and did not hide it. He was reported as saying, 'I do not think we can play compromise any longer . . . I am tired of babying the Soviets.' In 1946 Truman invited Churchill, now out of power, to Fulton, Missouri to give his view of the new Europe. In his Fulton Speech Churchill announced that 'an Iron Curtain has descended across the continent of Europe' from the Baltic to the Adriatic. It was a challenge to which the Western Allies had to respond. They should now work together to provide the west with 'an overwhelming assurance of security'.

American officials were returning from Europe with alarming reports of a continent weakened by poverty, lacking in leadership and facing an existential threat to its crippled democracies. Most prominent of these officials was George Marshall, America's former army chief of staff and now Truman's secretary of state. Marshall was an outstanding figure in post-war Europe. Hailed by Churchill as the man most responsible for defeating Hitler, he was both a soldier and a diplomat. He toured the continent in March 1947 and returned convinced of one thing – America had to take pre-emptive action if there was not to be another European catastrophe.

Marshall advanced a plan for Europe's economy that America would finance 'so far as it is practicable to do so'. In March 1947 Truman addressed Congress in its support, announcing what came to be called the Truman Doctrine. He said, 'Totalitarian regimes imposed upon free people, by direct or indirect aggression, undermine the foundations of international peace and hence the security of the United States . . . At this present moment in world history nearly every nation must choose between alternative ways of life.' He listed America's familiar freedoms and pledged that it would 'support free peoples who are resisting attempted subjugation by armed minorities or by outside pressure'. This identification of 'nearly every nation' as a possible threat to American security proclaimed a licence to intervene.

To Truman, in contrast to FDR, isolation from Europe at such a time bordered on the immoral. America should indeed police the world. This was a redrafting of Jefferson's Declaration of Independence but with global application. If its maxims were often vague, almost platitudinous, it required specific policies if they were to carry deterrent force. They were supported by a lengthy article, initially anonymous, in the magazine *Foreign Affairs* that appeared in July 1947.

The author of the article was later revealed to be the Russia expert and later American ambassador to Moscow George Kennan. While unequivocally hostile to the emerging communist empire, Kennan rejected a policy of western frontal aggression against it. A direct confrontation between two global powers, both from the late 1940s armed with atomic weapons, should not even be risked. Instead the article favoured 'vigilant containment' of Russia, to be achieved by 'counter-force at a series of constantly shifting geographical and political points'.

Kennan's thesis was confrontational but pragmatic, not belligerent. It offered a way forward and, as such, was widely influential among western governments. Vigilant containment came to be the ruling strategy of the 'Cold War' for the best part of half a century. This metaphor of frigidity had first been used by the English writer George Orwell in 1945, describing a country 'which was at once unconquerable and in a permanent state of "cold war" with its neighbours'. It was adopted by the American commentator Walter Lippmann and soon described the prevailing stance of east–west relations.

The dominant reality of the Cold War was that America, irrespective of the party or president in power, was rich and heavily armed. While the recent hot war had visited on the states of Europe a terrible destruction and much poverty, the raw fact was that America had hugely profited by it. The country was not encumbered by a costly welfare state yet its prosperity sent tax revenues rising sufficient to satisfy a spendthrift president. Truman duly gave to America's foreign outreach a full imperial subsidy. In April 1948 the Marshall Plan for western Europe was agreed by Congress and signed by the president at a price of $13.3 billion. Aid was offered to the Soviet bloc but rejected by Stalin as it would need vetting and accounting.

The Department of Defense in its mighty new Pentagon building was now matched by an overseas Central Intelligence Agency with a staff that soon grew to over 30,000. A National Security Council also brought the defence establishment into the heart of federal government, which it was never to leave. Furious that only twelve new atom bombs had been made, Truman ordered four hundred. He then established new USAF bases in Germany and located B-29 Superfortress bombers in Britain. He also secured from Congress permission to send four American divisions to be stationed in western Europe.

In June 1948 Kennan's policy of containment met its first challenge. Stalin's reaction to Truman's military reinforcement of Europe was to blockade the east–west flashpoint of Berlin, buried as it was inside East Germany. This denied West Berlin road and rail access and put it under effective siege, Stalin hoping that the west would retreat and leave Berlin to him. This was in clear violation of the 1945 settlement and America's reaction was immediate. It supplied the city with a highly publicized airlift of supplies. Planes were landing at Berlin's Tempelhof airport every two minutes and a complete power plant was imported and built. Stalin climbed down after a year and road access was resumed. Containment had passed its first test.

Truman now had to face his first election as president. His contribution to America's post-war stance had been the opposite of the return to normalcy that FDR had envisaged. He was opposed by a breakaway southern Democratic – or 'Dixiecrat' – party and by the Republican governor Thomas Dewey of New York. Dewey was very much the favourite. In a rare sign of political diversity, a Progressive Party candidate, Henry Wallace, also ran on a policy of appeasement towards Stalin. Truman embarked on a 'barn-storming and whistle-stop' tour of the country by train, and ended by crushing his opponents.

Thus encouraged, Truman took American foreign policy onto a new plane. The Berlin crisis had shown that peace was as yet tentative. The United Nations was vulnerable to Soviet veto. In 1949, such was the threat considered from Moscow that America, Britain, France, the Low Countries and later Scandinavia embarked on a North Atlantic treaty, NATO. This stipulated that America would develop 'such regional and other collective arrangements as are based on continuous and effective self-help and mutual aid as affect its national security'. Clearly aimed at the USSR and despite the opaque language, the treaty meant that an attack on any member would be considered an attack on all, and therefore a cause for war by all. NATO's most powerful member, America, was taking on an onerous military obligation. Congress agreed to it. It was America's first peacetime alliance with overseas military commitments, and would remain intact for seventy-five years.

NATO's headquarters were not in America but in Paris, though Eisenhower was recalled to duty as its first Supreme Allied Commander. At the end of the first year and with the Soviet Union now building an atomic arsenal, Truman authorized work on a far more powerful hydrogen bomb. This nuclear weapon was first tested in 1952, leaving a crater a mile wide. A year later the Soviets followed suit. The use of such a weapon was unthinkable, but that raised the question of how far they could be a practicable deterrent. Five years later in 1955 Stalin responded to NATO with a Warsaw Pact comprising eight east-European nations led by the Soviet Union. It effectively declared a Soviet empire behind the Iron Curtain and drew up the frontier line for the Cold War.

Truman's foreign policy was not idle elsewhere. In 1948 he recognized the new state of Israel. The Arab–Israeli War of 1948 had expanded Israel's UN-mandated territory by some 50 per cent into Palestinian land and was bitterly resented. Truman was supported by an already strong American Jewish lobby but opposed by an oil-funded pro-Arab one. He also backed aid to 'a new Garden of Eden' in Mesopotamia's Iraq and a new form of Tennessee Valley Authority on the Zambezi River in Africa. Billions of dollars in aid were now gushing from Washington across the world. It could hardly be less isolationist.

In the Far East, America's political and economic reconstruction of Japan was proving successful, as was the Allies' reconstruction of West Germany. Elections took place in Tokyo and a regime was installed that proved stable. Less happy was American support to the tune of $2 billion for the anti-communist Chiang Kai-shek, leader of China's Kuomintang party, which had ruled much of China since 1928. Chiang's defeat in a long civil war with communist forces led by Mao Tse-Tung made it clear that America had backed the wrong horse. As Chiang's forces retreated to the island of Taiwan in 1949, Truman had to direct America's Pacific Seventh Fleet to protect him. Truman's critics accused him of 'losing China'.

America had come out of the Second World War a star on the world stage, quite unlike its hesitant stance at Versailles in 1919. Its mighty army had a clear purpose. Less clear was under whose authority it would operate. At one level it seemed the quasi-mercenary arm of the United Nations. At another it was the military guarantor of NATO. Truman's justification to the American people was that this was all necessary for their nation's security. This in turn required the formulation of a plausible threat.

America's continent, let alone its existence, had never been threatened since independence, except briefly by Britain in 1812. Yet the rhetoric of insecurity and fear was rarely silent in the corridors of Washington. It was heightened by a booming defence lobby content to define security in the widest possible terms. These now extended beyond America's borders to embrace NATO, democracy, the west and 'the free world'. The cost was enormous. To America's friends, Pax Americana offered a reassuring alliance. To its enemies it was cover for an emergent neo-imperialism. The question was where the American people stood, when just a decade earlier a vast majority had rejected all such commitments.

22.

Hot Peace and Cold War

1950–1960

The Great Depression and the dictates of war had expanded the scope of America's federal government beyond all previous limits. They gave it a self-assurance and a bureaucracy that sprawled across the Washington plain, and the cost had become enormous. By 1955, with the war long over, the federal budget had almost quadrupled in real terms since 1941. The reason was an increase in the central government's intrusion into states' affairs to a degree that would once have been considered unconstitutional. Since the 1940s Washington had initiated policies on transport, education, health, welfare and employment. Hoover, Roosevelt and Truman had introduced programmes wherever circumstance – and politics – seemed to require them.

The budget of the Department of Health, Education and Welfare now ranked second only to defence. Few of its projects had the universalism of Europe's welfare states, being directed largely at specific groups such as cities, veterans or infrastructure. The impact was rarely efficient. Americans were to spend more per capita than any other nation on their health care, but the outcomes were behind almost all nationalized health services.

In the nineteenth century the most conspicuous recipient of federal largesse had been the railways. Now it was the roads, which before the war had been strictly a responsibility of the states. During the war the generals had complained of their difficulty in moving materiel around the country, itself enough to trigger federal action. In 1956 a carefully named National Interstate and Defense Highways

Act proposed to fund 90 per cent of the cost of building 40,000 miles of long-distance highways. American transportation shifted overwhelmingly from rail to road. Three-quarters of Americans now owned cars, driving 80 per cent of the world's motor vehicles. Trains lost their romance. Hollywood now produced road movies rather than rail ones, *The Wild One* and *The Hitch-Hiker*.

Cars had long helped make the suburb the defining American settlement, sprawling across the country's empty spaces. Cheap petrol liberated home-owners from polluted cities. The Henry Fords of housing, the brothers William and Alfred Levitt, designed and engineered a pre-fabricated building kit that came to define the suburban home. They even bid for government support by exploiting the language of security. 'No man who owns his own house and lot can be a Communist,' said Alfred. 'He has too much to do.' The federal government responded with a subsidy covering 95 per cent of building contractors' insurance.

America in the 1950s saw the consumerism of the interwar years reach a climax. While most of the world was struggling to return to pre-war economic equilibrium, the United States bred a newly prosperous working class. Televisions took over from radios, coverage doubling between 1952 and 1955. The aspiration to fill homes with consumer durables such as vacuum cleaners, cookers, washing machines and record players was fuelled by the television sitcom *I Love Lucy*, its semi-liberated housewife played by Lucille Ball.

This was accompanied by a cult of optimism. Dale Carnegie's *How to Win Friends and Influence People* (1936) was followed in 1952 by Norman Vincent Peale's *The Power of Positive Thinking*, books that sold in their millions. The theme was taken up by the charismatic evangelist Billy Graham, who travelled the country preaching to huge crowds, one crusade in Los Angeles attracting 350,000. Churchgoing in America peaked in the 1950s at 70 per cent of the population. Lest piety be thought universal, the era also saw the founding of *Playboy* magazine in 1953, the film *Baby Doll* in 1956 and the revelatory – to some shocking – reports on American sexuality by Alfred Kinsey. His most publicized finding was the spread of homosexuality and the need for 'not dividing the world into sheep and goats'.

The continuing migration of black people and their music north to St Louis, Memphis and Chicago produced a response in the boss of Sun Records in Memphis, Tennessee. Sam Phillips played a leading role in popularizing black music, in particular the new sound of 'rock and roll'. But he complained, 'If I could only find a white boy who could sing like a negro, I could make a billion.'

The answer came when a young man called Elvis Presley walked into his studio one day. Presley helped Phillips establish a new pool of white talent, including Johnny Cash, Jerry Lee Lewis and Roy Orbison. Presley signed up with RCA, his first single for whom, 'Heartbreak Hotel', entered the charts in 1956, and by the end of the decade he was America's highest-earning singer. At least in one respect, Presley answered orthodox America's prayer. When his turn for military service came in the 1958 – the draft had not yet ended – he felt he could not avoid it and served in West Germany for a widely publicized eighteen months.

America's relations with the outside world now settled into a pattern of alliances that held off any return to pre-war isolation. Kennan's doctrine of Soviet containment, strengthened over Berlin, was rooted in a theoretical nuclear deterrence and, more reliably, in the half-million American troops embedded in western Europe. It now faced a new challenge on the other side of the globe.

Stalin's initially tenuous relations with the new communist regime in Beijing were tested in 1950 by his stationing troops in the northern half of Korea. This country, occupied during the war by Japan, had been divided in 1948 after Japan's surrender. The north went to Russia's chosen leader, the communist Kim Il-sung, while the south was guarded by just five hundred American troops. Stalin firmly told Kim to respect the divide, since violation would involve a clear confrontation with America. In 1950 Kim chose otherwise, marching south to unify the country and swiftly capturing its capital, Seoul.

To Truman this was a clear breach of containment. The embryonic United Nations – boycotted at the time by the Soviet Union – agreed to approve a military response. Twenty-one nations enlisted, including Britain, though 90 per cent of the so-called UN force was American. The hawkish American commander in Japan, General Douglas MacArthur, decided on a dramatic counter-strike behind North Korean lines at Inchon. This did what Kennan had feared and caused an immediate escalation as China entered the war on Kim's side. Its army descended on MacArthur's force, taking it by surprise and occasioning a swift retreat.

America was presented with a crisis. A humiliated MacArthur demanded that he be allowed to confront China. He wanted to encourage the nationalists in Taiwan to invade the mainland and sought to deploy American nuclear weapons to the area. Truman refused to entertain any such confrontation. When the disagreement became public the traditionally non-interventionist Republicans in Congress played politics and sided with MacArthur, charging Truman with weakness. The prospect of starting a third world war appeared to hold no horror for politicians who, ten years before, had been violently opposed to joining the second. They wavered between isolation and belligerence on a whim.

War hysteria rose so swiftly that it was hard to imagine what might have occurred in the Pacific had Truman conceded MacArthur's – and Congress's – wish. As it was, the Joint Chiefs of Staff backed Truman and issued an ultimatum. An attack on China would 'involve us in the wrong war, at the wrong place, at the wrong time and with the wrong enemy'. MacArthur was sacked and the war dragged on into 1953, when it withered into stalemate on the original treaty border. The Korean people had lost three million dead, a higher proportion of a nation's population than any country in the Second World War. America lost 37,000. Containment had been applied, and succeeded, without escalating into a wider conflict.

The outcome of the Korean War at home was a virulent repeat of the 'Red Scare' seen after the First World War. The false rhetoric of national security bred a sense of an America besieged by communists. An Internal Security Act of 1950 sought to counter 'communist front' labour unions. It was followed in 1954 by a paranoid Communist Control Act, outlawing not just the Communist Party but any manifestation of pro-communist sentiment as 'an instrumentality of a conspiracy to overthrow the government'.

The legislation brought under suspicion anyone considered unconventional or 'un-American'. A competition to find communists 'under every bed' led to rivalry between two burgeoning Washington powers, the Central Intelligence Agency and the domestic Federal Bureau of Investigation under its boss, J. Edgar Hoover. The cause was taken up by a populist senator, Joseph McCarthy, who declared in 1950 that he had a list, never published, of 205 officials with communist sympathies working for the State Department. He even accused his president of being 'the prisoner of a bunch of twisted intellectuals'.

Hearings of McCarthy's Permanent Subcommittee on Investigations – the Senate equivalent of the House's UnAmerican Activities Committee – took on a ghoulish celebrity. McCarthy extended his suspicions from communists to homosexuals and Jews. He held what were in effect televised show trials, blacklistings, sackings and imprisonments. Julius and Ethel Rosenberg were executed in 1953 for leaking nuclear secrets to the Russians. There was certainly Soviet espionage activity in America, as there was in Europe, but in America the frenzy of suspicion spread deep into universities and the arts. Even to plead the first amendment in favour of free speech was taken as evidence of guilt. Lawyers who defended those blacklisted were prosecuted for contempt of court.

At the height of the hysteria 110 organizations, one of them a small Washington bookshop, were designated as having communist sympathies, their staff condemned or rendered unemployable. As for individuals, fame itself came to seem a crime. Artists and writers summoned before the committee included Charlie Chaplin, Leonard Bernstein, Aaron Copland, Albert Einstein, Lena Horne, Danny Kaye, Otto Klemperer, Gypsy Rose Lee, Arthur Miller, Robert Oppenheimer, Dorothy Parker, Jean Seberg and Bertolt Brecht. European artists were advised to avoid visiting America. Chaplin left Hollywood to live in Switzerland and never returned.

There were much-cited parallels with the seventeenth-century Salem witch trials. In 1953 the playwright Arthur Miller wrote an ill-concealed allegory on Salem entitled *The Crucible*, which led to his conviction for contempt of Congress. Within two years, in 1954, McCarthy's extremism had been punctured and he was disgraced. But the affair remains hard for outsiders to comprehend.

Washington's political community seemed as yet too introverted and immature to handle nonconformity. As yet, few Americans travelled abroad or experienced other democratic cultures. Public discourse was conducted through a handful of media outlets and rarely displayed the debating tradition that had guided the Founding Fathers. America in the 1950s flirted briefly with a despotic extremism.

Truman's last two years in office were blighted by Korea and McCarthyism. The Republicans shrewdly chose as their candidate to succeed him in 1952 the wartime commander and head of NATO, Dwight D. Eisenhower. He was genial, popular and instinctively moderate. In the election he faced a rare choice for the Democrats, an intellectual named Adlai Stevenson, whose bald head gave rise to the epithet egghead. His response was 'Eggheads of the world unite; you've nothing to lose but your yokes,' which went over the heads of many who heard it.

Eisenhower won and took office in 1953, when Korea was approaching armistice. He immediately refocused America's overseas attention on Europe, a theatre he knew well. He spoke of Europeans as 'blood and kin to us . . . now under the Soviet yoke'. America's conscience, he said, 'can never know peace until these people are restored again to be masters of their own fate'. Yet in 1956, when Soviet tanks suppressed an anti-communist uprising in Hungary, Eisenhower firmly refused to risk a military confrontation with the Warsaw Pact by aiding the rebels. Again, containment held.

The secretary of state was John Foster Dulles, an international lawyer of wide experience. Though passionately anti-Soviet, he also acknowledged containment while defining it in high-risk terms. In a nuclear age, he said, it meant an 'ability to get to the verge, without getting into war'. This led to him being accused of what was called brinkmanship. Such was the centrality of foreign policy to Washington at the time that Eisenhower insisted Dulles report to him by phone every day. His chief fear – and that of America's friends at the time – was that war might be caused not by communist aggression but by grandstanding senators and bellicose generals.

In October 1957 the entrenched assumption of American technological superiority over the Soviets was shattered. The Soviets announced the launch of a satellite, or sputnik, into orbit, its beeps made audible around the world. A satellite containing a dog, Laika, was sent up the following month, its triumph tempered by the animal dying in the process. The satellites were carried by a rocket with sufficient range to deliver a nuclear bomb to American shores, which made the impact on American public opinion all the more traumatic. The sputniks were described by a senator from Texas named Lyndon Johnson as 'another Pearl Harbor', one that meant 'we are in a race for survival'. He did not say how but the fear quotient was elevated.

A month later America launched an overhasty reply. A satellite was fixed to a Vanguard rocket, which exploded on the launch pad in Florida. The event was ridiculed variously as flopnik, kaputnik, dudnik and stayputnik. Eisenhower's White House was satirized as the tomb of the well-known soldier. A Soviet official at the UN asked an American counterpart if he would like a grant from Russia's underdeveloped countries programme. It was a rare moment of Soviet pride.

The result was a burst of federal investment. Eisenhower announced the setting up of the National Aeronautics and Space Administration (NASA) to initiate what was declared a 'Space Race'. The agency was formed in part to achieve 'a manned lunar landing' before the Soviets did so. This necessity was attributed 'to the strategic location of the moon for space travel and warfare'. A more dubious value would follow, 'that of claiming the moon for the United Nations of the Western World'. Large federal sums were also assigned to American scientific education. Yet again the expressed motive was security.

America was now led by a man who had seen war at close quarters and learned to detest it. Having refused to intervene in Hungary, he immediately condemned Britain's attack on Nasser's Egypt in 1956, forcing it to withdraw from the Suez Canal. Eisenhower, whose mother was a Jehovah's Witness, was a true president for peace. In his State of the Union Address of 1958, he said that Americans 'could make no more tragic mistake than merely to concentrate on military strength. For if we did only this, the future would hold nothing for the world but an Age of Terror.'

Eisenhower was rare among presidents in noting what he saw as a dangerous shift of power in Washington towards the now burgeoning defence establishment. Its sheer scale, he said in his farewell speech, meant that 'we must guard against the acquisition of unwarranted influence, whether sought or unsought, by the military-industrial complex. The potential for the disastrous rise of misplaced power exists and will persist.' For a general to draw attention to this so-called complex was widely noted and respected. But it was later revealed that in Eisenhower's original draft, the reference had been tripartite, to a 'military-industrial-congressional complex'. This comment was on the growing influence of corporations and their lobbyists on Capitol Hill and their capacity to distort policy in their own interests. Nothing indicated that influence better than Eisenhower's aides persuading him to drop the reference to Congress.

23.

The Kennedy–Johnson Years

1960–1967

The election of John F. Kennedy as president in November 1960 was widely seen as the start of a new chapter in America's history. Kennedy was neither a machine politician of the old school nor a self-made man of the provinces in the tradition of Harding, Coolidge or Truman. He was more a Teddy Roosevelt, a product of America's moneyed aristocracy. His father Joe was a Catholic-Irish tycoon with a reputation for fast dealing, not necessarily above board. He had virtually bought himself the American ambassadorship in London in 1938, but annoyed Churchill by moving out of the city when the bombing started.

Joe Kennedy was ambitious for his sons and secured John a Massachusetts seat in the Senate. There the majority leader, Lyndon Johnson, regarded him as a smart 'playboy', but his smartness won him the 1960 Democratic nomination, with Johnson as his running mate. There he confronted the veteran Republican Richard Nixon, former aide to McCarthy. Kennedy emerged the winner and Washington, long an artistic desert, was abuzz with the arrival of America's youngest president at forty-three, and his glamorous first lady, Jackie Bouvier.

Jackie converted the White House into a hotbed of cultural activity, dubbed 'Camelot' after the Arthurian court of wisdom and virtue: the poet Robert Frost recited at the inauguration and the cellist Pablo Casals played at the White House. This was accompanied by a new self-confidence in America's cultural life. An art that between the wars had seemed to be always a reflection of or reaction to European movements now marked out territory of its own. A vigorous Abstract Expressionism was displayed in the work of Willem de Kooning, Jackson Pollock and Mark Rothko, while Roy Lichtenstein and Andy Warhol kept representation alive in the Pop Art movement. All contributed to a sense of a new beginning.

Kennedy's cabinet broke new boundaries in being aggressively apolitical and meritocratic. The head of the Rockefeller Foundation, Dean Rusk, became secretary of state. The president of Ford Motors, Robert McNamara, was defence secretary. Eisenhower's able Treasury secretary, Douglas Dillon, was retained and Kennedy chose two distinguished intellectuals, McGeorge Bundy and Theodore Sorensen, as close aides. Though he was eager to match Eisenhower's mastery of Cold War diplomacy his early exploits were uncertain. His inaugural language bordered on a pastiche as he announced that the world was living 'at an hour of maximum danger'. He would 'pay any price, bear any burden, meet any hardship, support any friend, oppose any foe, to assure the survival and the success of liberty'. The call to arms concluded with, 'Now the trumpet summons us again . . . to bear the burden of a long twilight struggle – rejoicing in hope, patient in tribulation – a struggle against the common enemies of man: tyranny, poverty, disease and war itself.' There was no attempt to explain what all this meant in policy terms.

On entering office Kennedy was brought face to face with reality. In April 1961 the Russians repeated their sputnik coup by sending a human, Yuri Gagarin, into orbit and getting him safely home. Kennedy was furious and demanded his team at NASA catch up. They should put a laboratory into space or land a man on the moon and soon. Money was unlimited and was quickly spent, to the order of $5 billion.

A second humiliation was closer to home. In 1959 the Cuban leader, Fulgencio Batista, was toppled by a saloon revolutionary, Fidel Castro. He was not a Soviet agent but was openly communist in his leanings and was soon adopted by the new Soviet leader, Nikita Khrushchev. Though Eisenhower's policy towards Castro had been to live and let live, the CIA had already made plans to land some 1,500 armed Cuban exiles on the island's Bay of Pigs and stir up a counter-revolution. An initially wary Kennedy did not feel strong enough to kill the plan. Like MacArthur's landing at Inchon, the venture was ill judged and ill planned. The Cubans were ready and the invaders were killed or captured. The Bay of Pigs demonstrated that military planners are the worst predictors of their own success.

Eighteen months later Khrushchev enabled Kennedy to restore his reputation. He recklessly decided to ship forty-two medium- and intermediate-range nuclear missiles onto Cuba, under the control of Soviet soldiers apparently with discretion over when to use them. Kennedy felt he had no option but to push back. The Soviets were advancing missiles almost to within sight of America's beaches. He demanded that the ships carrying the missiles turn round or they would be sunk, while those missiles already installed should be removed, agreeing in return that Castro would be left in peace. He also agreed – but not publicly – to remove American missiles in Turkey from within similar range of Soviet soil. Khrushchev's ships turned back. Cuba was left alone, to become a showpiece of the economic failings of communism.

The Cold War was looking increasingly unstable. In little more than a decade, America had funded and lost a proxy war in China and fought another to a stalemate in Korea. It had practised brinkmanship in the Berlin Airlift, which had to be repeated in 1961 when Khrushchev built the Berlin Wall to stop a flood of migration from communist East Germany. In June 1963 Kennedy flew over to stand beneath it and declare 'Ich bin ein Berliner' to rapturous applause. He implied America's border was to begin at the foot of the wall, though Kennedy was explicit in seeking détente with the Russian leader.

Next in line was, again, Asia. Vietnam was a former French colony that had seen the rise in the north of a communist independence movement under Ho Chi Minh, supported by Mao's China. In 1954, after France's withdrawal, the country was divided between Ho in the north and an American-backed strongman, Ngô Đình Diệm, in the south. Eisenhower had supported Diệm lest the whole of south-east Asia fall to communism. This so-called domino theory held that Laos, Cambodia, Thailand and Burma would be next to go – as they had to Japan in 1941 – and what then of Malaya, Indonesia and even Australia?

Diệm was an autocrat threatened by a northern-backed insurrection of Vietcong dissidents. Back in 1956, Kennedy as a senator had declared that South Vietnam was 'a cornerstone of the free world . . . It is our offspring, we cannot abandon it.' As president he was warned by France's Charles de Gaulle to disengage from the country, or he would 'sink deep into the quagmire'. He did contemplate withdrawal from Vietnam, but the implication of foreign policy failure deterred him. He had once told Nixon that 'foreign affairs is the only important issue for a president to handle'. He rejected de Gaulle's advice and sent 7,000 troops to back Diệm. He embarked on mission creep.

Kennedy as leader relied heavily on rhetoric and charisma. He had the makings of a great president, another Teddy Roosevelt, but he lacked time and experience. Before he could acquire either, on a visit to Dallas in Texas on 22 November 1963 he was shot and killed. The dream of a new America under a young president dissolved. Kennedy's successor, the Texan Lyndon Johnson, was anything but a new chapter. He was a seasoned old-timer, a harking back to the old party values. It was left to Johnson to carry forward the next progressive cycle in American politics that Kennedy had proclaimed but not yet executed.

Determined to honour Kennedy's memory, Johnson kept his defence advisers, McNamara and Bundy. He also accepted their advice on Vietnam, that America should stop pretending South Vietnam could defeat the Vietcong merely with American aid. It was America's war to win or lose. The result was a devastating bombing of North Vietnam, intended to show that America meant business. It began in March 1965 and over the next ten years more American bombs fell on supposed Vietcong supply lines in south-east Asia than were dropped in the entirety of the Second World War. They were considered strategically ineffective and caused incalculable death and destruction. Thousands of unexploded examples litter the south-east Asian landscape to this day, causing three hundred deaths and injuries a year in neighbouring Laos, half of them to children.

By the end of 1965 there were 185,000 American soldiers on the ground in Vietnam, yet the Vietcong still seemed in control of half of the south. The US air force general Curtis LeMay declared his strategy towards the north as 'to bomb them back into the Stone Age'. Yet America's firepower had no deterrent value and seemed ineffective against jungle guerrillas fighting man to man with AK-47 rifles, and largely based underground. A total of 16,000 Americans had already died fighting an enemy they scarcely ever saw. Johnson reverted to preaching a doctrine of fear. Success for North Vietnam would leave Asia 'so threatened by communist domination that it would imperil the security of the United States itself'. The rhetoric was believed. No fewer than 85 per cent of Americans now favoured a war they were told was existential.

Vietnam was Kennedy's most dreadful legacy to Johnson, who resented the distraction from a domestic programme on which he came to set his heart. This was to revive the tradition of FDR's New Deal, which he extended into the twin fields of poverty and race under the title the Great Society. With America claiming to champion freedom and civil rights across the world, their continued neglect in its own backyard was all too apparent.

Johnson exploited Kennedy's death to take forward what he launched in 1964 as a 'war on poverty'. He asked Congress 'not only to relieve the symptom of poverty but to cure it and, above all, prevent it'. Later that year Johnson was elected president in his own right, and with a Congress overwhelmingly Democrat in his support he was determined to be the new FDR.

It had long seemed a contradiction to visitors to America that a country so boastful of its wealth could display such poverty on its city streets. A much-publicized book by an economist, J. K. Galbraith, *The Affluent Society* (1958), pointed out the reason. America's wealth had long been directed at meeting the demands of the middle-class majority, defined as the employed, the housed, the insured and the safe. But this put consumption ahead of other social goals. It produced what Galbraith described as 'private afflu-ence and public squalor'. It 'valued' a tube of lipstick ahead of a schoolbook. In doing so America had neglected any duty of care by society towards the poor, notably in education and welfare, and ever widened the gap between them and the nation's rich.

Johnson's determination to attack this gap was sincere. In 1965 Congress passed an Elementary and Secondary Education Act, empowering the federal government to fund schools in deprived areas, previously a strictly state activity. Johnson signed the act in the tiny Texas schoolhouse where he had himself been taught. It was followed by the equally ambitious – and intrusive on the states – Head Start Act, Higher Education Act, Equal Opportunity Act and even a Mass Transit Act.

In health Johnson achieved a real breakthrough, with Medicare for the over-sixty-fives and Medicaid for the very poor. Both had to overcome Washington lobbying by a profit-conscious medical pro-fession. Though the schemes were nowhere near as comprehensive as most European health services, they sought to end good health as a privilege of the wealthy.

The same to a lesser extent went for housing, with a Demon-stration Cities and Model Development Act and a Housing and Urban Development Act. The federal government even invaded arts and culture. In 1967 Johnson created a Corporation for Public Broadcasting – a modest version of Britain's BBC – and a National Endowment for the Humanities. The cost of these innovations was astronomical. In the thirty years following the Second World War American defence spending rose tenfold but welfare spending rose twenty-fivefold. Republicans might accuse the Democrats of social-ism, but it was socialism buoyed by the taxes of capitalism.

In the area of race Johnson faced a greater challenge. The battle against segregation had been left unfought throughout the twenti-eth century. Federal reform was hamstrung by the South's blocking minority in Congress. Short electoral terms and some southern states being electorally crucial 'swing states' made presidents reluc-tant to tackle reform. Teddy Roosevelt had not touched it, neither had Wilson or FDR. Kennedy before his death had done little more in three years than propose a bill. Race remained the sin against the constitution that dared not speak its name.

There had been some hopeful moves. Back in 1954 new ground had been broken by a Supreme Court decision in favour of a suit brought by the National Association for the Advancement of Colored People. Segregation had been considered legal as long as facilities were 'separate but equal'. The court now changed its mind. It ruled that separation of schools by race 'generates a feeling of inferiority as to their status in the community, which may affect their hearts and minds in a way unlikely ever to be undone . . . It is inherently unequal.' Segregation was declared unconstitutional and illegal.

Old wounds promptly reopened. Lobbyists for southern states' rights deplored 'paternalistic and totalitarian government', and the Supreme Court left it to state courts to implement its order. The consequence was that, for the first time, there was widespread direct action by black people. In December 1955 a black woman named Rosa Parks defied bus segregation in Montgomery, Alabama by refusing to vacate a front seat reserved for whites. She was jailed and black America erupted.

A young Montgomery minister named Martin Luther King led a boycott of the town's buses with rhetoric worthy of Lincoln. He declared that they had 'no alternative but to protest. If we are wrong, the Supreme Court of this union is wrong, the constitution is wrong, God Almighty is wrong.' A year later in 1956 the Supreme Court declared Montgomery's bus segregation illegal. Supported by a sympathetic national media, King became the unofficial leader of black America. He rode in the front seat of the first integrated bus in Alabama.

Progress was slow. In 1957 Arkansas refused to integrate its schools and it took federal troops to escort nine black children to a school in the state capital, Little Rock. They had to endure insulting chants of the n-word from white children. The schools were closed for a year and faced a Supreme Court order to reopen. Elsewhere, sit-ins at segregated lunch counters grew. Young black people proved more courageous than their elders. White sympathizers came south to join them, often occupying black facilities.

The most effective publicity was supplied by the southern states themselves. Unconcerned that the world was watching, Alabama's police used dogs and fire hoses against black children. Disorder erupted everywhere. Kennedy, who had at first been hesitant in addressing race, was still at the White House and was at last outspoken. He cited segregation as 'a moral issue as old as the scriptures and as clear as the American constitution'. In 1963 he sent a bill to Congress honouring the Supreme Court's banning of segregation in all public services and facilities.

Kennedy's bill was supported by some 250,000 demonstrators marching on Washington, white as well as black. They were addressed by King under the statue of Lincoln, where he echoed the Gettysburg Address in the centenary year of Lincoln's Emancipation Proclamation. King pointed out that it was a declaration yet to be realized. He ended with what became his best-known line: 'I have a dream that one day this nation will rise up and live out the true meaning of its creed . . . a dream that my four little children will one day live in a nation where they will not be judged by the colour of their skin but by the content of their character.' The words were a clear call to political action. But within weeks Kennedy was dead.

As soon as Johnson was in the White House, he treated Kennedy's bill as an act of remembrance. He saw it as atonement by a South from which he himself hailed. The proposed Civil Rights Act of 1964 banned 'all discrimination based on race, colour, sex, religion or national origin'. It specifically prohibited discrimination in employment, promotion and dismissal. The act was driven forward by demonstrations, often led by King, always with an emphatic instruction to avoid violence. Johnson's 1964 election victory made sure his reformism would hold. It was promoted by three fifty-mile Alabama marches in 1965 from Selma to Montgomery. The South was unrepentant and Johnson again had to send federal troops to defend the marchers both from white counter-demonstrators and from state police, who beat the marchers with sticks.

36. The world's most famous car: Ford Model T, 1910.

37. America arrives at last. The US Navy's battleship *Division Nine* being greeted off Scapa Flow in Scotland in December 1917 by British Admiral David Beatty and the crew of HMS *Queen Elizabeth*.

38. Hollywood's first celebrity couple. Douglas Fairbanks Sr and his second wife Mary Pickford in the 1920s.

39. Contestants at a Charleston dance contest being served food by musicians at a nightclub in New York City, c.1926.

40. Manhattan's Empire State Building (1931) and Chrysler Building (1930), signatures of America's inter-war wealth.

41. *Top right*: *American Gothic* by Grant Wood, 1930.

42. *Bottom right:* Dorothea Lange's photograph of a migrant mother, Florence Owens Thompson, during the Great Depression of the 1930s. She and her children were in a camp filled with field workers. The picture became a symbol of the plight of those caught up in the disaster.

43. American battleships exploding during the Japanese attack on Pearl Harbor in December 1941.

44. June 1944: American troops stand by with stores on Omaha Beach after the D-day landings.

45. Franklin Delano Roosevelt, 1944.

46. *Freedom from Want*, the third of Norman Rockwell's *Four Freedoms* series, 1943.

47. Louis Armstrong, 1946.

48. The Betty Grable 'pin-up' graced the B-17 Flying Fortress, America's four-engine bomber, during the Second World War.

49. American minister and civil rights leader Dr Martin Luther King Jr (1929–68) during his 'I Have a Dream' speech in August 1963 in Washington.

50. The Kennedys arriving in Dallas, November 1963.

51. A female demonstrator offers a flower to military police during an anti-Vietnam War march on the Pentagon, October 1967.

52. American helicopters evacuate Vietnamese civilians during an air raid, April 1975.

53. US President Ronald Reagan and Soviet leader Mikhail Gorbachev signing an arms control agreement in Washington, December 1987.

54. 9/11, September 2001. Photograph by Susan Meiselas.

55. The Funeral of George H. W. Bush, December 2018. Front row (l–r): Donald and Melania Trump; Barack and Michelle Obama; Bill and Hilary Clinton; Jimmy and Roslyn Carter. Second row (l–r): former Vice President Dick Cheney (behind Mrs Trump); Joe and Jill Biden (behind Mrs Obama).

The rest of America was outraged and supported Johnson and Congress in passing the Civil Rights Act in an unusual joint session of both houses. Johnson himself declared, 'We shall overcome.' An additional Voting Rights Act was passed in the summer of 1965, overturning the tests, qualifications and obstacles used to deprive 90 per cent of black Americans of their vote. At last America agreed with its independence and its constitution, that individual rights overrode states' rights.

As so often with America's periods of progressive change, a gulf remained between the will and the deed, between legislation and implementation. Incensed by continued instances of segregation in defiance of the new laws, black protesters took to the streets, often ignoring King's pleas against violence. Demonstrations were not confined to the South. In 1965 the Watts district of Los Angeles endured a week of rioting and burning of white-owned properties. The following year Chicago saw riots and marches through its white suburbs, highlighting the informal segregation of housing and jobs. Protests turned ever more militant, with a young activist, Stokely Carmichael, stressing the need for 'black power' and raising his fist in salute. The fist became the symbol of an overtly violent movement, the Black Panthers.

The mid-1960s undoubtedly saw a marked shift in the story of black advancement. Among other things it emphasized group identity as much as ethnic integration. The writer James Baldwin, an activist from Harlem, gained prominence with novels such as *Tell It on the Mountain*. Having lived in France and noted the status of black people in Europe, Baldwin saw their treatment in America with a new aggression. In 1965 he took part in a debate on racism at Britain's Cambridge University Union with the conservative intellectual William F. Buckley Jr. It was a display of eloquence on both sides, with Baldwin trouncing his countryman. However, back on the streets of urban America, the cause was advanced but still not won.

24.

Counter-Culture: Protest and Love

1967–1969

The 1960s in America mirrored the Roaring Twenties as a period of social upheaval. Across the western world, the conservatism of post-war politics turned dramatically progressive. A new generation, with no memories of the Second World War, came to the fore, less deferential to authority, more open to new ideas in politics and culture. To visit America at the time – I had a brief spell as a Senate intern in Washington – was to be acutely aware of the similarities, but also the differences, between America and Europe.

For a period there were signs that Europe was coming apart. In France persistent rioting in Paris came near to toppling the de Gaulle government. In Czechoslovakia the Prague Spring undermined the communist regime and prompted Soviet military intervention for its suppression. Demonstrations mostly but not exclusively of the young spread from Yugoslavia to Poland, Brazil, Japan and even to Russia. The relative stability of the post-war years no longer seemed certain.

Britain too was changing. Undoubtedly a closeness between Britain and America, sometimes tentative, sometimes troubled, had held for centuries since the earliest days of the union. Transatlantic contact was prolific and tourism was popular and easy. London and New York often seemed two sides of the same cultural coin. Their actors, dramatists, musicians, journalists and academics were almost conjoined. In the nineteenth century Bismarck had remarked that the most decisive factor in modern history was 'that the North Americans speak English'.

As the decade progressed differences also became noticeable. Britain in 1964 reversed thirteen years of Conservative rule and voted a Labour government under Harold Wilson into power. Washington was shocked at British opposition to the mounting war in Vietnam. Johnson was furious at Wilson's refusal to send even a token of support – not so much as 'a platoon of highlanders with bagpipes', he complained. Anger also greeted Britain's decision to withdraw from former imperial bases east of Suez, from Aden and the Gulf to Singapore. At home Labour proved itself ardently reformist. In just three years after 1964 it abolished capital punishment, legalized homosexuality, allowed abortion and reformed divorce. Even politically aware Americans would ask visitors, always with politeness, 'Have you become some sort of communists?'

To visit America at the time was to see a country still conservative. Its self-consciousness as the global harbinger of freedom and democracy was incanted in presidential speeches. The Stars and Stripes was saluted by children at school and flown in front gardens. God was recruited to the cause. The Christian faith was nowhere as strong as in America. Such sentiments were regularly supported in opinion polls.

A parallel difference from Britain was cultural. America rightly regarded itself as in the vanguard of popular entertainment and music, which was certainly the case in film and television, where Hollywood still reigned supreme. But in April 1964 its music industry was swept aside by Britain's Beatles. The group overtook Presley in popularity and attained twenty hits at No. 1 on the Billboard Hot 100, a record to this day. Tours by them and the Rolling Stones caused such crowd frenzy – rendering some concerts inaudible – that the Beatles chose to return only once. When the group appeared on *The Ed Sullivan Show* the ratings far outstripped those for any other guest, again including Presley, the programme being watched by a record television audience of 73 million.

Life magazine wrote that same 1964 month, 'in 1776 England lost her American colonies. Last week the Beatles took them back.' *Time* went further. In a special issue it declared that London was where the 1960s were now 'happening'. A city of anti-war demonstrations and social reform was also 'the swinging city' of rock music, Carnaby Street, mini-skirts, flared trousers, coffee bars and trendy tourism. By implication America should watch out.

In reality, America was about to see the same generational change. The number of college graduates rose from 15 per cent in 1950 to 25 per cent in 1960 and a new class of American was born. They displayed radicalism in dress, leisure, music and politics. They also showed a marked change in attitude towards race. Both white and black opinion now demanded desegregation. During 1966 Black Power and other movements began demonstrating for black rights. Then in April 1968 events took a traumatic turn when the man who had towered over black protest for a decade, Martin Luther King, was assassinated. His rhetorical talent and stress on non-violence had so far set the tone of black advancement. Many white Americans saw him as having saved them from a violent uprising. His death brought one closer.

The streets of America erupted. The worst demonstrations broke out over two days in Chicago and led to an overreaction by the city's mayor, Richard Daley. He mobilized his police and National Guard, leaving eleven dead, 2,000 arrested and a three-mile swathe of the city looted and in ruins. The message was clear. Black Americans would no longer wait for whites to deliver their constitutional rights. King had shown that taking to the streets did have some effect, even if it was not one that had yet worked.

The trigger for a different area of protest came later in 1968 from those of student age who were now being conscripted in their thousands into a Vietnam War that few of them supported. That year in January had seen a turning point in the war with the North Vietnamese launch of the so-called Tet Offensive. This displayed the Vietcong's strength by penetrating American bases throughout the south, even the embassy in Saigon. A marine forward post near the northern border saw the Battle of Khe Sanh. A barrage of B-52 bombers reduced vast areas of jungle to desert, yet failed to remove the encircling Vietcong.

Tet undermined any plausible optimism for America's presence in Vietnam. The war seemed unwinnable and pointless. America's leading journalist, CBS's Walter Cronkite, visited Saigon afterwards and wrote that the war was unwinnable and that 'the only rational way out then will be to negotiate not as victors but as an honourable people who lived up to their pledge to defend democracy and did the best they could'. Johnson remarked afterwards that 'if I have lost Cronkite then I have lost the American people'.

In May 1968 American military deaths in Vietnam peaked at 2,371, exhausting the patience of both America and its allies. Demonstrators took over college campuses, the most high profile being that of New York's Columbia University. US embassies around the world were under siege. In October the worst London disturbance in living memory occurred when 3,000 people laid siege to the American embassy in Grosvenor Square. Twenty-five police officers ended up in hospital.

Opposition to the war now surfaced in Congress and even in the judiciary. In a remarkable move, the Supreme Court redefined conscientious objection to the draft as including moral as well as religious belief. The number of objectors soared, as did the number of draft-dodgers fleeing abroad. Conscripts were now making up half of America's land forces in Vietnam, and suffering half the fatalities. Two leading organs of opinion, the *New York Times* and the *Washington Post*, both declared that enough was enough.

Johnson had no answer but to send more troops. They descended into depths of violence. In March a unit of US infantry went berserk in the Vietnamese village of My Lai, killing four hundred women, children and old men. The footage was horrific. The only comfort for the government was that 60 per cent in opinion polls – mostly older people – were still in favour of the war and 70 per cent opposed anti-war demonstrators. But in the course of 1968 an American president who four years earlier had been among the most popular in history became the least popular, his approval falling to 26 per cent.

The long-standing defence secretary, Robert McNamara, lost

faith in the war. He had to endure the daily opposition of his wife and son and, at a February cabinet meeting, minutes record him losing his temper. He blurted out, 'This goddamned bombing campaign, it's worth nothing, it's done nothing. They dropped more bombs than on all of Europe in all of World War II and it hasn't done a fucking thing!' He resigned, but his successor, Clark Clifford, agreed with him.

Johnson's spirit broke. He announced that America would stop bombing North Vietnam and seek negotiations to reach a peace. He himself would not stand for re-election at the end of the year. The man who decided to run in his place was JFK's brother, Bobby. But no sooner had Kennedy been selected at the June California primary than, like his brother and like King, he was gunned down by an assassin. To the outside world, America appeared to have lost control of itself.

An obsession with guns and bombs at home and abroad seemed a senseless play on violence. In response to Kennedy's death Johnson demanded a gun-control bill from Congress, pointing out that there were 6,500 gun killings in America annually, against thirty in Britain. It was 'mail-order murder'. Yet so powerful had the Washington gun lobby become that the bill failed. Roughly half of Congress was recorded as being in receipt of the lobby's election donations.

This contributed to what was a tense build-up to the Democratic convention in Chicago in August 1968, an event usually of interest only to political addicts. This year it was partly hijacked by anti-war demonstrators and partly by a repeat of the 1967 'summer of love', a congregation of some 100,000 young people in San Francisco's Haight-Ashbury district. Led by two activists, Abbie Hoffman and Jerry Rubin, it celebrated folk and rock music, psychedelic drugs, sexual freedom and opposition to the war. Wearing flowers in their hair, the so-called 'hippies' could hardly be further removed from conventional American mores.

The bible of the new movement was Jack Kerouac's *On the Road* (1957), a book that gave a romance to escapist nonconformity. He was joined by other leaders of the 'age of dissent' such as the singer

Woody Guthrie, the novelist Norman Mailer, the poet Allen Ginsberg and the prophet of narcotic psychedelia, Timothy Leary. Guthrie satirized the patriotic chant God Bless America in the song, 'This Land is Your Land, This Land is My Land', protesting that in truth it was 'made for you and me'. The young Bob Dylan summed up this 'alternative' generation in what became its anthem, 'The Times They Are a-Changin' '(1964). Born Robert Zimmerman in 1941 but a fan of the Welshman Dylan Thomas, his 'protest songs' were not so much political as societal, bearing witness to his age and its transformation, rather in the manner of Walt Whitman a century before. They won him an eccentric Nobel prize for literature.

These personalities converged on Chicago in the heat of mid-summer for what was called a Festival of Life. California's hippies became 'Yippies' – of the Youth International Party – and more specifically anti-war. As in the racial disturbances earlier in the year, Chicago's Mayor Daley again overreacted, deploying 12,000 police and armed National Guardsmen as if facing a military uprising. The outcome was a conference of dissent such as America had not seen before. Thousands of young people came to Chicago to join the protesters from across the country. There were riots everywhere. Hundreds were injured, though there was only one fatality.

Chicago 1968 left one unintended legacy. This was the concept of the summer music festival. The following year young America reassembled in a more peaceful frame of mind at Woodstock in upstate New York. Here, with an attendance of almost half a million, the 'Woodstock generation' came to life, to become the 'counter-cultural society'. A decade born amid the novelty of the Kennedy age ended in a very different novelty, sexual and narcotic permissiveness and a new movement of political dissent. What the Beatles had sown, America's youth unquestionably reaped. It was redeemed by the extraordinary popularity of the duo Simon and Garfunkel, whose hit 'Bridge Over Troubled Waters' became the anthem of a new generation.

Inevitably there was a reaction to the events of the late 1960s as there had been to the innovations of the 1920s. The counter-culture was highly publicized but involved a relative minority of American society. A poll showed that 56 per cent of Americans had no sympathy with it. What was undeniable was that a year of assassinations, rebellions and the ongoing agony of Vietnam left a widespread feeling of a nation approaching a crisis. The response was that the presidential election of 1968 served to tilt the electorate to the right. The Democratic candidate, Hubert Humphrey, was confronted by Kennedy's defeated 1960 opponent, Richard Nixon. This time Nixon won.

Nixon had explicitly styled himself against the 1968 generation. He identified with the 'small-town' Republicanism of Harding and Coolidge, the 'Middle America' of the silent majority, the left-behinds and the patriots. Nixon was an intelligent lawyer but a difficult, lonely figure, his life consumed by relentless ambition. But in one respect he wasted no time after his 1969 inauguration. He answered Johnson's departing plea to extricate America from Vietnam. He handed the task to a German refugee and Harvard politics academic, Henry Kissinger.

Rarely have two such dissimilar men been thrown into so crucial an embrace. Kissinger at one point described Nixon as 'the most dangerous of all men running' for president, and 'one who appears not to like people'. He shared Nixon's personal sensitivity, noted for chewing his nails to the quick. He also shared Nixon's ambition, leading the new president to say of him, 'I don't trust Henry but I can use him.' Whatever his views, Kissinger applied for and became Nixon's national security adviser. He was a rare example of an academic theorist given the opportunity to put his ideas into practice, those of realpolitik, détente and 'shuttle diplomacy'. His influence was to be immense over the remainder of the Cold War.

25.
Defeat and Victory

Fortune gave President Nixon an early stroke of luck. In July 1969 two Americans landed on the moon. Where Kennedy had been welcomed to office by a Russian sputnik, Nixon was greeted by news that America's eight-year-old moon-landing programme was well in advance of any similar venture by the Soviet Union. The astronaut Neil Armstrong's 'one small step for [a] man, one giant leap for mankind' was overleaped by Nixon in his ecstasy. He declared the mission 'the greatest week in the history of the world since the Creation'. It was certainly an epic achievement, though of dubious utility. The Apollo missions, once completed, were still not repeated half a century afterwards. The exploration of space, like that of the polar regions, was largely a matter of national machismo.

As for leaving Vietnam, Nixon remarked to an aide, 'I am not going to end up like LBJ, afraid to show my face in the street . . . I will stop that war, fast.' It was not to be fast. At the time two hundred Americans were dying every week and college campuses were in revolt. The war was costing American taxpayers $30 billion a year. Nixon knew Vietnam was now politically toxic and he wanted no part in it. Unlike his predecessors, he at least did not pretend there was any victory in sight. He did what he said he would do and began withdrawing America's troops.

Nixon also recognized that North Vietnam's chief supporter was communist China. Beijing was still 'a sleeping giant' but before entering the White House Nixon had written that China needed 'pulling back into the world community – as a great and progressing nation, not as the epicentre of world revolution'. This insight resulted from an improbable encounter with the French intellectual André Malraux. Meeting Nixon, the French cultural affairs minister had remarked on the tragedy that 'the richest and most productive people in the world' should be so at odds with the 'poorest and most populous people in the world'. Nixon got the point.

Kissinger was soon engaged in seeking informal contacts with China. In July 1971 he flew covertly to Beijing, leading to a formal invitation to Nixon for a visit the following year. At the same time Washington put intense pressure on both Moscow and Beijing to push Hanoi to a settlement. Nixon stressed that he was looking for an 'honourable withdrawal'. He faced re-election at the end of 1972 and was desperate for almost any deal before then.

Progress was not helped by America resuming the bombing of Cambodia, Laos and North Vietnam, supposedly to reassure Saigon that America was still committed. This infuriated Hanoi and immediately stalled talks. Not until January 1973 were the so-called Paris peace accords signed. America then signalled it would still aid the southern regime but would itself leave altogether, with the South Vietnamese left to their fate. Nixon had already reduced America's military presence from 500,000 in 1968 to just 24,000. By March 1973 all American troops had returned home.

The war lasted a further two years. On visiting Saigon at the time, I found it eerily quiet, with Japanese businessmen buying property, hoping the city might one day become Vietnam's Hong Kong. It had briefly reverted in part to its French past, particularly in its superb restaurant wine lists. Everyone who could leave was trying to do so. Saigon was like a city waiting for Armageddon. Eventually in early 1975 the Vietcong broke through its defences. American officials made an undignified helicopter escape from their embassy, with their Vietnamese staff desperately trying to climb aboard. The Vietcong flag was soon flying from the building's flagpole. America's humiliation could not have been more visible.

The Vietnam War had festered for almost twenty years, longer than any conflict in American history. Over its fruitless course 58,000

Americans had died, along with some 2 million Vietnamese. In one respect the conservatives were right. The North's victory was followed by two dominos falling, with communist coups in Laos and Cambodia in a matter of months. For Cambodia the consequence was horrific: a civil war with the slaughter of over 2 million of its population. No one suggested America should intervene. A nightmare chapter in the attempted containment of world communism was over.

Under Johnson, America's security bureaucracy in the Pentagon, the CIA and the FBI had dramatically expanded. So too had the White House staff. President Hoover in the 1930s had three personal secretaries; Johnson had grown a presidential staff of 1,200. Under Nixon it was 5,395. Recruitment seemed uncontrolled, with staff appointed afresh by each new incumbent, inevitably inexperienced and mostly temporary.

Washington lacked a cadre of professionals whose job was to oil the machinery of government whoever was in power. While Britain has its civil service, an incoming American president has no such asset to hand, arriving with a patronage army of courtiers, expected to hit the ground running and within two years to start worrying about re-election.

Nixon had gathered round him associates of uncertain loyalty and ability. Two of the closest, Bob Haldeman and John Ehrlichman, made Nixon's 1972 re-election their ruling obsession. As the date grew closer, a group of contractors known as the White House plumbers were recruited to plug hostile leaks to the press. They were instructed to break into the Watergate complex to bug the Democratic Party's offices, in the course of which they were caught and prosecuted.

There now unfolded one of the most bizarre scandals in the history of the presidency. The cover-up of Nixon's role in Watergate survived his November re-election, but from the start of his new term in 1973, rumours of White House involvement were flowing in all directions and Nixon was unable to stem them. The media, increasingly hostile to the president, were on the hunt. In May a

Democratic Congress appointed a special prosecutor, Archibald Cox, to investigate. A Senate Watergate Committee contrived to indict forty Nixon officials, its proceedings broadcast daily across the nation.

The last straw for Nixon was being ordered to surrender tapes he had made of conversations in his own office. A president who had posed as a respectable, Quaker-educated, Middle American was revealed as mendacious, corrupt and foul-mouthed. His friend the evangelist Billy Graham was so appalled he admitted to bursting into tears. Then, in the summer of 1974, a detailed account of Watergate was published by two *Washington Post* reporters, Carl Bernstein and Bob Woodward, under the title 'All the President's Men'. Nixon was about to be the first president to be found guilty in an impeachment. To avert this humiliation he resigned in disgrace.

Nixon was succeeded by his vice-president, Gerald Ford, a nonentity who had been chosen, as so often, not as a 'next best president' but merely to balance the ticket. Never had the nineteenth-century historian James Bryce's puzzlement been more true, that a meritocratic nation 'open to all talents' should find it so hard to be led by one.

In the backwash of Watergate the institution of the presidency went into decline. The system of checks and balances saw radical adjustment as the long drift of power from Congress to the White House was reversed. Already in 1973 a War Powers Resolution had been passed, 'to fulfill the intent of the framers of the Constitution' and ensure that 'the collective judgment of both the Congress and the President will apply to the introduction of [US] Armed Forces into hostilities'. In other words the protocol was enforced that the president could not declare war without Congress's permission. Further measures limited the president's freedom to arm foreign powers, make treaties or conduct covert operations. The days of White House wars seemed at an end.

The Nixon debacle coincided with a diminution in America's leadership of the western world. The Yom Kippur War in the Middle

East precipitated a surge in oil prices in 1973–74, leading in turn to a global recession. America in 1974 saw something previously unimaginable, queues outside petrol stations as supply disrupted a third of America's oil. The dollar was losing its international pre-eminence and the last elements linking it to the price of gold were removed.

At the same time Europe's Economic Community, founded in 1956, was helping that continent to recover from the toils of post-war reconstruction and work towards the creation of a single market. It was further strengthened when Britain joined in 1973, together with most western European states. Europe was now close to being a market big enough to compete with America, whose share of world output of motor vehicles fell in the 1970s from 32 to 19 per cent. America's per capita GDP, for so long a talisman of its economic supremacy, was now well behind those of Japan, Germany and Scandinavia.

It was thus to a weakened presidency that the Democrats nominated an outsider and governor of Georgia, Jimmy Carter, to run against Ford in 1976. He won, and continued a period of faltering American power and an upturn in the self-confidence of the Soviet Union. Carter sought to shift America's international leverage away from military intervention and in the direction of 'soft power', notably a championing of human rights. He openly deplored America's image as 'the most warlike country on earth'. He later pointed out that of its 242 years of existence, only sixteen had seen it not fighting someone, four of which he was proud to say were under his presidency.

The results of this policy were mixed. Nicaragua saw its right-wing regime toppled with American tacit collusion, only to be replaced by a Marxist one. In 1979 the Iranian monarchy fell, with America dithering over how far to support the Shah's opponents. He was replaced by a hostile Islamist hierarchy. Carter's term was then dominated by the plight of American citizens held hostage in Tehran, including a botched attempt to free them. Carter argued that a waning of America's global interventionism was realistic. His secretary of state, Zbigniew Brzezinski, said, 'We can no more stop change than Canute could still the waters.' The world was always to be 'under the influence of forces no government can control'.

This was a far cry from the usual presidential bombast. Where Carter felt he could reasonably achieve beneficial change, at least in the direction of peace if not democracy, he was successful. He initiated talks at his rural base, Camp David, in September 1978 between the Egyptians and the Israelis, leading to the Camp David Accords. It was to establish a difficult but lasting peace between the two nations, even as Israel's relations with its other neighbours worsened. It was an example of American soft power sensitively deployed.

At the same time America was seeing a radical change to its economic geography. At the end of the Second World War, the north-east remained the dominant region of the union. With just 8 per cent of America's land area, it had played host to 42 per cent of its population and 68 per cent of its manufacturing output. Smoke-stack industry decline, new tech employment and, above all, air conditioning meant that, over the 1970s, the north-east lost 2.4 million people and the south-west gained 3.4 million. In 1964 California became America's most populous state, with New York second, but with Texas and Florida third and fourth. By 1980, the so-called 'sun-belt' could outvote the 'frost-belt' in the electoral college.

The late 1970s now delivered a periodic shift in America's political cycle, following Nixon's shift to the right against the liberal 1960s. A victory in the Supreme Court in 1973 found in favour of a woman's constitutional right to abortion in *Roe* v. *Wade*. But an Equal Rights Amendment failed to secure states' ratification. A similar hesitancy faced the implementation of the 1960s laws against racial segregation in schools and elsewhere. In southern schools it remained ubiquitous; attempted enforcement simply impelled 'white flight' to the suburbs, leading to segregated housing instead. These echoes of segregation survive to this day.

Across America the championing of states' rights remained what it had always been, an entrenched article of constitutional faith. Americans seemed to sense that, if the union was to hold together, its component states must retain the right to stand apart. This was not merely an archaic tradition; it seemed as important in the twentieth century as it had in the eighteenth. It reflected the fact that America embraced a diversity of peoples harbouring a diversity of ethical and social habits and beliefs. They had to feel that, whatever the nature of the union of which they were a part, they had a democratic right to have those beliefs honoured locally, be they progressive or conservative. I cannot stress too strongly this theme in American history.

This diversity found expression in the growth of evangelical Christianity. The preaching of Billy Graham was followed by Jerry Falwell and his Moral Majority movement, founded in 1979. This orchestrated opposition to the counter-culture's espousal of abortion, homosexuality and recreational drugs in a number of states. Likewise individual states took divergent views on capital punishment, gun control and compulsory helmets for motorcyclists. New Hampshire did not even force drivers to wear seat belts. Freedom under the constitution had many interpretations.

The conservative politician who championed this reaction against Carter in the 1980 election was an improbable Republican, Ronald Reagan (1981–89). He had been a Hollywood actor, a trade unionist, a corporate executive and then a two-term governor of California. He was relaxed, personable and seemingly disengaged from day-to-day politics. His chatty style disparaged the liberalism of the 1960s and adopted a familiar populist antipathy to north-eastern elites and Washington grandees. Whatever the issue, he said, 'Big Government is the problem not the solution'. He considered the most terrifying words in the English language were, 'I'm from the government and I'm here to help to be.'

Reagan not only defeated Carter but helped the Republicans to win control of the Senate for the first time since the 1950s. He peddled America's founding clichés and loved bad jokes. 'Sometimes,' he said, 'our right hand doesn't know what our far right hand is doing.' Averse to hard work, he slept a lot and concerned himself only with what he felt mattered. In office, Reagan cut taxes, increased defence spending and was unapologetic about a federal budget that surged into the red. When the national debt doubled, he remarked that it was 'big enough to take care of itself'.

So far as foreign policy was concerned, Reagan came to office breathing opposition to the Nixon–Carter era of détente and, within two years, was declaring the Soviet Union to be an 'evil empire'. Yet he was a long-standing sceptic of nuclear weapons and preferred to concentrate on his project for Star Wars, an orbital anti-missile umbrella across America. He ignored Russia's 1979 invasion of Afghanistan. Ten years later the CIA were to assist the forerunners of the Taliban in that country to oust Moscow and themselves take power. The CIA was more adept at toppling governments than at installing new ones.

A test of America's commitment to its alliance with Britain came in 1982 when that country was under a Conservative prime minister, Margaret Thatcher, with whom Reagan had formed a close ideological and personal relationship. Washington had devoted much effort to building up anti-communist regimes in South America, including that of the Argentinian dictator General Leopoldo Galtieri. In spring of 1982 Galtieri brazenly invaded the British dependency of the Falkland Islands off the coast of Argentina, assuming America would stay neutral. This was a miscalculation. In the event, Reagan gave Britain both an Atlantic base and missiles, ensuring the islands' recapture, and the fall of Galtieri soon after. As someone said of America at the time, blood was thicker than salt water.

After his re-election in 1984, a different Reagan came to the fore with the arrival in the Kremlin of a new Soviet leader, the extrovert Mikhail Gorbachev. The two men met in Geneva in 1985 and immediately developed a personal rapport. Though they failed to agree on nuclear disarmament, they privately agreed to aid each other if attacked by aliens from outer space.

The Cold War, now forty years old, entered a period of enhanced collaboration. Diplomatic channels were maintained. The prospect of a nuclear arms treaty had been first mooted as long ago as 1967 under Johnson, when a tentative agreement for nuclear non-proliferation was signed. It was taken forward under Kissinger, to counter what Kennedy's McNamara had graphically termed 'the insane road to mutual assured destruction'. The goal was to halve the build-up of nuclear missiles and limit their spread, manufacture, testing and deployment.

Kissinger had opened a Kremlin 'back-channel' in order to build confidence, and the technique worked. Talks on what became the Strategic Arms Limitation (SALT-I) had begun in November 1969 and were signed in 1972. They were followed in 1972–9 by SALT-II on the size of arsenals. Clearly the two sides wanted agreement. When Congress, largely on partisan grounds, failed to ratify SALT-II, both governments informally agreed to adhere to it until its expiry in 1985.

Reagan and Gorbachev met again in 1986 in Reykjavik and reached an accord on the reduction in stocks of nuclear weapons. But Reagan's fixation on Star Wars, with which Gorbachev could not agree, remained a sticking point. Finally, in 1987 Gorbachev visited Washington and a modest deal on removing nuclear missile arsenals from Europe was reached. When Reagan paid a return visit to Moscow a year later, he declared Russia no longer an evil empire. Détente was back on the agenda. The role of personal chemistry in diplomacy was never more evident.

Gorbachev at the time was the subject of 'Gorbymania' both in the west and among many in Moscow's progressive establishment. His programme of Russian perestroika and glasnost, reorganization and openness, emphasized the new mood. The opportunity seemed ripe for a redrawing of ideological and perhaps strategic boundaries. In 1987 Reagan performed a theatrical stunt beneath the Brandenburg Gate in Berlin. He exhorted his Soviet friend in direct terms, 'If you seek peace and prosperity, Mr Gorbachev . . . Come here to this gate! Open this gate! Mr Gorbachev, tear down this wall!' No one supposed it was anything but bombast.

America's rapprochement with the Soviet Union in the 1980s undoubtedly eased the path of progressives within the now ailing

Soviet empire. War seemed inconceivable. In May 1988, on a visit to Moscow, Reagan could address a gathering of Soviet 'dissidents' in the American embassy and tell students at Moscow University, 'Your generation is living in one of the most exciting, hopeful times in Soviet history . . . leading to a new world of reconciliation, friendship and peace.' Glasnost had begun to loosen the cruder disciplines that had bonded the Soviet empire together for over half a century. In retrospect these were indeed special times, which George Kennan's policy of containment and, finally, Kissinger's and Reagan's personal diplomacy had brought to pass.

Reagan's term ended in 1989, when he handed over the White House to his Republican vice-president and former UN ambassador George H. Bush. It was therefore a new face in the White House who oversaw the culmination of détente, the ending of the Cold War. When popular dissent took to the streets of communist Poland and Hungary, Gorbachev declared that 'we will respect their decision whatever it is'. The words were the most significant to emerge from Moscow since the Second World War.

Without a murmur of opposition from those in power and without a drop of blood being shed – other than against the regime in Romania – the iron curtain buckled. On the night of 8/9 November 1989 the Berlin Wall was breached and crowds swarmed over it from both sides. I went two days later to visit a friend's farm in Germany's Brunswick region that had been cut in half by the Iron Curtain's barbed-wire fence for thirty years. We were to witness its floodlit demolition late one night, and the reuniting of both the farmland and tearful family members. It was a deeply moving witness to the end of the Cold War. This end was a victory for Europe, but above all it was a victory for America, marking its unquestionable ascendancy as a global power.

26.

An Uncertain Policeman

1989–2001

A president is never off duty. On Christmas Day 1991, two years after the fall of the Berlin Wall, President Bush was in Camp David when he took a call from Gorbachev, then about to retire as president of the dissolving Soviet Union. The transcript survives and is touchingly personal. It opens with Gorbachev saying, 'George, my dear friend,' and admitting that the new-born Russia was not one he had favoured. He said that the choice of 'what kind of state to create took a different track from what I thought right'. Gorbachev none the less asked Bush to support the new 'Russian Commonwealth' and its elected leader, Boris Yeltsin. They bade each other a courteous and final farewell.

Russia now saw a period of turbulent introversion as it came to terms with the loss of its Soviet empire. Most members – from the Baltic republics to the Black Sea – went their own way, freed from Soviet dictatorship. Others such as Belarus and Ukraine lingered on in a reordered Russian sphere of interest. Russia itself was still a nuclear-armed power with immense natural resources, but it could not be described as an existential threat to America or the west generally. Gorbachev had remarked amiably to Bush's chief of staff, Colin Powell, 'General, I am very sorry. You'll have to find another enemy.'

The remark could serve as a text for students of American foreign policy over the following decades. That policy too entered a period of turbulence. Presidents had grown used to referring to the Soviet Union and thus the outside world in terms of enmity, power, strength and fear. As Gorbachev had implied, at the very least these abstract nouns would now need redefining. Many Russians were eager to do this. Visiting Moscow at this time was an eerie experience. At two conferences I attended I found the Russians assuming themselves now part of a collective Europe. An age of darkness and misunderstanding was over and they hoped normal relations could resume, as between friendly powers eager to collaborate in global affairs.

A leading American academic, Francis Fukuyama, chose to declare this a moment of supreme historical achievement. The west's victory in the Cold War was not just the passing of an era, it was 'the end of history as such'. To Fukuyama it was 'the endpoint of mankind's ideological evolution and the universalization of Western liberal democracy as the final form of human government'. This analysis was interpreted by some as a sign of American arrogance. But optimists more generously saw it as indicating a confidence in the future, a challenge to America and its allies to secure the hallowed moment and not waste it.

In this spirit American policy adjusted itself from confrontation with a specific enemy to a more generalized ambition against a vaguer set of evils. Presidential speeches were generalized to render America synonymous with freedom and democracy and thus, as Gorbachev had suggested, confronting a more variegated cast of opponents. These were no longer 'communists' but regimes variously terrorist, extremist, anti-democratic, autocratic or just evil. Washington was also home to a colossal vested interest, a state within a state, the multi-billion-dollar enterprise that was America's defence establishment. Something was needed to justify America retaining the greatest assemblage of weapons of war on earth. What nobler purpose could there be than to devote it to the policing of freedom? Something must be found to keep the dogs of a resurgent isolationism at bay.

Something was found. In 1988 a war in the Persian Gulf between Iran's ayatollahs and Iraq's dictator, Saddam Hussein, had reached an exhausted end. Since Saddam was a foe of America's enemy

Iran, he had been backed by the CIA. A blind eye was therefore turned to his oppression of his Kurdish minority, with such atrocities as bombing them with chemical weapons. Then in August 1990 a Saddam deeply in debt went too far. He decided to invade and occupy his neighbour Kuwait, to grab oil revenues that were twice his own.

The unprovoked conquest of an independent state was condemned by the UN Security Council, though with no expectation of a military response. This was a regional dispute between two authoritarian regimes. Yet in Washington President Bush offered to intervene with main force. He argued implausibly that an American ally, the equally autocratic Saudi Arabia, was under threat and America's oil interests with it. The UN did not demur.

A proposed military operation in the Gulf was treated with some scepticism by Democrats in Congress. The ever cautious Colin Powell, Bush's military chief of staff, insisted on using a massive force to ensure swift victory. Bush seemed almost messianic. Using language that might have been the answer to Gorbachev's question, he compared Saddam to Hitler. He announced, 'We have before us the opportunity to forge for ourselves and for future generations a new world order, a world where the rule of law . . . governs the conduct of nations.' He went further and warned, 'We must resist aggression or it will destroy our freedoms.' Saddam might almost have felt flattered.

Under a UN resolution Powell was instructed to summon allies and prepare for war. Saddam was given an ultimatum to withdraw from Kuwait, which he ignored. An extraordinary army of 950,000 French, British and some thirty other allied states was assembled in the Gulf in a congregation of western militarism. Operation Desert Storm commenced in January 1991. It was utterly one-sided and cleared Kuwait of Iraqis inside a week. The operation was effectively over in a month. Just under three hundred American and coalition soldiers were killed in action, against more than 20,000 Iraqis.

The UN had not given America the authority to follow this action with an invasion of Iraq, nor with the removal of Saddam from power. Powell was adamant that 'if you break [a country] you own it', and America had no plan for owning Iraq, at least not then. Bush was elated. He announced what appeared to be a new chapter in American foreign policy, 'We can see a very real prospect of a new world order . . . It's a proud day for America. We've kicked the Vietnam syndrome once and for all.' Whatever this meant it was hardly a victory for democracy. Kuwait's hereditary emir was restored to power, while Saddam suppressed another Kurdish uprising with extreme violence, and no American objection.

Immediately after the war, Bush's Gallup poll rating soared to a near unprecedented 89 per cent. There was no question, military intervention once undertaken was popular. A year later came a corrective. In 1992 a civil war in Somalia degenerated into chaos and famine. As in Kuwait, Bush again informed the UN he was ready to intervene. Nearing the end of his term, he offered to send American forces to protect UN aid workers. Some 25,000 troops landed in Somalia and embarked on an ill-conceived mission in an anarchic land, from which it became increasingly hard to disengage. In the so-called Battle of Mogadishu, eighteen Americans lost their lives in a downed helicopter, their fate related in the film *Black Hawk Down*.

Somalia wiped out Bush's electoral popularity. America was passing through a recession and he faced a lively Democrat, the governor of Arkansas Bill Clinton, teamed with his wife Hillary. Both were fresh-faced and new. Also in the running was an outsider from Texas, Ross Perot, who in the pre-election summer was leading both Bush and Clinton in the polls. His appeal was similar to Reagan's, a populist attack on 'a political nobility immune to the people's will . . . a little group of Washington insiders, lobbyists and professional politicians'. He ended with 20 per cent of the popular vote, splitting the right of the spectrum. Clinton was elected, but Perot's populist appeal lingered in the political air.

Clinton was the first president to preside over what was to become a repeat of the innovative explosion seen in America at the end of the nineteenth century. The transistor and the silicon chip had for some time captured the technology of the machine from metal and plastic. Micro-computing now moved from the laboratory and the factory into every office desk, briefcase and handbag in the land. Printing was succeeded – at first it seemed it might be replaced – by instant electronic communication.

The mobile phone and the internet took the world by storm. The global internet had 3 million users in the 1990s, 70 per cent of them American. Ten years later the figure was 360 million. A technological revolution had taken place. The postal service was superseded, the wired telephone upstaged. Exchanges between humans became instant and ubiquitous. The Library of Congress was at the press of a button in every home.

Existing computer firms such as IBM, Xerox and Intel found themselves overtaken by Apple, Microsoft and a stage army of start-ups. Many settled under the shadow of Stanford University near California's Silicon Valley. From the 1990s the west coast offered American investors what the east coast had offered the previous century: enterprise, talent, innovation, risk and reward. It also offered another feature shared with the robber barons of the 1890s, an absence of regulation. As the east coast rusted, the west coast glistened.

Apple Corporation's Steve Jobs imitated Herbert Hoover's boast of 'a car for every garage', promising 'a computer for every person'. By 2006, 70 per cent of Americans were carrying mobile phones, doubling as hand-held computers. Social media soon followed and a new meaning was given to friendship. There was agony and delight in every teenage pocket and a third person in every marriage. The transformation in lifestyle extended even to children, not least with a controversial impact on their mental health. The industry found its Andrew Carnegie in Microsoft's Bill Gates. He became the world's youngest and richest billionaire in 1995, going on to retire and give much of his money to medical charities.

Micro-computing and its brainchild, artificial intelligence, were to throw up problems as well as solutions. The digital revolution soon displayed the familiar corporate evils of monopoly and regulatory failure. But at no point, at least initially, did America show any

vulnerability to rivals to its west or east. Europe, Japan and the surging Chinese economy followed behind but could not compete with
the creative mass that fuelled America's digital upheaval. The start
of the twenty-first century demonstrated the extraordinary robust-
ness of America's capitalist model.

America in the 1990s was on course for what was to be the longest period of economic expansion in its modern history. Clinton's
first term of office saw a growth rate of 4 per cent a year, rising
tax revenue and a balanced federal budget. But he was unable to
achieve his fondest ambition, which was to take forward Johnson's
medical reforms to give all Americans a universal health service on
a European pattern. In 1993 he appointed his wife Hillary as head
of a task force to steer the relevant legislation through Congress.
It was an illustration of the power of Washington's lobbying industry that the doctors, pharmaceutical companies and insurance firms
succeeded in killing it inside a year. The insurance industry was
never to give way to a public service.

Clinton had no greater success than Bush in converting operations in Kuwait and Somalia into a coherent policy of intervention.
An early test came in April 1994 when the regime in the small African country of Rwanda instructed its Hutu majority to exterminate
its Tutsi minority in cold blood. UN peacekeepers were murdered
and a humanitarian catastrophe loomed. If anywhere on earth cried
out for policing, it was Rwanda.

With dead Americans so recently dragged through the streets
of Mogadishu, Clinton was more than reluctant to intervene. He
simply refused, even as the bodies of 600,000 massacred Tutsis
were filling streets and choking rivers. Given that America's power
projection was now virtually universal, the world was demanding
that 'something must be done' and only America could do it. As
Powell was later to remark, 'A policeman cannot pick and choose
the crimes he confronts.'

This theme lay at the root of the conflicts over intervention that
were to pockmark America's post-Cold War experience. Clinton's
aides dismissed Rwanda as 'a local thing' and asked all-comers to

concentrate on 'where do America's true interests lie'. This was not the language of Bush in Iraq. Why did America have fleets of warships all over the globe, laden with fighter-bombers, if not to intervene at will?

This same question was asked as the international spotlight now turned from Africa to Europe. A tangential result of the fall of the Iron Curtain was the break-up of once-communist Yugoslavia. By 1993 Slovenia and Croatia had freed themselves from the Serbian regime in Belgrade, but the province of Bosnia, with a mixed Christian/Muslim population, also wanted independence. This Serbia could not tolerate. In the course of 1992 the Serbian army began crudely clearing Bosnia of its Muslims to secure a Christian majority in favour of remaining Serbian.

Atrocities not seen in Europe since the Second World War were committed, including starvation camps, rape centres and the mass murder of thousands of Muslim men. Over a million people were driven from the country into neighbouring states. The Bosnian capital of Sarajevo had been under continuous siege since 1992 and what was legally judged a genocide was occurring on the mainland of Europe. Then, in the summer of 1995, the Serbs massacred 8,000 Bosnian Muslims in cold blood in the town of Srebrenica.

America had a navy with planes and missiles cruising the Mediterranean supposedly in honour of Bush's much-vaunted new world order. Clinton was at first adamant against intervention but finally cracked. He announced, 'There are times when America and America alone can make the difference.' Bombs pounded Serb positions round Sarajevo and in a matter of days the siege was lifted. The Serbs agreed to an independent Bosnia in negotiations at Dayton, Ohio. Intervention worked, but the question remained: what took the policeman so long?

The same question was to recur two years later in yet another Yugoslav territory, Kosovo. An overwhelmingly Albanian majority also wanted to free itself from Serbian control. As Belgrade began to drive a million Kosovans over the mountains into Macedonia, America could hardly now claim that Kosovo was not its business.

In March 1999 American planes under the umbrella of NATO began hitting Serb positions as well as civic buildings in Serbia itself. The bombing seemed almost random, including of the Chinese embassy in Belgrade. In the event it was Serbia's ally, Moscow, that pressured its leader, Slobodan Milošević, into retreat. Both Bosnia and Kosovo became de facto NATO protectorates.

There was no doubt the world needed a policeman, and the moral authority for such a role lay with the UN. In 1998 the UN sponsored the setting up of an International Criminal Court, but it was one that America declined to join as Congress refused to recognize an alien authority. This was bizarre, given America's support for just such authority in setting up the UN and its assumption of a right to intervene since then. Besides, there was little point in a court without an enforcer.

The ICC was followed in 2005 by the UN's new doctrine of 'responsibility to protect' (R2P). This was an extension of the authority to intervene, recognizing the culpability of member states in matters such as genocide and crimes against humanity. But again, who would be the enforcer? The UN was starting to look as had the pre-war League of Nations, dependent on the changing outlooks of American presidents.

For Clinton the Kosovan crisis had come at an opportune time. His second term was approaching its end and, as with Nixon, his presidency was distracted by personal crises. His popularity waned amid persistent inquiries into his sexual and financial concerns. These ended with the start of impeachment over his affair with an aide, Monica Lewinsky. At the turn of the new century in 2000, he limped over his second term's finishing line, but with the White House grabbing the attention of gossip columnists rather than political analysts.

27.

The Wars of 9/11

2001–2016

No date is so embedded in America's modern history as 11 September 2001. On that morning Clinton's successor as president, George W. Bush, son of George H., was visiting a Florida primary school when two hijacked jets flew into New York's World Trade Center. A third plane crashed into the Pentagon in Washington and a fourth in a Pennsylvanian field. More than 3,000 people died. The world's reaction was horror at the act itself and America's was a sense of national defilement. The country's territory had been violated as never since the 1814 burning of Washington, and in its holiest of shrines, downtown Manhattan. America's reaction was to dominate the presidency of the second George Bush (2001–9).

Initially New York's mayor, Rudy Giuliani, adopted the response so often advocated to acts of terrorism, which is to downplay them. He asked his fellow citizens to continue about their normal business and not disrupt the life of the city. He understood the maxim that the power of terrorism lies 10 per cent in the deed and 90 per cent in the reaction.

The attack was soon known to have been committed by an Islamist terror group, al-Qaeda, under its leader Osama bin Laden, operating from a hideout in Afghanistan. Washington immediately demanded that the ruling Taliban in Kabul hand him over. A meeting of senior Afghan figures in Kandahar was divided over complying. It was clear many of them did not know of bin Laden's presence – the Afghan foreign minister sent America his sympathies for 9/11. Kabul initially refused America's request but agreed to negotiate. It was not enough. America was a nation straining for revenge, with its president in the lead. It was rarely a sound basis for foreign policy.

The 9/11 outrage was not an act of war by a foreign power or an existential threat to America's security. It was an act of terror so awful that not a single country expressed support for it, with only Iran failing to offer its condolences. Such was the response that, with help from Pakistan, there is little doubt al-Qaeda could sooner or later have been hunted down and its leader arrested or killed.

The American president was confronting a national trauma and had to make decisions fast. He was being advised by a group of neo-conservatives led by the defence secretary Donald Rumsfeld, the vice-president Dick Cheney, and three activists – Paul Wolfo-witz, Richard Perle and John Bolton. They formed what amounted to a lock on White House foreign policy. To them 9/11 was an event that could be exploited, above all, to project American power in the Middle East. That it involved doing exactly what the terrorists most wanted – antagonizing Islam seemed beside the point.

Bush now did all he could to enhance the horror, turning 9/11 into a global threat, publicizing its cause and demanding the world support him in whatever he might do. This, he said, 'begins with al-Qaeda but it does not end there. It will not end until every terrorist group in global reach has been rounded up, stopped and defeated . . . This is the world's fight, this is civilization's fight.' Speaking in 2002 in his 'axis of evil' speech, Bush characterized particular regimes as collaborators, as 'warriors of terror', naming Iran, Iraq and North Korea. Bin Laden was awarded serious allies.

This response elevated a group of well-heeled bandits in a moun-tain hideaway into champions of Muslim extremism against the west. Even the conservative historian of American foreign policy Paul Schroeder found the White House's response to 9/11 baffling. Washington was driving supporters into bin Laden's embrace. Amer-icans were threatening 'bloody reprisals so as to destroy the vital centre and force everyone to choose between them and a national or religious enemy'. Indeed, 9/11 was turned into what seemed a religious war. Bush's every decision seemed directed to this end. At one point he even used the emotive word crusade, as if to provoke Muslims to oppose him.

Within a month and with only Britain initially as a committed ally, Bush was bombing the Afghan capital of Kabul. On the ground, American special forces joined with Afghanistan's anti-Taliban Northern Alliance and advanced south on Kabul, from which the Taliban retreated in November. By December, America had assembled an international army of occupation under NATO auspices, though its relevance to NATO was obscure. That month a puppet ruler, Hamid Karzai, was installed in Kabul and the Taliban were formally driven out, mostly over the border to Pakistan.

Even as America wrestled with how long it should stay in Afghanistan – Rumsfeld was adamant it should get out fast – the White House team shifted its attention to a different goal, Iraq. Using false intelligence supplied by an exiled Iraqi dissident, Ahmed Chalabi, the team persuaded Bush that Iraq's Saddam Hussein was behind 9/11. One member was reported as saying that, after 9/11, 'America has to conquer a country' to show its strength was unimpaired. The claim was disseminated that Saddam had weapons of mass destruction and intended to use groups such as al-Qaeda to attack America with them. Bush became fixated on this supposed menace. He announced, 'I will not permit the world's most dangerous regimes to threaten us with the world's most destructive weapons.' It was what Kennan had called 'the blind egotism of an embattled democracy'.

Voices of sanity in Washington were few and far between. Colin Powell, now Bush's secretary of state, pleaded with him to get the UN to investigate if Saddam really had weapons that threatened America. He warned against another Vietnam, one that would 'suck the oxygen out of everything' that Bush wanted to do domestically. In the event the UN inspectors found nothing in Iraq. Bush, a prisoner of his advisers, refused to believe them. He stated that 'the United States will if necessary act pre-emptively'. He said invasion would be a 'preventive war'.

The run-up to the Iraq war illustrates how critical is the chemistry of leadership elites at such times. It was always assumed that civilized regimes would not unleash nuclear holocaust because sanity would prevail. Yet a near fanatical group of Americans was able to browbeat its allies into believing that Iraq was an imminent threat to western democracy and war must be declared to prevent it.

Corrupted intelligence led the CIA to persuade Britain's normally robust MI6 of this fact. The British government published what was later dubbed a 'dodgy dossier', designed to justify a pre-emptive war on Iraq. It claimed that 'Iraq could assemble nuclear weapons within months of obtaining fissile material from foreign sources'. As for chemical and biological weapons, these 'could be deployed in 45 minutes . . . capable of reaching UK bases in Cyprus'.

This dubious thesis was accepted by Britain's Tony Blair and overwhelmingly by the House of Commons, though the foreign minister, Robin Cook, resigned in disagreement. A statement along similar lines by Powell to the UN also sounded sufficiently plausible to win the support of NATO members. America's strategic authority over the western 'bloc' was awesome. Powell was later to admit, 'I regret that a lot of it turned out to be wrong.'

The world now saw a war in search of a justification rather than a justification in search of a war. Despite frantic attempts at making peace, in which Iraq offered Washington everything short of Saddam's exile, Washington was adamant for war. As Gorbachev had foreseen, when deprived of the Soviet menace, Washington's defence establishment would yearn for something to do. Rumsfeld complained that 'there aren't any good targets in Afghanistan and there are lots of good targets in Iraq'. America was the inverse of threatened. It seemed badly in need of a threat.

Bush's failure to convince a number of European countries – including Germany and France – led him to invite 'a coalition of the willing' to join him. Some thirty pro-American nation-states did so to a limited degree. American satirists attacked the French as 'cheese-eating surrender monkeys'. Rarely has democracy so conspicuously failed to penetrate a fog of mendacity and prejudice as over Iraq.

In March 2003 a coalition of initially 300,000 American and allied forces invaded Iraq from Kuwait after subjecting Baghdad to a month of bombing, described as inflicting 'shock and awe'. Iraq's army collapsed in the face of massive pressure and Saddam was soon toppled and executed. On 1 May, Bush stood on a warship off the Californian coast and declared 'mission accomplished', though he added that he still had 'to bring order to parts of that country that remain dangerous'.

Bush now extended his 'ownership' of Afghanistan to Iraq, just as for twenty years his predecessors had owned South Vietnam. This was remarkable in that, before taking office, Bush had declared himself emphatically against just such interventions. He wanted military deployment only 'in our vital national interests' and was explicitly against becoming a 'nation builder'. His national security adviser and later secretary of state Condoleezza Rice was equally averse. It was not America's job, she said, to be 'the world's 911 call center', a reference to the American emergency phone line.

This was not a view shared with the White House advisers, who saw Kabul and Baghdad as ideological client states at the heart of a new pro-American Arab world. Sceptical State Department Arabists were not allowed near Iraq for the duration. Guided by Chalabi, the American occupation authority dismantled Saddam's administrative apparatus on the grounds that it was composed mostly of his Ba'ath Party members. A swathe of the country's governing class was thus sacked, with police, civil servants and university staff alike rendered unemployed.

I visited Iraq in 2003 shortly after the invasion and saw bizarre sights. Trestle tables were erected in Saddam's old Green Zone palace, labelled with the names of government departments that had been destroyed by American bombs or rendered ineffective by sackings. Some were manned by youths from America's right-wing Heritage Foundation. Volunteers tried to direct the Baghdad traffic. A young British aid worker was put in charge of Baghdad's rubbish collection, at which he was briefly impressive. But the country was near ungovernable and soon anarchic.

The overall result was lawlessness and chaos. The ancient site of Babylon was occupied as an army base. The national library and archive in Baghdad were gutted by fire. To go round Baghdad's National Museum, looted of Mesopotamian treasures, was heart-breaking. Despite the efforts of staff to protect its contents, American soldiers refused to guard it as 'we are not policemen'. Thousands of pieces found their way onto the international antiques market. I could have climbed the remains of Ur of the Chaldees and picked up anything I wanted.

The American occupation of Iraq lasted until 2011 amid growing instability. American military deaths rose to 4,150 a year while an estimated 150,000 Iraqi lives were lost in civil insurgencies, in a country supposedly under American control. Serious atrocities were committed in Baghdad's Abu Ghraib prison. Apart from removing a dictator, the invasion achieved nothing that its champions had advocated.

Stephen Graubard, in his biographical survey of twentieth-century presidencies, is most scathing of Bush over Iraq. The president had promised that Saddam's destruction would mean 'a democratization of Iraq, greater American influence throughout the Middle East and a final peace settlement between Israel and Palestine'. Graubard concluded, 'Never in the twentieth century had so fundamental a foreign policy error been made and rarely had so much been promised and so little achieved.'

The British historian Niall Ferguson was a rare commentator to be well-disposed to what he called the Colossus, the new American empire 'that dare not speak its name . . . an empire in denial'. He argued that no one could take exception to its ambition, to use American power to promote values of freedom, civil rights and democracy round the world. But Ferguson contrasted America's means of achieving it with the British Empire's efforts to establish a similar sovereignty of values in the nineteenth century.

Ferguson argued that Britain had the courage of its convictions, which required the long haul. 'When Britain went into a country, it stayed', as indeed had America in Japan and Germany after the

Second World War. America's twenty-first-century empire, nervous of being thought imperialist, lacked commitment. It neglected the non-military requirements of nation-building in favour of holding one election followed by a date for leaving. By promising its imminent departure, it gave the relevant insurgents no incentive to collaborate. Iraq's Shi'ite militias could be seen in Baghdad and elsewhere, watching and waiting for America to leave.

This was why, Ferguson concludes, 'this vastly powerful [American] economy with its extraordinary military capability, has had such a disappointing record when it has sought to bring about changes of political regime abroad'. Even the Russians in Afghanistan in the 1980s built schools and colleges to last. As for Iraq, to watch inexperienced young Americans trying to reconstruct a Baghdad they had just smashed to bits was like watching a think-tank on a weekend team-bonding exercise.

Meanwhile, back home there were signs that the long-booming American economy was at last under strain. The cause was specific: an excess of mortgage lending to poor homeowners, described as 'sub-prime' and even 'predatory and toxic'. Federal subsidies had encouraged relatively low-earning buyers to take on variable-rate mortgages which they could not safely afford. The market became awash in debt. The preliminary to the crisis was thus similar, if not identical, to that of 1929. When confidence collapses, so do credit and investment.

In September 2008 the Lehman Brothers bank failed and debts were called in everywhere. The knock-on effect saw the American stock market crash and other highly geared world markets follow suit. Unlike in previous recessions, financial authorities now at least understood what to do, which was to print money. Swift central action propped up the principal banks. Huge sums of money were fed into the system, to the tune of an estimated $2,000 for every living American. By the spring of 2009 this had achieved stabilization. While the crash certainly affected a large number of homeowners and investors and produced a short recession, it was nothing like as severe as those of old.

At the end of 2008 a new page was turned in American history, the election of Barack Obama as the country's first black president. The Harvard-educated lawyer and son of a Kenyan father and white American mother, Obama was remarkable. He did not merely win 53 per cent of the popular vote but he won in southern states such as Florida, Virginia and North Carolina. The election also showed the emerging power of the internet and its social-media platforms. Obama's crowdfunding site accumulated 1.5 million members who between them raised $600 million. It suggested that the new American politics was not, as so often alleged, only for the rich.

Obama's inauguration recalled the heady days of the Kennedys. He arrived in Washington in a vintage train, after addressing crowds en route. The event itself was witnessed by an estimated one million people in Washington's Mall, and by the largest broadcast audience in American history. It was followed by ten inaugural balls, including six 'neighbourhood' ones for local people. There were readings from the Founding Fathers, concerts and a service in memory of Martin Luther King. Obama swore his oath on Lincoln's personal Bible. He claimed that 'I have brothers, sisters, nieces, nephews, uncles and cousins of every race and every hue scattered across three continents . . . in no other country on earth is my story even possible.'

Although Obama was an intelligent and liberal personality, his inaugural message did not get a good press. It was as clichéd as the catchphrases of his campaign, full of 'Yes we Can' and 'Change we can believe in'. One critic dismissed it as 'all hopey-changey stuff'. But the fact of his election offered a new promise to millions of Americans who had long felt excluded from public life. It was also a collective release from a contorted and uncertain period in the presidency. A bridge from the past appeared to have been crossed. The political pendulum had swung back to progressivism.

Like Clinton and other Democrats before him, Obama set his domestic sights firmly on removing the greatest stain on American social policy: the lack of a free health and social care service for its poor. First steps had been attempted under Johnson, and Obama's proposal was hardly radical, further to extend free insurance on a means-tested basis. In this he succeeded. What was called the Affordable Care Act – or Obamacare – was passed in 2010. Its effect was to reduce the number of Americans lacking insurance cover from about 20 per cent of the population to under 10 per cent. It was Obama's most substantial domestic achievement.

As for resolving the legacy of Bush's 9/11 wars, Obama was less successful. America departed Iraq in December 2011 on an arranged schedule, but it was left increasingly in thrall to its neighbour and member of Bush's 'axis of evil', Iran. This in turn saw the rise of a Sunni affiliate of al-Qaeda known as Isis or Daesh, which, by 2013, had taken control of some 40 per cent of northern Iraq and a third of adjacent Syria. One result was that the ancient Christian population of Iraq, 1.5 million strong when America invaded in 2003, was within a decade massacred, tortured or driven into exile by Islamists. Just 150,000 remained. This was the price of anarchy.

Afghanistan was if anything even less fortunate. America's occupation was now a decade old and most of its coalition allies had gone. British troops occupied the southern province of Helmand in 2006, boasting that they would drive out any remaining Taliban, suppress the opium trade and pacify it 'without firing a shot'. They left eight years later with 457 British troops dead and the Taliban on the brink of ruling the province. At the end of 2009 Obama, who had wanted to withdraw, was persuaded to 'surge' America's military presence, finally to wipe out the Taliban. An army of 30,000 Americans was sent to Kabul, declaring the intention to pacify the country in two years and leave by 2014. The plan, like similar efforts in Vietnam, was to avoid conspicuous failure. The puppet regime in Kabul was corrupt and diverted millions in American aid to fuel Dubai's property boom. In 2014 security was supposedly handed over to the Afghans, but the Taliban was soon in control of the bulk of the country. A half-hearted American presence remained in Kabul for a further seven years.

America's three principal attempts in half a century at imposing its will on poor nations by military aggression had seemed a travesty of the manifest destiny advocated by the Founding Fathers. Two of them, in Vietnam and Afghanistan, became the longest wars in American history. Those in Afghanistan and Iraq were estimated by the economist Joseph Stiglitz to have cost $3 trillion, a fortune that might otherwise have been devoted to philanthropy, whether abroad or at home.

What Gorbachev had described as necessary enemies of America's military outreach fell into two categories. The first were the victims of the quasi-imperialism of Afghanistan and Iraq, the other the victims of the policing function on which Bush Senior had explicitly set America's sights after the Cold War. It is hard to see the first as anything but fiascos. But for the second there was no shortage of calls. After Kuwait, Somalia, Bosnia and Kosovo a new challenge arose in the so-called 'Arab Spring' of 2011. This was a burst of uprisings against authoritarian regimes across the Muslim world, from Tunisia to Libya and Egypt to Syria. The invitation to America's manifest destiny could hardly have been more blatant.

In Muammar Gaddafi's Libya, Britain and France requested Obama urgently to intervene on the side of the rebels, in particular to prevent a threatened massacre in Benghazi. It was a classic policing task but Obama, who had forces available in the Mediterranean, was reluctant, understandably fearing that he would be expected to underwrite the whole Arab Spring. Like Clinton in Yugoslavia, he did finally concede. He authorized air strikes on Benghazi's attackers as well as on targets in Tripoli. The people of Benghazi were saved and by the autumn Gaddafi was dead. But there was no plan for what should happen next and the result was anarchy. The American ambassador was killed and Libya became a conduit for thousands of African migrants to Europe across the Mediterranean.

A consequence of Libya was, as Obama feared, immediate pressure for America to do likewise in Syria, whose ruler Bashar al-Assad was bombing his own citizens. This time Obama adamantly refused, though he did warn Assad that the use of chemical weapons would be 'a red line'. When Assad crossed that line, Obama still refused. This time his officials argued that it was unnecessary as Assad's regime was on the point of collapse. With Russia and Iran then coming to Assad's aid, it took thirteen years for that to happen.

By 2016 America's military reach was global and unprecedented. It had some 150,000 military personnel located in forty 'friendly' countries round the world. Not even the British Empire had seen anything comparable. Yet the purpose of such a dispersal remained obscure. Presidents of both parties from Kennedy to Obama had declared themselves champions of a new world order. Obama emphatically declared America to be 'the one indispensable nation in world affairs'. But this assumption of moral imperialism was bereft of practicalities. The values supposedly to be enforced were nowhere defined in detail. The context of their enforcement was not explained, nor were its possible limits. There was no attempt to explain America's right to unleash extreme violence against sovereign states who were fellow members of the UN. And when, as was the case in Rwanda or Syria, America declined to intervene, it would be as 'not in America's strategic interest'. What was the world supposed to make of that?

28.

The Long Twentieth Century

2016–2025

The twenty-first century opened with America on a high. The end of the Cold War and a decade of comparative world peace saw it advance further to international pre-eminence. Its military superiority was unchallenged, if at times uncertain in outcome. Its economy was driven in large part by ever freer global trade and a fast-evolving digital revolution. At home, the nation's political community was increasingly polarized between Republican and Democrat, but they held a common vision for their country, that of America as a force for good and with a role to play in the world. Pax Americana was in the ascendant.

In this, America's domestic politics was uncannily balanced. Apart from Obama in 2008, by 2024 no presidential election in the twenty-first century had been won by a margin of more than 4.5 per cent of the popular vote. Yet polarization was ever more apparent. Media outlets were patently either conservative or progressive. The proportion of Americans averse to their children marrying into an opposing political camp rose from a minimal number in the 1960s to a third of Democrats and a half of Republicans in the early 2020s. Property agents even classified residential districts by dominant voting intention.

In most democracies the number of floating voters was rising, but in America the reverse was happening. Just seven of the fifty states represented in the Electoral College were considered 'swing', or evenly balanced, with capacity for change often measured in just a few thousand votes. In 2000 George W. Bush lost the nationwide ballot but won all Florida's Electoral College delegates, and thus the presidency, by 537 votes. Following Obama, in 2016 Donald Trump lost the popular vote but won in the Electoral College. The son of a New York property magnate with no government experience, he was able to turn his status as an outsider to his advantage. Widely greeted as a populist, his calling card was an expressed hatred for any form of elite power, and for any person or institution to whom or to which he took a personal dislike.

This was ironic. The Electoral College had been devised specifically to guard against such populist intruders. Hamilton wrote in Federalist Paper no. 1 that the union should not be led by those who had 'begun their careers by paying an obsequious court to the people, commencing demagogues and ending tyrants'. His safeguard was that state delegates to the College should be free to vote for the candidate they thought best, not as mandated by their electors. This was soon discontinued as undemocratic. But equally so was that all a state's delegation should vote according to their winning candidate. Only in Maine and Nebraska did they split according to the balance of their popular vote.

Trump's initial targets were those familiar to America's political outsiders in the tradition of Andrew Jackson and William Jennings Bryan. They were east-coast liberals, the Washington 'swamp' of machine politicians and the so-called 'liberal elite'. Despite his plutocratic background, Trump spoke the direct, simplistic language of the 'left-behinds' and the 'silenced'. Audiences saw him as 'one of us' and flocked to his rallies.

In office, Trump displayed no ambition for world leadership and no trace of moral or philanthropic crusade. He pledged to 'make America great again', but it was an introverted greatness dubbed 'America first'. It would seek an end to costly foreign alliances and 'interventionalism' (sic). Trump had a businessman's fixation with 'the deal'. It might be to end some overseas conflict by high-profile personal involvement – though his patience was quickly exhausted – or to regulate America's trade with competitor countries. In the latter case his chief weapon was the import levy or tariff, which he called 'the most beautiful word in the dictionary'.

The 2017 presidency saw a chaotic sequence of gestures, staff hirings and resignations. It lasted just one term and coincided with the Covid-19 pandemic. America had an additional outbreak of vaccine denial and a proportion of Covid-related deaths above the world average. Trump was true to his pledge to withdraw America from international agreements, including those on climate change, human rights, Iranian weapons inspection and UNESCO. He even hinted he would disband NATO if its other members did not pull their weight financially. Trump's often expressed aversion to war was sincere. He approved no substantial 'policing' interventions during his term and even attempted a personal détente with North Korea's autocrat Kim Jong Un, without success.

An echo of past divisions and a sign of growing polarization concerned gender and race. In 2017 a feminist movement known as #MeToo arose following the conviction of the film producer Harvey Weinstein for sexual assault. A measure of the power of social media was that the movement received immediate publicity and support on both sides of the Atlantic. The same was true three years later when a black Minnesotan, George Floyd, was killed by a white police officer. Black Lives Matter (BLM), a movement formed in 2013 to protest anti-black violence, now became another world-wide campaign, this time against race discrimination. Cities across America saw BLM demonstrations, leading to 200 imposed curfews, while at team sports events players 'took the knee', even at British football matches.

In 2020 Trump sought re-election but was defeated by a veteran Democrat, Joe Biden, a defeat he refused to concede, claiming vote rigging. On 6 January 2021 his supporters reacted in a violent riot that stormed and ransacked the Congress building on Capitol Hill, clearly encouraged in a speech by Trump himself. There followed a series of attempts to reverse the election result, unprecedented in the history of the presidency. They led in turn to multiple prosecutions of Trump and his team for electoral fraud. He appeared finished, and possibly facing jail.

America's retreat into isolationism, such as it had been under Trump, proved half-hearted. The first half of the 2020s was dominated by two of the fiercest international conflicts since the Cold War, with America overtly aiding one participant in each. In 2022 Russia's Vladimir Putin launched an unprovoked invasion of his neighbour Ukraine. This was checked when Ukrainian forces were aided in large part by weapons from America and other western powers. Though Ukraine was not a NATO member the assistance was a gesture of outrage at Russia's aggression against an independent state. Biden was scrupulously careful not to escalate the conflict by contributing troops on the ground, instead adhering to the Cold War discipline of restraint by containment.

A year later, in October 2023, another conflict erupted. It began with a massacre by Palestinian terrorists at an Israeli settlement and music festival, resulting in the deaths of 1,200 Israelis and the taking of around 250 hostages. The Israeli response was ferocious and out of all proportion, bombing to devastation the urbanized Gaza strip. Some 45,000 Palestinian civilians were killed within a year, a quarter of them believed to be children. The unprovoked killings continued. Charges of war crimes, ethnic cleansing and genocide were made against the Israelis but at no point did America voice any criticism. The two conflicts together stirred a widespread sense of a world descending haphazardly into a new Cold War, with America drawn in as more than just policeman.

In 2024 Trump returned to the public eye to seek a second White House term. He repeated his former platform of anti-immigration, protectionism and 'America first'. He found a new self-confidence, reinforced by his fortunate survival of an assassin's bullet during the campaign. This time his victory was unquestioned, though only by a narrow 1.62 per cent of the popular vote. He was aided by the now-frail Biden's tardy replacement as Democratic candidate by a weak vice-president, Kamala Harris.

Unlike in his first term, Trump came prepared for probably the most dramatic first hundred days of any president in history. His inaugural ceremony was graced with a bizarre guard of honour of America's tech billionaires. They included Elon Musk of Tesla and X (formerly Twitter), Mark Zuckerberg of Facebook, Jeff Bezos of

Amazon and Tim Cook of Apple. Far from adhering to the customary inaugural patriotism, Trump's speech was a blistering rant against his opponents, many sitting uncomfortably before him.

The new Trump cabinet was unlike any other. Virtually devoid of experience or intellectual distinction, it was composed of devoted supporters. The new vice-president, J. D. Vance, was a forty-year-old lawyer and writer from Ohio. He had once likened Trump to Hitler and called him a 'reprehensible idiot', though he had since deftly changed his allegiance. A Cuban senator from Florida, Marco Rubio, became Secretary of State; a Fox News presenter, Peter Hegseth, was made defence secretary; and a vaccine denier, Robert Kennedy, was appointed health secretary. The most remarkable member was Musk, who was to head a new Department of Government Efficiency, with a pledge to cut the federal budget by $2 trillion. He accepted the post at a rally with an apparently fascist salute and waving a chain saw.

Trump celebrated his first hundred days in April with a televised cabinet meeting in which members took turns to eulogize him. It was a monarchical performance that would have had Benjamin Franklin turning in his grave. The president had come armed with an unprecedented 130 executive orders emanating from the White House. The incumbent's right to make such orders independent of Congressional oversight was supposedly limited to emergencies. Trump duly declared eight 'national emergencies', including ones involving immigration and America's balance of overseas trade.

Some orders were blatantly unconstitutional. Trump denied citizenship guaranteed to a foreign child born in America. He deported without trial to an Ecuadorian jail an American he claimed to be a gang member. Other orders were authorized by Republicans in Congress, though their majority would be vulnerable to midterm elections in 2026. Trump's orders were considerably aided by a Supreme Court whose majority comprised judges he had selected and appointed in his first term.

Trump's first hundred days proved to be an extraordinary display of centralized power, in anything but a Republican tradition.

It included roughly a third of the 300 'objectives' listed before the election by a conservative think-tank, the Heritage Foundation, in its Project 2025. They included a ban on new federal hirings, a resumption of oil and gas drilling, no more leases for wind farms, a pardon for the Capitol rioters and no federal contact with any law firm that had ever crossed Trump's path. A declared 'war on woke' included closing all federal diversity, equality and inclusion offices, banning federal funds to universities with such offices and the arrest of critics of American support for Israel. Trump also took time to lay down the law on architecture. He deplored 'Brutalism and Deconstructivism' in federal buildings, which should in future be in a 'classical architectural style'. He also ordered the reopening of the long-closed Alcatraz island prison off San Francisco.

Most drastic was Elon Musk's assault on government efficiency. Two million civil servants were offered 'a fork in the road', with payments made if they did not return to work. Agency chiefs were dismissed 'for being disloyal to President Trump'. The entire Department of Education and its 4,400 staff was disbanded, leaving Washington awash in lawyers waving employment contracts. Many judicial rulings Trump simply ignored, leaving them in executive limbo. Musk lasted in office barely four months, after a bitter row in which he called for Trump's impeachment. He went on to found a new party committed to defeating the President's fiscal policies.

Turning his gaze overseas, Trump was equally radical. He implied that America had lost patience with the outside world. To him, a sequence of ill-considered interventions and costly conflicts had gained no advantage. It was as if the Founding Fathers had ordered America to return home and attend to its own affairs. Trump was agreeing with Britain's Lord Palmerston in his warning that powerful nations should not climb pulpits. They should have 'no eternal allies and no perpetual enemies'. They should rather understand that 'it is our interests that are eternal and perpetual, and those interests it is our duty to follow'.

In that spirit, Trump repeated his first-term decisions and again withdrew America from international institutions. He pulled out of the World Health Organization, UNESCO and the Paris climate change agreement. He ordered the immediate cessation of America's overseas aid programme, USAID, the biggest national agency of charitable relief on earth. Staff on the ground had to stand aside from a devastating earthquake in Myanmar, while famine-relief ships in Africa were unable to unload their cargoes, though this refusal was later rescinded. Almost as an aside, Trump declared his desire to make Canada America's fifty-first state. He also wanted to annex Greenland and invade Panama to improve America's security.

Most sensational was Trump's intervention in Russia's invasion of Ukraine. He bluntly switched sides. America and the whole western community had been solidly behind Kyiv, but Trump stopped all arms shipments to the country and denied it intelligence support. He chatted with Putin for an hour over the phone, subsequently blaming Ukraine for starting the war and declaring its elected president Volodymyr Zelensky 'a dictator'. He and his vice-president then humiliated the Ukrainian leader in a White House meeting with an audience and the media present.

The implication for NATO of this lurch towards the Kremlin was clearly traumatic. Trump refused to recognize Russia's action in Ukraine as a threat to Europe's security. He also declined to see why America should carry the lion's share of Cold War levels of defence. He protested, 'Why are we in it for billions, and Europe is not?' His defence secretary, Hegseth, piled on the pressure, telling a NATO meeting in Munich that America was no longer 'a primary guarantor of European security'.

As if to crown his hundred days, Trump in April upstaged even himself. He held a press conference at which he listed some seventy-five nations with trading surpluses with America. On them all he proposed to impose import tariffs ranging from 10 to 45 per cent, or, in China's case 145 per cent. The reason was their 'cheating, pilfering, plundering and raping' of American business over the years. Prominent in the audience were not financiers or corporate bosses but leaders of America's trade unions in working attire.

Trump's list of nations was near meaningless as the surpluses took no account of services. It also disregarded the role of imports in America's own manufactures, notably Asian computer chips. The president was eventually persuaded by his Treasury secretary, Scott Bessent, to ease the higher tariffs, leading him to gloat that 'these countries are all kissing my ass. They are delighted to make a deal. Please, Sir, please.' Amid chaos on world financial markets – some losing as much as 15 per cent in value – deals were indeed made to reduce the imposts. To Trump, the deal was all.

The president clearly rejected the constitution's entrenched concept of checks and balances, its separation of powers. Partisan politics, his dominance of Congress through a Republican majority, was his most effective weapon. Trump felt able bluntly to assert, 'I have the right to do whatever I want as president.' This egotism and the absence of consultation or debate was rapidly authoritarian. The victims of what amounted to Trump's rage embraced every corner of America's establishment, federal departments, courts domestic and international, universities including Harvard, cultural institutions and the media. Scientific research was starved of federal funds. Trump's dictatorship of revenge and whim crippled America's global outreach and saw tourism to America plummet by a third.

The aversion to overseas entanglements was in itself not new. The tradition stretched back to George Washington's attitude to Europe, if rarely so explicit. In the Middle East in May, Trump told a delighted audience of undemocratic Arab states that the days of 'western interventionalists flying in with lectures on how to live or how to govern your own affairs' were over. Despite his supposed aversion to internationalism, Trump revelled in strutting the world stage with leaders of whom he approved.

The contrast was marked with a 2022 BBC documentary series, *Corridors of Power: Should America Police the World?*, which invited a series of White House officials to recall twenty years of foreign interventions. Each portrayed a Washington beset by ambivalence in acting out its role as world policeman. Even apart from Afghanistan and Iraq, crises seemed endless, from Kuwait to Somalia, Yugoslavia, Libya, Syria and Sudan. At every turn presidents, Republican and Democrat, were sincerely eager to promote peace and liberty, yet most promotions ended in disarray and a clash with self-interest. Time and again moral leadership fell foul of pragmatism and reality.

In however crude a fashion, Trump sought to end this ambivalence. Though the longer he was in office the more he was tempted to get involved – as between India and Pakistan in 2025 and later in bombing Iranian nuclear facilities – it was as a deal-maker, not a policeman. He never spoke of America's duty to freedom or democracy. He abused allies as 'pathetic freeloaders'. This was despite the fact that the only NATO member ever to activate the treaty's Clause 5 requesting allies to come to its aid was America after 9/11. To Trump, Russia posed no existential threat to the west as a whole. If Putin menaced his immediate neighbours, that was their business, or at least Europe's.

In April 2025 the president of the European Commission, Ursula von der Leyen, declared enough was enough. She said, 'The West as we knew it no longer exists.' She called for 'a major realignment' of the former western powers. This shift had been decided by no war, no treaty, no conference or Congress. The president of America had merely announced that his country, at least as long he was its leader, was no longer a reliable ally. He had abandoned Ukraine and possibly even NATO. Collective security was a twentieth-century concept and it appeared over.

In reality, Trump was calling NATO's bluff. Within six months he was expressing exasperation with Putin and resuming military aid to Ukraine. It was hardly a secret that few people expected America to risk a nuclear exchange for the defence of a few square miles of Poland or a Baltic state. Such American champions of NATO down the years as George Kennan and Henry Kissinger had viewed the alliance's 1990s advance to the Russian border as a high-risk provocation of the Kremlin's historic paranoia. But that advance was now a fact. Nuclear deterrence duly was held in reserve should Russia's border belligerence stray too far.

Von der Leyen had warned that this reserve was now in doubt, which could only involve an urgent reassessment of NATO strategy. That in itself was no bad thing. The immediate consequence of the Trump crisis was that all European countries other than Hungary announced increases in their defence spending. Most now promised to move towards the 2 per cent of GDP they had in 2014 pledged to spend but, as Trump implied, failed to honour. Britain even promised 3 per cent and then an implausible 5 per cent. None the less, the automatic assumption of American leadership was now clearly in question.

If America's commitment to Europe was vulnerable to a new realism, so too was the other arm of America's outreach: its commercial supremacy. By the 2020s, the G7 economies had declined from two-thirds of global wealth in 1990s to under a half. Their global exports fell from 45 per cent to under a third. The alternative BRICS group – Brazil, Russia, India, China and South Africa – was expanding to include countries from Africa, the Middle East and South America. This 'BRICS-plus' group was about to overtake the G7 in its share of world trade. The promotion of the global economy that America had championed for some seventy years was about to be transformed.

World trade had already been thrown into turmoil by Trump's predecessor Biden in his sanctions of unprecedented severity against Russia in 2022 over Ukraine. Russia had been able to gather together a sanctions-busting coalition involving China and other Asian powers including Iran and India. A BRICS-plus conference in 2024 in the Russian city of Kazan was attended by no fewer than thirty-two countries. It was clearly galvanized both by sanctions and by Trump's threatened trade militancy. The world seemed to be changing all of a sudden, with China emerging as the dominant rival to America.

Trump's return to the White House was perhaps best seen as the termination of one of Arthur Schlesinger's cycles of American history. The twenty-first century had seen many short cycles, as earlier from Carter to Reagan and Bush to Obama. At the time of writing, six months into his second term of office, Trump was still a mercurial figure. His fixation on treating every policy issue as a threat subject to a deal made his responses unpredictable. But as his term progressed and opponents increased in number, Trump appeared more chaotic than sinister. It seemed more likely that his presidency would in time test the constitution's strength rather than prove its weakness. Trump appears more as the conclusion to a longer cycle of American history, that of 'the long twentieth century'.

It had begun in 1900 with Theodore Roosevelt's quasi-imperial arrival on the world stage and his Great White Fleet circumnavigation. America then proceeded to be the dominant player in twentieth-century conflicts. After the First World War it instigated the League of Nations, after the Second the UN. It formulated and guaranteed the west's security against communist dictatorship. During and after the Cold War it purported, however uncertainly, to act as de facto policeman, if not ruler, of the world. Its greatness was undeniable. Now it appeared that the Great White Fleet was returning to harbour. Possibly Trump may one day be succeeded by a President eager to reassert America again as the champion of world democracy in collaboration with its historic European partners. But for now, America's military outreach and its economic ascendancy could no longer be taken for granted. If Trump performed any useful task, it was to inject a needed scepticism into that ascendancy. A curtain was at last coming down on the twentieth century, and a new one rising, to reveal who knows what?

Conclusion: The Final Achievement

The American constitution was born of a belief that individual liberty should be sought in a new land across the Atlantic. Europe's rulers had for centuries proved unable to resolve conflicts within or between their borders without resorting to often bloodthirsty violence. America's Founding Fathers would avoid that resort through democracy, through principles learned from Europe's classical civilizations. Their chosen framework was a federal union of thirteen previously separate British colonies, a union under a constitution they cautiously described as experimental.

By the twentieth century the experiment had spectacularly succeeded. The United States had emerged as a rich and stable nation with a political structure that honoured its creators' acumen. It had become a refuge for the enterprising and the oppressed, a cradle of freedom and a breeding ground of capitalism. But the constitution itself had fallen short. It did not grant equality to black people or fairness to Native Americans. The states were frequently in dispute and, as long ago as 1861, the constitution failed its most crucial test, that of maintaining peace. But the resulting Civil War did not destroy the union, which remained intact to sustain the onward march towards liberty and equality.

Over the next century America matured as the world's preeminent power, economically and then militarily. By the second half of the twentieth century it had accepted this power as implying the role of the world's leading nation. But, like Icarus, America flew too close to the sun. From Korea and Vietnam to the Middle East, South America and even the Mediterranean, it found itself acting not as honest broker but as unpredictable participant in military conflicts, often of limited international relevance. America's motives became confused, whether self-interested or philanthropic, and its use of military force bordered on the imperial. Its defence establishment seemed to crave war. Yet throughout this time, America's constitution proved robust. Designed in the eighteenth century for a nation of 4 million, it was still serving 300 million two centuries later.

I firmly believe that critical to this success was the mechanics of union. Holding together very large countries often lapses into the iron grip of centralized authoritarianism, as evidenced by Russia and China. Such states are vulnerable to rebellion, secession and dictatorship. The liberation of Spain's South American empire never came near the unity achieved by Britain's in the north. Nor was a politically mature Europe able to offer examples in federal harmony. In the twentieth century Austria–Hungary, Germany, the United Kingdom, Czechoslovakia and Yugoslavia all failed in some degree as unions.

America, on the other hand, managed to combine in a common enterprise what became fifty potentially divergent states and groups of people spread over a vast land mass. It persuaded them that their interest lay in a joint geographical, political and linguistic identity, in a 'union of states'. This union often lagged behind other developed countries in progressive reform but it sustained relentlessly the ambition of its original constitution. It did so by securing the consent of all Americans, a consent long in the consummation.

The art of political federation is notoriously elusive. It requires the central power to deny itself authority, to decentralize and compromise. As we have seen, compromise lay at the heart of Jefferson's and Madison's union. It was party to the continual acceptance of slavery, to the separation of power in Washington and to the conquest and colonization of the American west. Emerson called America a land of antagonisms, 'an impossible whole'. He accepted that any person might abuse another, but 'in a true society, as in a true man, both must combine'. They must live together in peace. In the 1770s Hamilton was right that it needed a strong union to bind the thirteen colonies into one nation, but the other Founding Fathers were right to counsel that this held true only up to a point. The president could override Congress only so far, and Congress could override the president only so far. To effect fundamental change also required the agreement of two-thirds of the states.

America is also a nation of neighbourhoods and communities as well as of cities and states. Each tier has its gradations of autonomy, with the very word 'state' implying a degree of sovereignty. I recall the pride that a mere Connecticut village took in its own fire service, school, police and local court house, a pride long disallowed to Britain's local councils, for instance. In the Senate, mighty California and Texas each have the same two votes as tiny Rhode Island. Localism is the lifeblood of American democracy; witness the divergence of states in matters such as abortion and drug use.

The balance of federal power now being abused by Donald Trump has been abused by presidents throughout history. The issue is not whether presidents are arrogant and self-serving – that was a decision for the electorate – but whether the constitution can call such arrogance to account. This has happened before. Andrew Johnson tried to reverse the outcome of the Civil War and was impeached. Theodore and Franklin Roosevelt both strained the criteria required of executive orders. So did Richard Nixon. America has often flirted with autocracy. But Congress and the courts have eventually come to the rescue. When the protocol of the two-term limit was abused by FDR, the constitution was amended in 1947 to entrench it.

The constitution remains defective. The Electoral College borders on democratic travesty when it permits losers in the popular vote to enter the White House. The Senate's bias towards small states may have guarded their autonomy but it plainly distorts democracy. Longevity has rendered the Supreme Court a gerontocracy, its membership a political gift for presidents. The constitution itself is hard to amend. Yet reformers confronting its failings have usually conceded, 'Better the devil you know.'

The result is an America that can be deeply conservative. In a 2024 Commonwealth Fund report its health service, entombed in special interests, ranked bottom of the ten highest-income countries. The average American's lifespan is actually declining. Inner cities are plagued by drug addiction and homelessness. Annual gun-related deaths in the early 2020s reached an all-time high of over 45,000, largely due to a third of Americans personally owning a weapon. For a country facing no real threat to its existence, its grotesque military spending is dictated by the power of the defence industries. Commercial lobbying has become one of Washington's most lucrative services, reckoned to spend twice its declared $3 billion a year.

At the same time, America can be excitingly progressive. At least until the Trump presidency, USAID was the biggest national donor to famine, disease and disaster relief. In scientific research America leads the world. Despite – or perhaps because of – its citizens' poor health, it spends more on medical research than the next ten countries combined. Thirty of the fifty top research centres are in America, and in academic citations it outranks the entire rest of the world. Its businesses, universities and creative enterprises are open to global talent. Americans were second into space and first to land on the moon. Half its states are libertarian towards recreational drugs. America's film and television productions keep the world entertained day and night.

Many historians have described America's principal weakness as its vulnerability to myth. It was the challenge of myth, that of the theological 'city on the hill', that enticed the Pilgrim Fathers across the Atlantic. The myth of a 'new' continent drew early colonists to the repression of Native America. The myth of the frontier sent millions to journey westwards, challenging every horizon, geographical, intellectual, even moral.

In the twentieth century Americans basked in the myth of being God's chosen agents of salvation. Woodrow Wilson claimed for them 'a superior energy which no other nation can contribute to the liberation of mankind . . . the infinite privilege of saving the world'. Lyndon Johnson at one point said he sought victory in Vietnam because 'history and our own achievements have thrust upon us the principal responsibility for the protection of freedom on earth'. To Ronald Reagan, 'this anointed land was set apart in an uncommon way . . . a divine plan, to be found by people from every corner of the earth'.

In the 1960s Arthur Schlesinger warned against such talk as 'a delusion of a sacred mission and a sanctified destiny'. It alarmed him that such talk might turn sour, ushering in a terrible fate. He described this as the moment when 'a rough beast, its hour come round at last, may be slouching towards Washington to be born'. In the nineteenth century that beast was de Tocqueville's tyranny of the majority. Schlesinger viewed Nixon as such a beast, though he was correctly sure the constitution would thwart him. Many Americans regarded Trump's re-election in 2024 as the beast returned.

Trump's self-image was as an iconoclast, a demythologizer. He was a corrective after decades in which America had seen itself as the world's 'indispensable nation'. To Trump and those who voted for him, America should be 'made great', not on the world stage but rather within itself. As with Palmerston's claim that nations have no duties, only interests, Trump offered a return to interests, albeit strictly as interpreted by him and with him as interest number one.

To this extent, America is now being asked only to speak not so much truth to power as reality. It can be no bad thing for a nation to be asked occasionally to question its place in the world, to review its strategies. However ham-fistedly, a nation should re-examine its sovereign independence, and perhaps tell others to do the same.

Pessimists often predict that the American union will one day decay and break apart, riven by populist uprisings. This book was written at a time when such talk had some currency. I see Trump's presidency rather as an example of the constitution releasing a safety valve. A sufficiency of Americans had clearly lost faith in those purporting to be their leaders. They saw a nation distracted by the politics of identity at home and by posturing abroad. They seemed unsure what they wanted except that they wanted something different. In 2024 they made their point. The next question was whether the constitution could satisfactorily perform its other function, of acting as a bulwark against its own undermining by autocracy. Could its checks and balances avert another beast that appeared to be slouching towards the gates of power?

New technology's social media, artificial intelligence and digital insecurity offer the world unknown challenges and dangers. I can only leave my own tentative vision of optimism. What Jefferson, Madison and Hamilton called an experiment – born of British political experience – has so far proved resilient. It has been a strength, not a weakness, that America has seen many false starts and hesitant finishes. But its constitution was born not of vanity but of the determination of good people to see if they could live together through compromise and prosper through energy. They have shown that they can, and have done so for two and a half centuries. I regard this as nothing short of astonishing. However battered and blemished, the achievement stands as an example to the world. If today's United States ceased to exist, it would be a global catastrophe. There is no other nation imaginable that could take its place.

Acknowledgements

This book arose from a lifetime's fascination with the United States. I spent a year of my childhood there and my father taught there for many years. My first wife, Gayle Hunnicutt, was American and we visited annually New York, Texas and California. There have thus been far too many Americans to name who have given me of their country's history. Their insights and conversation were always stimulating. The same applied to successive, always impressive, members of the American press corps in London.

The stimulus for the book came from Daniel Crewe and Connor Brown at Viking Penguin, where I also thank Trisha Mendiratta, Sara Granger, Leah Boulton and Annie Lucas. The text owes much to the copy-editor, Trevor Horwood, and Cecilia Mackay's picture research is as always incomparable.

Of readers and checkers I greatly appreciate the thoroughness of Louise Clare, Andrew Fearnley, Peter Furtado and Lucy Haire, Anthony Hippisley and Stephen Ryan, and of the stern critics, Tom Jenkins and Hannah Kaye. The book was written at a turbulent time in American history. I welcome comments and corrections, for what may be dramatic changes ahead.

Further Reading

The following books are either cited in the text or have been used as sources of reference:

Black, Jeremy, *A Brief History of America*, 2024

Burk, Kathleen, *Old World, New World: The Story of Britain and America*, 2008

Burke, Jason, *The 9/11 Wars*, 2011

Davidson, James West, *A Little History of the United States*, 2015

Ferguson, Niall, *Colossus: The Rise and Fall of the American Empire*, 2004

Fraser, Rebecca, *The Mayflower: The Families, the Voyage, and the Founding of America*, 2017

Freedland, Jonathan, *Bring Home the Revolution: How Britain Can Live the American Dream*, 1998

Graubard, Stephen, *The Presidents: The Transformation of the American Presidency from Theodore Roosevelt to Barack Obama*, new edn, 2009

Haass, Richard, *A World in Disarray: American Foreign Policy and the Crisis of the Old Order*, 2017

Halper, Stefan and Jonathan Clarke, *The Silence of the Rational Centre*, 2007

Hämäläinen, Pekka, *Indigenous Continent: The Epic Contest for North America*, 2022

Johnson, Paul, *A History of the American People*, 1997

Lepore, Jill, *These Truths: A History of the United States*, 2018

Lieven, Anatol, *America Right or Wrong: An Anatomy of American Nationalism*, 2004

Perkins, Dexter and Glyndon van Deusen, *The United States of America: A History* (2 vols), 1968

Reynolds, David, *America, Empire of Liberty: A New History*, 2009

Schlesinger, Arthur, *The Cycles of American History*, 1986

Slotkin, Richard, *A Great Disorder: National Myth and the Battle for America*, 2024

Winchester, Simon, *The Men Who United the States*, 2013

Appendix: Presidents of America

George Washington	1789–1797
John Adams	1797–1801
Thomas Jefferson	1801–1809
James Madison	1809–1817
James Monroe	1817–1825
John Quincy Adams	1825–1829
Andrew Jackson	1829–1837
Martin Van Buren	1837–1841
William Henry Harrison	1841
John Tyler	1841–1845
James K. Polk	1845–1849
Zachary Taylor	1849–1850
Millard Fillmore	1850–1853
Franklin Pierce	1853–1857
James Buchanan	1857–1861
Abraham Lincoln	1861–1865
Andrew Johnson	1865–1869
Ulysses S. Grant	1869–1877
Rutherford B. Hayes	1877–1881
James A. Garfield	1881
Chester A. Arthur	1881–1885
Grover Cleveland	1885–1889
Benjamin Harrison	1889–1893
Grover Cleveland	1893–1897
William McKinley	1897–1901
Theodore Roosevelt	1901–1909
William H. Taft	1909–1913
Woodrow Wilson	1913–1921
Warren G. Harding	1921–1923

Calvin Coolidge	1923–1929
Herbert Hoover	1929–1933
Franklin D. Roosevelt	1933–1945
Harry S. Truman	1945–1953
Dwight D. Eisenhower	1953–1961
John F. Kennedy	1961–1963
Lyndon B. Johnson	1963–1969
Richard M. Nixon	1969–1974
Gerald R. Ford	1974–1977
Jimmy Carter	1977–1981
Ronald Reagan	1981–1989
George H. Bush	1989–1993
William J. Clinton	1993–2001
George W. Bush	2001–2009
Barack Obama	2009–2017
Donald J. Trump	2017–2021
Joseph R. Biden Jr	2021–2025
Donald J. Trump	2025–

Index

Index